Pope Francis and Mercy

GILL K. GOULDING, CJ

Pope Francis and Mercy

A DYNAMIC THEOLOGICAL HERMENEUTIC

University of Notre Dame Press
Notre Dame, Indiana

University of Notre Dame Press
Notre Dame, Indiana 46556
undpress.nd.edu

Published in the United States of America

Library of Congress Control Number: 2023937773

ISBN: 978-0-268-20644-4 (Hardback)
ISBN: 978-0-268-20646-8 (WebPDF)
ISBN: 978-0-268-20643-7 (Epub)

Ad majorem Dei gloriam, and with gratitude to Pope Francis and all who have shared with me the depths of the loving mercy of our most gracious God—a Trinitarian ontology of mercy.

CONTENTS

Thirty seconds . . . a miniscule amount of time to effect such a drastic change. Within thirty seconds I passed from being a fit, active, energetic woman to being unable to sit, to stand, or to walk without excruciating pain. The cause: a spinal fracture, compression of the spine, and bone fragments pressing on nerves. The consequence involved two spinal surgeries and a significant recovery period. Yet alongside the physical deprivation there was a deep recognition of vulnerability. I had taken a vow of poverty many years previously, but during this Summer of 2018 I experienced a depth of poverty previously unknown to me. I was dependent on others to an extent I had not previously experienced, and in this state of vulnerability I encountered the goodness, kindness, and generosity of others, many of whom I had never met before, but all of whom showed a compassion that was the face of God's mercy to me at that time. As Pope Francis once said, "God immerses himself in our miseries, he approaches our wounds and heals them with his hands; it was to have hands that he became human," and God acts in this way "with tenderness and with caresses."[1] For mercy is not only a response to human sin; it is, more generically, God's tender and compassionate response to the human condition in all its complexity, brokenness, and beauty.

As I struggled to live well in the present moment, I was called to both a deep awareness of my limitations and a deep transformation; I was more profoundly aware not just that I was being shown mercy but that I was encountering the God who is himself mercy. It was a time reminiscent of Pope Francis's words concerning an experience when the Lord touched his heart with mercy. "Contemplating that heart," he said, "I renew my first love, the memory of that time when the Lord touched my soul and called me to follow him."[2]

Recalling how I received mercy during that summer impels me to commit myself to be what Francis has called an "artisan of mercy."[3] Indeed, the most powerful witness to Christian faith that an individual and the Church collectively can give is to let ourselves be transformed by the very gospel we proclaim, namely, the good news of God's mercy. As Archbishop Donald Bolen has written, "Mercy is God's way of changing the world, transforming us, that the world might be transformed."[4]

Mercy, I suggest, is the hermeneutical lens through which Pope Francis views all things, because mercy is at the heart of the Christian faith, revealed most clearly to us through the incarnation and the paschal mystery of Jesus Christ.[5] Indeed, in Pope Francis's homily at the supposed closure of the Jubilee of Mercy he invited all present and all the Church "to entrust the life of the Church, all humanity, and the entire cosmos to the Lordship of Christ, asking him to pour out his mercy upon us like the morning dew, so that everyone may work together to build a brighter future."[6] It is to further that aim that I have written this book.

ACKNOWLEDGMENTS

It is important to acknowledge the Henry Luce III Fellowship that enabled me to spend a full year researching and writing this book. I am grateful to the Luce Foundation and to the Association of Theological Schools for their choice of my project and for the generous funding they provided. My gratitude also extends to Professor Jennifer Newsome Martin, who first suggested that I send this manuscript to the University of Notre Dame Press and to Marilyn Martin, who undertook the onerous task of editing. Mention must also be made of the significant efforts of Michael Rogers and Joseph Schner, SJ, who also assisted with editing copy.

I also own my indebtedness to Cardinal Arthur Roche, Bishop Jose Bettencourt, Bishop Paul Tighe, and Frs. John Cihak and Tad Oxley for their kind encouragement and facilitation of my meetings with various curial officials. Fr. Servais, SJ, generously allowed me to use the Von Balthasar library at Casa Balthasar and gave me time and encouragement as I shared ideas.

Frs. Larry Gillick, SJ, Dermot Mansfield, SJ, and John Wauck assisted me to engage more contemplatively with the profound depths of mercy and enabled me to remain sane in the writing process.

My sisters in the Congregation of Jesus and the Institute of the Blessed Virgin Mary lived with me in the writing of this work, and the Sisters of Maria Bambina graciously welcomed me into their accommodation close to the Vatican.

Above all I wish to acknowledge with gratitude Pope Francis and the manner in which he has elevated the discourse on mercy, engaging with it as a dynamic hermeneutic and challenging us all by his example to live, pray, and work, with merciful hearts.

INTRODUCTION

On the ceiling of the Sistine Chapel in Rome, amidst all the beauty and splendor, there is an image of God stretching out his hand in the creation of a human person.[1] God points with his finger, and it forms and creates the reality of history in a gratuitous act of divine generosity. All particular historicity is established in that moment, and temporal reality has continued to be marked by the presence of God at work in the world, forming a covenant with his chosen people to which he faithfully adheres despite the infidelities of the people.[2] With the incarnation, the presence of God among his people becomes a personal encounter in Jesus Christ. His life, Passion, death, and resurrection mark God's definitive engagement and irrevocable commitment to human persons. In the growth of the early Church we see a community growing in faith and understanding amid the trials of persecution and exile.[3] Across many generations there have been significant moments of history in the life of the Roman Catholic Church. In the elevation of Cardinal Bergoglio to the pontificate of Pope Francis we encountered another such moment.[4] Here was a man "from the ends of the earth," the first Latin American and the first Jesuit pope.[5]

It was not just the manner of his being announced to the crowd outside St. Peter's Basilica, where six thousand accredited journalists had waited patiently for a puff of white smoke,[6] that made us conceive we were touching history. It has been the way that Pope Francis has lived out his papacy, in a manner such that he has been seen to put into action the words he has spoken.[7] Central to this enactment was the way he called the Church to a radical encounter with Christ and a re-appropriation of the gospel message.

A man of gestures both large and small, the Holy Father has commanded respect even from those who have profoundly disagreed with him. People have been attracted to him and intrigued by him, perhaps especially those who would designate themselves non-believers. His statements and gestures have been simple, direct, and profound. At times they have seemed to be passionate enactments of the gospel. His leadership has been novel. He has been the first pope for centuries to believe in the fruitfulness of tension and disagreement within the leadership of the Church, and he has advocated the principle of dialogue and the operative tool of discernment as key skills for governance.[8] It is also noteworthy that in the Church's relations with international nations, in his first three years in office Pope Francis met with every head of state with whose countries the Holy See has diplomatic relations, most of whom trod the path to Rome to greet him.[9] In this new papacy world leaders have seen a figure willing to engage with international issues and speak out in favor of the poorest members of society. Essential to the mission of the Church is the need to reveal the compassion of God for all, particularly those most vulnerable, who exist on the margins of society.

Facing global problems of climate change, terror, unemployment, political destabilization of an unprecedented international order, refugees, and dire poverty, Pope Francis has given shape to his compassion through endorsing a clear trajectory of mercy, love, and forgiveness as pre-eminently the mission of the Church to contemporary cultures and communities of faith. He once said, "Mercy cannot become a mere parenthesis in the life of the Church; it constitutes her very existence, through which the profound truths of the Gospel are made manifest and tangible. Everything is revealed in mercy; everything is resolved in the merciful love of the Father."[10] This could not be a more distinctive assertion of the importance of mercy. The pope was saying that it is in no way a mere appendage; rather, it is the operative dynamic of the Church's existence, revelatory of the good news of the merciful love of God. In addition, for the Holy Father, the mercy of God has a concrete face and a generative heart in the incarnate Word—Jesus Christ. Here we see the central consistent importance of Christology for Pope Francis's thought in terms of both his teaching and his preaching.

In this book I aim to re-appropriate the theological foundations of mercy, the Christological and Trinitarian roots, and the ecclesiological ramifications of that call to exercise mercy both within and without the parameters of the Church. I draw on two primary interlocutors to whom Pope Francis has owned his own indebtedness very significantly, Hans Urs von Balthasar and, to a lesser extent, Romano Guardini.[11]

I will also examine how Pope Francis has elevated Christian discourse about mercy, endeavoring to draw from the Christian tradition and to bridge the destructive polarizations, such as those that particularly mark church life in North America and Europe,[12] to focus Christian energies on fecundity in the mission. The potential ramifications for ecumenical and inter-faith dialogue are significant. At the most profound level, Pope Francis has issued a challenge to re-appropriate an understanding of the Church configured to Christ journeying with him toward Trinitarian life. From the heart of the Trinity and the depths of the mystery of God, the tide of God's mercy never ceases to flow.

The central dynamic of his pontificate from the very first days was Pope Francis's proclamation of the importance of the mercy of God, a mercy that imperatively calls for a human response and imitation. "Let us abandon a language of condemnation and embrace one of mercy," he said in a tweet.[13] It is this language of mercy that has prompted me to write the current book. In the closing months of 2015, having completed my work on *A Church of Passion and Hope: The Formation of an Ecclesial Disposition*,[14] I realized that the imperative for my future work was a consideration of the importance of mercy with regard to the mission of the Church. Awarded a Henry Luce III Fellowship, I was enabled to pursue my research during a year's sabbatical leave from my home institution.[15]

We receive the mercy of God to adopt this attitude toward others. The work of mercy is a visceral love that brings knowledge of the goodness and kindness of God to all. Mercy is the Lord's most powerful message. Mercy is not one divine attribute among many, but the central lens through which we may glimpse the love of God. For Pope Francis, Jesus Christ reveals the infinite mercy and love of the Father and calls those who would follow him to express that dynamic of merciful love in the life of the Church. In terms of ecclesiology, I will indicate how mercy is the foundation of the Church's life and a force that both reawakens the Church to new life and energizes her members with the courage to look to the future with hope.

The way in which I inter-relate the areas of ecclesiology, Christology, and Trinity in this book is of major significance. There has been much contemporary scholarship in these discrete areas, but within the theme of mercy it is possible to see the profound co-inherence of these distinct parts of theology into an organic whole. One way of doing this will be to explore mercy in dialogue with Hans Urs von Balthasar's understanding of kenosis and the kenotic event within the Trinity. We can consider Balthasar's thinking as a radicalization of the more traditional language of "self-gift" in the Trinity. The Father "has" nothing apart from what he "is," so his gift to the Son is an act of total "self-expropriation." The Son is the perfect image of the Father who returns the Father's self-gift in an act of thanksgiving that likewise involves his whole self. And the Spirit is the fruitfulness of this mutual gift that always exceeds and overflows both, so much so that it is not only object but also its own subject vis-à-vis the others.

God is not merely another ontic being whose positive attributes exist only relative to their negations; we might think of Cusanus's notion of God as *non aliud*, not another,[16] when Balthasar writes that "in God, poverty and wealth (that is, wealth of giving) are one and the same."[17] There is, then, a primal or *supra*-kenosis within the Trinity that encompasses God's various economic acts of kenosis from creation itself to covenant and, above all, the cross of Christ. Creation, covenant, and the cross are all features traceable in the discourse of Pope Francis, and the common link between them is more often than not the way in which they are associated with the leitmotif of this pontificate, namely mercy.

Yet what has come to be known as the "Francis effect" or the "Francis phenomenon" was not a sudden irruption in time. It is also important to have a sense of where Pope Francis drew on his predecessors for inspiration. Indeed, I shall argue that Pope Benedict XVI prepared the way for Francis both theologically and through his noble humility and courage in resigning, thereafter voluntarily placing upon himself a vow of prayer and silence.[18] There is a certain theological continuity that is, as Walter Kasper clearly indicates, "most clearly expressed by the fact that Pope Francis, with only two short additions, adopted as his own the encyclical *Lumen Fidei* that had been written by Pope Benedict before he left office."[19] We do know that Pope Francis often spoke with Pope Benedict, because the former declared it.[20] There are significant references in Pope Francis's encyclicals, allocutions, and addresses to the work of Pope Benedict. In addition, clearly an encyclical of Pope St. John Paul II, *Dives in Misericordia*, is a foundational document for perusal.[21]

In chapter 1 I lay the foundation of the book, which is built on the first years of Pope Francis's pontificate, quarrying from his homilies, allocutions, encyclicals, and addresses to gain a more profound sense of the breadth of the meaning of mercy as he understood it. In those years the Holy Father's supreme ability to make gestures that reached out to the hearts of individuals, groups, and nations laid a truly fervent foundation for his acts of mercy and his thought related to it. In this chapter I clarify the dialogical principle that he espoused and the operative tool of discernment that he employed.

Discernment forms the bridge into chapter 2, where there is a necessary focus on the Ignatian formation of Pope Francis, which underpins his work. His Ignatian formation, particularly his profound appropriation of the Spiritual Exercises of St. Ignatius of Loyola, have had a significant effect on his manner of life and his way of acting.[22] His way of showing discerning love—*discreta caritas*—which he also espoused for all members of the Church, is clearly grounded in his experience of the Spiritual Exercises and in the profundity of his own personal prayer and contemplation.

In the following three chapters I consider the Christological lynchpins, the Trinitarian horizon, and the ecclesiological ramifications of mercy. Here there is substantive dialogue with the interlocutors Balthasar and Guardini. In chapter 5 I also explore the impact of the re-appropriation and elevation of the discourse of mercy by Pope Francis on the work of the Curia in Rome. Here it becomes apparent that Pope Francis well understood that any crucial reform must begin with a conversion of hearts and minds if institutional change is to have any lasting effect.

Accordingly, in this last chapter I also indicate how all Catholics are challenged to faithful adherence to the principle of mercy as the impelling characteristic of dialogue in all relationships. Finally, in the conclusion I indicate possible implications of the work for future research and a potential renewed hermeneutic for theological scholarship as the twenty-first century progresses. I also make further pragmatic suggestions for a wider appreciation, and indeed appropriation, of the tools necessary to enable an engagement with mercy in our contemporary world.

CHAPTER I

Foundations for a Dialogue on Mercy

"God's love must take primacy over all else,"[1] Pope Francis stated in his apostolic letter issued at the conclusion of the Extraordinary Jubilee of Mercy, November 20, 2016. For the Holy Father, the awareness that God is animated by a truly passionate love for human beings and that this love is always inclined toward us in tenderness is the fundamental determinant for the lives of all Christians. He believes that an authentic knowledge of the God of mercy and divine love reveals God as radically, recklessly vulnerable: "What delights and attracts, humbles and overcomes, opens and unleashes is not the power of instruments or the force of the law, but rather the omnipotent weakness of divine love, which is the irresistible force of its gentleness and the irrevocable pledge of its mercy."[2]

The extraordinary discovery that God in Christ overcomes evil through self-surrender, even to death on the cross, can inspire human persons to desire that ongoing conversion to God that is the prelude to authentic union. The fruit of such conversion can be a life lived from a disposition of gratitude and a spirit of radiant contemplation. This is the good news of mercy that Pope Francis desired to share, and indeed what he, himself, exemplified. It is a recognition that in and through the Church Christ desires to bring us once more to the Father by the transforming grace of the spirit. As the pope wrote: "The Son of God, by becoming flesh, summoned us to the revolution of tenderness."[3] It is this tenderness that lies at the heart of mercy because it is a tenderness that "never disappoints but is always capable of restoring our joy," always making it possible "for us to lift up our heads and to start again."[4] This is why the pope desires to generate a "culture of mercy" in the Church, and he draws his own fervor from the transforming power of this tender love of Christ.

The gift of God's mercy informs the dynamic program of the mission of the Church because it is the very breath of life of the Church. According to the pope: "Mercy cannot become a mere parenthesis in the life of the Church; it constitutes her very existence, through which the profound truths of the Gospel are made manifest and tangible. Everything is revealed in mercy; everything is resolved in the merciful love of the Father."[5] This gift of merciful love can be most profoundly embraced only through sharing. When received as gift, it does not become a possession, but always remains, and indeed flourishes, as a gift to be shared.

MERCY AND HOPE

The overflowing nature of this gift of mercy brings with it a certain fortitude that enables Christians to take risks, to grow in the virtue of hope—to "hope against hope," to share the joy of the gospel. As Pope Francis insisted: "Hope is struggling, holding onto the rope, in order to arrive. . . . In the struggle of everyday, hope is a virtue of horizons, not of closure! Perhaps it is the virtue that is least understood, but it is the strongest. Hope: living in hope, living on hope always looking forward with courage."[6] Hope, thus identified, is also a source of significant energy and enthusiasm for acting in the present, looking toward an open horizon with a merciful gaze.[7]

Pope Francis's passionate commitment to mercy is clearly evident in so many of his homilies and allocutions. "The truth of mercy," he stated in his homily for the Mass and Canonization of Mother Teresa during the Jubilee Year of Mercy, "is expressed in our daily gestures that make God's actions visible in our midst."[8] He continued: "In the different contexts of the "need of so many people, your presence is the hand of Christ held out to all and reaching all. The credibility of the Church is also conveyed in a convincing way through your service to abandoned children, to the sick, the poor who lack food or work, to the elderly, the homeless, prisoners, refugees and immigrants, to all struck by natural disasters."[9] It is in the pragmatic reality of the small, ordinary interactions of daily life that the work of mercy is undertaken, the gospel truly lived, and the God of mercy glorified.

This chapter focuses first on the scope of Pope Francis's witness to mercy in his words and deeds from the earliest days of his pontificate. This scope includes the dimension of accompaniment as the necessary pastoral outreach of mercy particularly necessary for bishops and priests; Mother Teresa as a personal expression of mercy and exemplary for the many workers of mercy and volunteers; the significant questions posed by mercy; and priests as operative instruments of mercy. Then I consider the continuity of Pope Francis's words and witness to mercy with those of his most immediate predecessors, Pope Emeritus Benedict XVI and Pope St. John Paul II.[10] Central to Pope Francis's exposition of mercy is the dialogical principle he espouses, which impels him to reach out to all—across boundaries of faith, age, poverty, sickness, and citizenship. This principle is also apparent in his style of leadership. Finally, as a bridge into chapter 2, I clarify the operative tool of discernment and reveal it to be rooted in the Ignatian spirituality that lies at the heart of all Jesuit formation and continues to influence Pope Francis, himself a Jesuit. It is in the light of discernment that we come to understand also the Ignatian vision of living in the world as a continual struggle about the very destiny of human life.[11] It is clear that Pope Francis believes that members of the Church are called to be at the forefront of this struggle.

THE SCOPE OF POPE FRANCIS'S PROCLAMATION OF MERCY

Pope Francis's words during the Jubilee Year of Mercy were addressed to all people in society: "The jubilee year is a time of grace and mercy for all, the good and the bad, those in health and those who suffer. It is a time to remember that nothing can separate us from the love of God (Rom. 8:39)."[12] To new bishops at a meeting in Rome in 2016 he stated: "Make mercy pastoral, for you have experienced the thrill of being loved by God." This is the mission of bishops, Pope Francis stated, especially those who are new pastors of the church. He reminded them that the holy door of the Jubilee of Mercy was Christ himself.[13] To pass through the door that is Christ should help the new bishops to live "an intense personal experience of gratitude, of reconciliation, of total entrustment, of delivering your life without reservation to the Pastor of Pastors." He continued by stating: "The most precious richness you can take from Rome at the beginning of your episcopal ministry is the awareness of the Mercy with which you were looked at and chosen." The result of this, he asserted, is that "Mercy should form and inform the pastoral structures of our Churches."[14] Pope Francis then indicated three ways that could assist them in making mercy pastoral. He suggested that the men be bishops capable of attracting others and that they should make of their ministry "an icon of mercy" so that men and women may be attracted to God. Secondly, they should initiate others into the truth of faith.[15] Such a focus on initiation, Pope Francis indicated, should be included in schools and seminaries, as well as the parishes. The reformation of the way of life of the bishop has had its consequent effects on the structures throughout his diocese. Thus the realization of the gift of mercy in the renewed life of the bishops calls for a pastoral outworking of this gift of mercy in the way of "accompaniment." Consequently, the pope's final injunction to the new bishops was that they should be bishops capable of accompanying.

Accompaniment: The Pastoral Outworking of Mercy

With great poignancy, Pope Francis elucidated the depths of what it means to render mercy pastoral by using the parable of the Good Samaritan as an illustration of how

> to contemplate the heart of the Samaritan that is torn like the womb of a mother, touched by mercy in face of that nameless man who had fallen into the hands of brigands. First he let himself be lacerated by the vision of the wounded, half dead man and then comes the impressive series of verbs we all know. Verbs, not adjectives, as we often prefer, verbs in which mercy is conjugated. This is precisely what it means to render Mercy pastoral: to conjugate it in verbs, to render it palpable and operative.[16]

One of the most important verbs the pope emphasized is the verb "to accompany." The Samaritan accompanies the man he had come across to an inn and provides for him. As Pope Francis said to the new bishops: "Mercy, which had broken his heart, needs to be poured out and to gush forth. It cannot be plugged. It cannot be stopped. Although he was only a Samaritan, the Mercy that struck him participates in the fullness of God, therefore, no dam can hold it back."[17] In like manner, the pope exhorted the bishops to be tireless "in the humble task of accompanying the man that 'perchance' God has put on your way." In particular, Pope Francis urged them to realize the importance of accompanying clergy and families.[18]

At World Youth Day in Rio de Janeiro in 2013, Pope Francis, in speaking to the Bishops of Brazil, had already mentioned the importance of the Church accompanying people: "We need a church capable of walking at people's side," he said, a church that does more "than simply listening to them: a church that accompanies them on their journey."[19] Later that same year, Pope Francis reiterated the importance of the art of accompaniment in the apostolic exhortation *Evangelii Gaudium* when he stated: "The Church will have to initiate everyone—priests, religious and laity—into this 'art of accompaniment' which teaches us to remove our sandals before the sacred ground of the other (cf. Ex. 3:5). The pace of this accompaniment must be steady and reassuring, reflecting our closeness and our compassionate gaze which also heals, liberates and encourages growth in the Christian life."[20] The whole aim of spiritual accompaniment, Pope Francis emphasized, is to lead people ever closer to God.[21] As the pope elaborates his understanding of accompaniment it is clear that key characteristics are prudence, understanding, patience, and a sensitive docility to the Holy Spirit. Listening is a key component of any accompaniment—listening in depth, an exercise of the art of listening that is more profound than merely hearing words: "Listening, in communication, is an openness of heart which makes possible that closeness without which genuine spiritual encounter cannot occur."[22]

Pope Francis has returned to this theme of a church that mercifully accompanies people time and time again, in various settings—always emphasizing the mystery of a person's situation before God and the work of grace in their lives[23]—but especially when talking to pastors. This appears to be the way the Holy Father envisions being a pastor, namely, being a priest who accompanies people. In particular, the pope draws attention to the importance of "genuine spiritual accompaniment," which, he has said, "always begins and flourishes in the context of service to the mission of evangelization."[24]

Mother Teresa: A Personal Expression of Mercy

The saint of mercy, so prominent during the year of mercy and canonized by Pope Francis on September 4, 2016, was Mother Teresa. In her the pope saw exemplified a personal expression of mercy. The story of her life, from her vocation to be a Loreto sister to her later call to found the Missionaries of Charity, has been well documented.[25] This new order—founded to care for the poorest of the poor, initially on the streets of India and gradually, as the order expanded, throughout the world—gave exemplary witness to the gospel injunction to show mercy to the poorest members of society. The Mass of Teresa's canonization was also used by the pope as a moment to celebrate the Jubilee for Workers of Mercy and Volunteers.[26]

Pope Francis said of Mother Teresa that "in all aspects of her life [she] was a generous dispenser of divine mercy, making herself available for everyone through her welcome and defence of human life, those unborn and those abandoned and discarded." Mother Teresa put into practice, in concrete actions, what she invoked in prayer and professed in faith. She understood that hers was a vocation to charity and this was the expression of her growing love for Christ and for those to whom he called her. She was committed to defending life, ceaselessly proclaiming that the unborn are the weakest, the smallest, the most vulnerable. As the pope said:

> She bowed down before those who were spent, left to die on the side of the road, seeing in them their God-given dignity; she made her voice heard before the powers of this world, so that they might recognize their guilt for the crime of poverty they created. For Mother Teresa, mercy was the "salt" which gave flavour to her work, it was the "light" which shone in the darkness of the many who no longer had tears to shed for their poverty and suffering.[27]

Pope Francis called on the faithful not just to revere Mother Teresa as a saint but to see her as exemplary of an attitude toward the most vulnerable members of society that all Christians should embrace. He saw her mission to what he called the "urban and existential peripheries" as a most eloquent witness to God's tenderness and closeness to the poorest. The pope also indicated that he saw her as an emblematic figure of both womanhood and consecrated life who could be a model of holiness for all volunteers. He saw in the way Mother Teresa freely expressed her love for the poorest a certain criterion for action that all could follow: "May this tireless worker of mercy help us increasingly to understand that our only criterion for action is gratuitous love, free from every ideology and all obligations, offered freely to everyone without distinction of language, culture, race or religion."[28]

The Questions Posed by Mercy

Pope Francis drew attention to the fact that at the heart of our understanding of mercy lie key questions that challenge our very understanding of the nature of human life. He suggested that these questions were ones we all need to consider at any time of life: "Where do I look for security? Is it in the Lord or in other forms of security not pleasing to God? What direction is my life headed, what does my heart long for? Is it for the Lord of life or ephemeral things that cannot satisfy?" In prayerfully responding to such questions the Holy Father insisted that it is important to take note that the surest realities that the world puts before us do not last forever.[29] The pope emphasized that there are only two realities that remain when all else may disappear; these are God and our neighbors.[30] Such prioritizing stands in stark contradiction to the contemporary predilection for exclusion, whereby human persons are often discarded in favor of ephemeral things. Pope Francis warned that it is ominous when our consciences have become anaesthetized and therefore we cease to acknowledge such rejection of persons.[31]

In his homily for the end of the Jubilee of Mercy, Pope Francis raised further challenging questions. He reminded those present that we are called to follow the tangible humble love of Christ, our king. In imitation of Christ, then, we are called to ask ourselves each day: "What does love ask of me, where is it urging me to go? What answer am I giving Jesus with my life?"[32] This encounter with Christ in a living relationship that gives form and direction to life, and consistently draws from the source of divine love, is the dynamic impulse of mercy. It is both an inspiration for individual living and a source of communal endeavor. It calls us to resist the temptations to seek out the comforts and certainties offered by the world and the lure of power and success.[33]

Rather, "Mercy, which takes us to the heart of the gospel, urges us to give up habits and practices that may be obstacles to serving the Kingdom of God; mercy urges us to orient ourselves only in the perennial and humble kingship of Jesus, not in submission to the precarious regalities and changing powers of every age."[34] When such an orientation forms the dynamic of our lives we come to understand that God "is ready to completely and forever cancel our sin, because his memory—unlike our own—does not record evil that has been done or keep score of injustices experienced. God has no memory of sin, but only of us, of each of us, we who are his beloved children. And he believes that it is always possible to start anew, to raise ourselves up."[35]

Priests as Operative Instruments of Mercy

Pope Francis stated with great clarity, in his introduction to the retreat for priests on the occasion of the Jubilee for Priests during the Year of Mercy, "Mercy is the fruit of a covenant; that is why God is said to remember his covenant of mercy. At the same time, it is an utterly free act of kindness and goodness rising up from the depths of our being and finding outward expression in charity."[36] Indeed, so imperative is this movement of God's love from the depths of our being to engage in merciful acts that Pope Francis insists, "Nothing unites us to God more than an act of mercy—and this is not an exaggeration: nothing unites us to God more than an act of mercy—for it is by mercy that the Lord forgives our sins and gives us the grace to practice acts of mercy in his name."[37] The one who receives mercy becomes in that very moment the possible instrument of mercy for others.

Thus it is the fact that we have received mercy ourselves that makes us able and desirous of showing mercy to others. So mercy, said the pope, "impels us to pass from [the] personal to the communal. . . . [And] the bread of mercy multiplies as it is shared."[38] Indeed, the very way Pope Francis uses the word "mercy" indicates the outward active dimension of the word. As we have seen already, he understands the word "mercy" as a verb, not as a noun.[39] The Holy Father insists that mercy, "joins a human need to the heart of God and this leads to immediate action." Here, we encounter "evangelical simplicity," which is attentively attuned to undertaking all through the key of mercy. And mercy is always linked with hope, as indicated above.

Indeed, Pope Francis has spoken of mercy as the mother of hope. And the clear indication that we have encountered the reality of mercy is that we desire to be merciful ourselves and in this way we enable others to pass from exclusion to inclusion from the estrangement of sin to the celebration of mercy.[40] A particular example of this movement is when a priest goes to confession himself and then later is the instrument for other penitents receiving the grace of reconciliation. For Pope Francis such an act has an inherent beauty: "One of the most beautiful things, and which moves me, is a priest's confession: it is something great, beautiful, because this man who comes to confess his own sins is the same who will listen to the heart of other penitents who come to confess their sins."[41] In this way he becomes God's instrument for the celebration of mercy and an impetus for penitents to enact mercy in their relating to others.

Many saints have been cited by Pope Francis as exemplars of mercy—those who received mercy and therefore were able to let their hearts be re-created so that they might show mercy.[42] Supreme among the saints is Mary, Mother of God, whom Pope Francis sees as a vessel of mercy in the way she both receives and bestows mercy. Here he especially focused on Mary's gaze and the way in which the tenderness of her look gives courage to us to open our own hearts to God's mercy. It is a gaze of attentive integral concern, he has said: "It brings everything together: our past, our present and our future. It is not fragmented or partial: mercy can see things as a whole and grasp what is most necessary."[43] This is most often a deeper love and care for the poor: "The good odor of Christ—the care of the poor—is, and always has been, the hallmark of the Church."[44] Also: "Unless we can see into people's suffering and recognize their needs, we will have nothing to offer them."[45] It is this distinctive trait of the Church that has drawn many to faith and, particularly in our contemporary era, has attracted many young people to the Church, as they see the tenderness of God made visible through that reaching out to the poor and the fact that, in the pope's words, "when it comes to serving the poor by the works of mercy, as a Church we have always followed the prompt-ings of the Spirit."[46] And the way of the Spirit is neither coercive nor abrasive; rather, it is a gentle yet dynamic impulse. As Pope Francis reiterated: "God forgives not by a decree but with a loving touch and with mercy. . . . Jesus also goes beyond the law and forgives by gently stroking our sins' bruises."[47] It is, however, the comprehensive nature of God's mercy that draws us to deep conversion: "So it is not about God showing me mercy for this or that sin, as if I were otherwise self-sufficient, or about us performing some act of mercy towards this or that person in need. The grace we seek in this prayer is that of letting ourselves be shown mercy by God in *every* aspect of our lives and in turn to show mercy to others in all that we do."[48]

CRITICAL COLLABORATIVE CONTINUITY

For Pope Francis mercy is always a gratuitous act of our heavenly Father, an unconditional and unmerited act of love. "Mercy," he has written, "is this concrete action of love that, by forgiving, transforms and changes our lives. In this way the divine mystery of mercy is made manifest."[49] Concomitantly with this assertion the Holy Father emphasized the way in which Jesus reveals this loving mercy of God in the action of forgiveness: "Forgiveness is the most visible sign of the Father's love, which Jesus sought to reveal by his entire life."[50] God is merciful, and, as the psalmist corroborates in song, his mercy endures across all generations (Ps. 136). This mercy "gives rise to joy, because our hearts are opened to the hope of a new life. The joy of forgiveness is inexpressible, yet it radiates all around us whenever we experience forgiveness."[51] Though the depths of mercy are a mystery to human perception, the pope writes, "it is a wellspring of joy, seren-ity and peace."[52]

IN CONVERSATION WITH POPE BENEDICT XVI

The centrality of mercy as espoused by Pope Francis has clear reso-nance with the words of his predecessors. Cardinal Ratzinger, in his homily at the Mass for the election of the pope in April 2005 stated: "Jesus Christ is divine mercy in person: encountering Christ means encountering the mercy of God."[53] Later in that same homily he emphasized the overwhelming importance of mercy in the struggle against evil. "The mercy of Christ is not cheap grace; it does not presume a trivialization of evil. Christ carries in his body and on his soul all the weight of evil, and all its destructive force. He burns and transforms evil through suffering, in the fire of his suffering love."[54] Like Pope Francis, Pope Benedict XVI emphasized the importance of an encounter with Christ. At the Synod of Bishops in 2012 he emphasized that everyone has a right to an encounter with Christ.[55] As I have written, "This indicated something of what became a key trajectory within the Synod: the movement from encounter with Christ through conversion to mission."[56]

In his homilies Pope Benedict eloquently shared his understanding of what the mercy of God involved: "God loves us in a way that we might call 'obstinate' and enfolds us in his inexhaustible tenderness."[57] He emphasized the importance of trusting in God's mercy, made evident both in the Word of God and in the sacraments, and then going forth to share with people who are in search of divine mercy a message that may touch their hearts and minds. So his injunction to Catholics in the Roman parishes was that they should seek "to understand and accept God's merciful love: May this be your commitment, first of all in your families and then in every neighborhood milieu."[58]

In a most poignant farewell address to the College of Cardinals, Pope Benedict emphasized: "We must trust in the mighty power of God's mercy. We are all sinners, but His grace transforms us and makes us new."[59] The underlying dynamic of this mercy of God is the divine love "which God mysteriously and gratuitously offers" to each human person and "which we in turn must share with others"[60] It is an ecstatic love, "not in the sense of a moment of intoxication, but rather as a journey, an ongoing exodus out of the closed inward-looking self towards its liberation through self-giving and thus towards authentic self-discovery and indeed the discovery of God."[61] It becomes clear from Pope Benedict's discourse that the very possibility for such a way of loving exists because of the continual replenishment of love we receive from a rooted relationship in Christ.[62]

In Pope Benedict's understanding of the Old Testament, it became clear over time that "God's passionate love for his people—for humanity—is at the same time a forgiving love."[63] In Christ this is brought to ultimate fulfilment on the Cross as "he gives himself in order to raise man up and save him."[64] As Pope Francis later stated, "Every page of the Gospel is marked by this imperative of a love that loves to the point of forgiveness."[65] This is "love in its most radical form."[66] In addition, Christ gives this self-oblation as an enduring presence in the Church through the institution of the Eucharist, which draws those who receive him into "the very dynamic of his self-giving."[67]

Central to our participation in Christ's self-giving is a growing communion of will, with merciful action the habitual outworking of this communion. So, as Pope Francis indicated, "In God and with God, I love even the person whom I do not like or even know."[68] This is to see from a divine perspective, seeing with the eyes of Christ, and being enabled to love and serve others—even those who may be hostile. Accordingly, acting mercifully to others no longer seems impossible but rather "a freely-bestowed experience of love from within, a love which by its very nature must then be shared with others. Love grows through love. Love is 'divine' because it comes from God and unites us to God; through this unifying process it makes us a 'we' which transcends our divisions and makes us one, until in the end God is 'all in all' (1 Cor. 15:28)."[69] The dynamic movement empowered by divine grace impels the individual through encounter with divine love to a communal horizon, perspective, and action.

It is Benedict XVI's focus on this divine initiative of love that aroused great joy in the mind and heart of his successor, as the latter stated in *Evangelii Gaudium*: "I never tire of repeating those words of Benedict XVI which take us to the very heart of the Gospel: 'Being a Christian is not the result of an ethical choice or a lofty idea, but the encounter with an event, a person, which gives life a new horizon and a decisive direction.'"[70] It is, as previously stated, this personal encounter with the loving mercy of God that impels us toward merciful action, and an integral part of this is the experience and attraction of joy. Thus the proclamation of the gospel becomes a sharing of joy, an invitation to see and taste the beauty of the good news. In this way the Church grows, in Benedict's words, "by attraction."[71]

Pope Benedict also insisted that "[the Church's] joy in communicating Jesus Christ is expressed both by a concern to preach him to areas in greater need and in constantly going forth to the outskirts of its own territory or towards new sociocultural settings."[72] And always, Benedict XVI emphasized that the mercy of God finds a particular fullness in outreach to the poor: "The poor are the privileged recipients of the Gospel."[73] It is easy to hear the resonance of this idea in the words of Pope Francis.

The exercise of mercy, both pontiffs have insisted, is linked to the reality of a faith lived and expressed with great-hearted generosity. Pope Francis has spoken of a "spiritual desertification" evident in some societies.[74] Cardinal Ratzinger spoke of the "grey pragmatism of the daily life of the Church, in which all appears to proceed normally, while in reality faith is wearing down and degenerating into small-mindedness."[75] In this kind of desert Pope Benedict asserted: "People of faith are needed who, by the example of their own lives, point out the way to the Promised Land and keep hope alive."[76] We find an echo of this same call to hope in Pope Francis's vigorous challenge: "Let us not allow ourselves to be robbed of hope!"[77] We have already seen that hope is an essential ingredient of the practice of mercy, as it enables acts of mercy to be truly life-giving in their execution. Through such actions there is clear witness to the faith in what Pope Benedict referred to as a new "language of parables,"[78] one that was best exemplified in the life and teaching of Jesus.

Within the demesne of mercy, Benedict wrote, there is a fundamental priority of "going forth from ourselves towards our brothers and sisters," and such going forth reveals a spiritual maturity in response to the free gift of the mercy of God. This is why "the service of charity is also a constituent element of the Church's mission and an indispensable expression of her very being."[79] Pope Benedict consistently asserted that merciful charity "is the principle not only of micro-relationships (with friends, with family members or within small groups) but also of macro-relationships (social, economic and political ones)."[80] He was concerned to emphasize that "closing our eyes to our neighbor also blinds us to God."[81] We are all called to share the divine loving mercy received from God, which is the light that "can always illuminate a world grown dim and give us the courage needed to keep living and working."[82]

THE HERITAGE FROM POPE ST. JOHN PAUL II

Both Pope Francis and Pope Benedict also owned their own indebtedness for their understanding of mercy to the person and writings of Pope St. John Paul II. His writings were redolent of references to the importance of the mercy of God offered in and through Jesus Christ: "It is 'God who is rich in mercy' whom Jesus Christ has revealed to us as Father: it is His very Son who, in Himself, has manifested Him and made Him known to us."[83] Perhaps *Dives in Misericordia* is the most substantial presentation of Pope John Paul II's thinking on mercy. After comprehensive scriptural chapters, he considers the sources of uneasiness in the world, focusing on the increase of existential fear and the acceptance of the "primacy of things over persons,"[84] which leads to a moral uneasiness.[85]

In the face of this reality Pope John Paul II emphasized the need for the Church to bear witness in all parts of her mission to the mercy of God revealed in Christ. Indeed, the Church that remains faithful to the mission of mercy has the responsibility to prayerfully implore that same mercy "in the face of all the manifestations of physical and moral evil, before all the threats that cloud the horizon of the life of humanity today."[86] The Church is honor bound to proclaim the truth of God's mercy, and is only truly authentic when she professes what is "the most stupendous attribute of the Creator and Redeemer—and when she brings people close to the sources of the Savior's mercy, of which she is the trustee and dispenser."[87] Accordingly, the Church consistently calls her members to conversion to God that his mercy may be discovered and shared.[88]

Such conversion involves a spiritual transformation, and again we have a prefiguring of Pope Francis's words in this encyclical as Pope John Paul II spoke of such a transformation being an evangelical process that transforms a whole lifestyle and is essentially the appropriation of the Christian call to love God and one's neighbor: "It consists in the constant discovery and persevering practice of *love as a unifying and also elevating power*[89] despite all difficulties of a psychological or social nature: it is a question, in fact, of a merciful love which, by its essence, is a creative love."[90]

Pope John Paul II also desired to emphasize that merciful love always overflows to the good of the one who gives as well as the one who receives.[91] This is because the nature of this love has deep roots in the divine initiative of mercy. Indeed, "an act of merciful love is only really such when we are deeply convinced at the moment that we perform it that we are at the same time receiving mercy from the people who are accepting it from us. If this bilateral and reciprocal quality is absent, our actions are not yet true acts of mercy."[92] So it becomes clear in Pope John Paul's thinking that mercy is an indispensable element in building mutuality in relationships such that there can exist a profound respect for the human reality of the other(s).

Within the most intimate relationship of marriage, John Paul thought, merciful love becomes an indispensable element for the flourishing of the marriage and family life. Again we can find echoes of this same emphasis in Pope Francis's apostolic exhortation *Amoris Laetitia*.[93] For Pope John Paul, this merciful love is most clearly revealed in the "moment of forgiveness," since "forgiveness demonstrates the presence in the *world of the love which is more powerful than sin.*"[94] Accordingly, Pope John Paul emphasized that the Church is bound to consider it a principal duty to "*proclaim and to introduce into life* the mystery of mercy, supremely revealed in Jesus Christ."[95] He concluded this encyclical with a fervent plea for the mercy of God on the present generation: "Everything I have said in the present document on mercy should therefore *be continually transformed into an ardent prayer*: into a cry that implores mercy according to the needs of man in the modern world."[96] It is clear that both of Pope John Paul's successors have taken this admonition to heart and contributed their own proclamations of the mystery of mercy,[97] through the rich theological tropes of Pope Benedict XVI's pontificate and through the compelling gestures of Pope Francis and his elevation of the discourse on mercy.

A Principle of Diligent, Dynamic Dialogue

Central to Pope Francis's proclamation of the importance of mercy is a clear principle of the importance of diligent dynamic dialogue. Dialogue is always, by implication, a reaching out to others; it is dynamic in that such approaches are positive, affectionate, and life-giving; and it is diligent because there is a consistency about such an approach and a continued willingness to engage with others whether the others are friendly or hostile in response: "All Christians are called to go out to encounter others, to dialogue with them, without fear."[98] Indeed, there is a significant responsibility for the Church, in particular those who minister in the Church: "The ministers of the gospel must be people who can warm the hearts of the people, who walk through the dark night with them, who know how to dialogue and to descend themselves into their people's night, into the darkness, but without getting lost."[99]

In an address to the Congregation for Catholic Education, Pope Francis emphasized the importance of teaching young people how to engage in dialogue. "Dialogue," the Pope said, "is constructive when it takes place in an authentic atmosphere of respect, esteem, sincere listening, without the need to blur or mitigate one's identity. So it is encouraging," he continued, "to hope that the new generations, who are brought up to know how to engage in Christian dialogue, will leave school and university classrooms with the motivation to build bridges and find new answers to the many challenges of our time."[100] Such engagement in dialogue is an outworking of mercy, for it is to look at the other with a merciful gaze. In this same address, Pope Francis emphasized the need for a culture of dialogue, saying: "Our world has become a global village in which each person belongs to humanity and shares in the hope for a better future for the whole family of nations."[101] He continued: "Within this context, Catholic educational institutions are called to be on the front line in practicing a grammar of dialogue," which, he said, "is the basis of encounter and of the enhancement of cultural and religious diversity."[102]

This focus on dialogue is another characteristic of previous papacies and a priority for papal communication. During the pontificate of Pope John Paul II, Archbishop Pablo Puente, the apostolic nuncio to the United Kingdom, gave an unequivocal endorsement of the need for dialogue when he stated: "Dialogue with God. Dialogue [is vital] within the Church; dialogue amongst yourselves; dialogue with the world, with people, with the culture of our day, with the poor, with those who have no hope, with those who are seeking a pathway and a meaning for their lives. Without a broad-based dialogue we run the risk of closing ourselves in a museum, as yet another memory of the past."[103] The active movement toward engaged dialogue has produced a dynamic momentum across the recent papacies.

Fundamental to all dialogue, David Schindler asserts, is the call made present in Christ himself, the Word of God, in whom God initiates the dialogue.[104] Accordingly, Schindler understands that the mission of all Christians is to enter into this dialogue that God has initiated. The terms of this dialogue are found in Christ, who is "both the objective truth and the subjective way." This reality, made present in the incarnation, excludes no one from the conversation but rather draws all into the mystery of redemption. Therefore, Schindler concludes that each human being is created with this vocation to communicate, which can be fully realized only through an experience of forgiveness and conversion from sin. In consequence, within such dialogue, since all are forgiven sinners, there is no room for any abusive exercise of power. Instead, in imitation of Christ, there is a clear call to incorporate the voice of suffering as a key participant.[105]

In a not dissimilar manner, addressing a group from the Foundation Scholas Occurrentes,[106] Pope Francis emphasized that dialogue involves certain key characteristics, "of listening, of not arguing immediately, of asking questions: this is dialogue, and dialogue is a bridge. Do not be afraid of dialogue. . . . It is about agreeing on proposals for forging ahead together. In dialogue everybody wins, and no-one loses."[107]

Pope Francis also insisted on the indispensable nature of dialogue for marriage and family life in the experience, expression, and fostering of love. He did not underplay the demanding nature of such dialogue if it is to bear fruit in a merciful, loving exchange, particularly as it involves communication between men and women, the young and the old, all of whom communicate differently. The pope's advice here is relevant to all forms of interacting in families, communities, and professional relationships: "Our way of asking and responding to questions," he wrote, "the tone we use, our timing and any number of other factors condition how well we communicate. We need to develop certain attitudes that express love and encourage authentic dialogue."[108]

Foremost among these attitudes, the pope asserted, is the willingness to give to the other the gift of quality time: "This means being ready to listen patiently and attentively to everything the other person wants to say. It requires the self-discipline of not speaking until the time is right."[109] It is a patient waiting until the person has said everything he might want to say without trying to offer advice or an opinion prematurely. Such self-discipline requires a mature interiority: "This means cultivating an interior silence that makes it possible to listen to the other person without mental or emotional distractions. Do not be rushed, put aside all of your own needs and worries, and make space."[110]

Another key characteristic of dialogue espoused by Pope Francis is the attitude of giving real importance to the other person by valuing her contribution to the exchange, recognizing the unique nature of the other's life experiences along with the different insights and concerns that accompany this. Even in the face of seeming hostility, "we ought to be able to acknowledge the other person's truth, the value of his or her deepest concerns, and what it is that they are trying to communicate, however aggressively."[111] Giving a clear sense of value to the other in any dialogue enables an exchange in which there can be the possibility of a change in thinking and even of a new synthesis emerging. This requires, however, the willingness to have an open mind and to move beyond narrow-mindedness to be able to recognize the value and importance of unity in diversity or, as Pope Francis suggests, "reconciled diversity." As he writes: "Fraternal communion is enriched by respect and appreciation for differences within an overall perspective that advances the common good."[112]

Merciful love as expressed in dialogue is able to deal sensitively with difficult feelings that emerge within the exchange without allowing it to disrupt the dynamic of communication. Such love is also never patronizing but rather warmly affectionate, unfearful of the other and uncompetitive, not needing to "win" the discourse. Rather, the maturity of merciful love encourages ongoing interior growth in prayer, reflection, and study, in openness to the contemporary world, so that what is brought to the dialogue is the fruit harvested from such internal richness. At the heart of such dialogue is that positive orientation of heart and mind that is so clearly a feature of the predisposition of the Spiritual Exercises of St. Ignatius of Loyola.[113] Dialogue, Pope Francis continued to insist, is created by humility and self-discipline that prevent the walls of resentment and hatred from arising in any exchange. The way of dialogue, he asserted, is "the way of approaching and clarifying the situation," and this is how "the way of peace begins with dialogue."[114]

Clearly dialogue is not easy; it is difficult. Nevertheless, Francis said, "It is only by dialogue that we build bridges in a relationship rather than walls that separate us."[115] Humility and gentleness are important for any real dialogue, and, as the Pope indicated, this sometimes involves galling humiliation: "It's not written in the Bible, [but] we all know that doing these things means swallowing many bitter pills. We have to, because that's the way to make peace!"[116] At the heart of the dialogue is a constant willingness to remember that the other person or persons are made in the image of God; for this reason we are "always trying to see God's image in the other person."[117] In this way we promote a culture of encounter. In addition, when it comes to inter-Christian and inter-faith dialogue, Pope Francis has indicated that the best way forward is through undertaking works of mercy together: "To do something together is a high and effective form of dialogue."[118] Pope Francis is profoundly convinced that there is a need to overcome barriers and walls of all kind so that all can co-operate for the common good. This conviction lies behind his promotion of a culture of encounter.

THE OPERATIVE TOOL OF IGNATIAN DISCERNMENT

Promoting a culture of encounter is a key ingredient of the Spiritual Exercises, and it is evident that Pope Francis's long formation as a Jesuit and his own deep familiarity with the Exercises as a retreatant, as a spiritual director, and as a professor of spiritual theology informs his elevation of the discourse of mercy. He is profoundly aware of the struggle for the human heart and mind that is ongoing in contemporary society. Significantly, he has spoken on many occasions of needing to be aware of and pray to be free from "the idolatry of vanity, the idolatry of pride, the idolatry of power, the idolatry of money."[119] There is a need to be attentive, to understand and to take action against "the impediments the enemy of our human nature puts before us when we are moving forward in God's service, rising from good to better."[120] Such awareness, understanding, and action form key steps in Ignatian discernment.

Pope Francis has emphasized the quintessential importance of discernment throughout his papacy. The heart of discernment is a constant disposition of openness to the movement of the spirit of God at work throughout the concrete reality of everyday life. This is why an interior awareness and understanding of the spirits at work within the heart is vital as a preliminary to action. "The church today needs to grow in the ability of spiritual discernment,"[121] Pope Francis told a group of Polish Jesuits on his visit to Poland for World Youth Day in the summer of 2016. Indeed, so important does Francis consider the reality of discernment that he urged the Polish Jesuits to teach this art to diocesan priests and seminarians. The situation is grave in some seminaries, he noted: "We run the risk of getting used to 'white or black,' to that which is legal," he said. "One thing is clear: today, in a certain number of seminaries, a rigidity that is far from a discernment of situations has been introduced. And that is dangerous, because it can lead us to a conception of morality that has a casuistic sense."[122]

By contrast, Pope Francis called for a recovery of moral reasoning that follows the example of St. Thomas Aquinas and St. Bonaventure, who "affirm that the general principle holds for all but—they say it explicitly—as one moves to the particular, the question becomes diversified and many nuances arise without changing the principle."[123] He identified this "scholastic method" as being present both in the *Catechism of the Catholic Church* and in his encyclical *Amoris Laetitia*. For Pope Francis it is quite clear that moral considerations must take into account the rigor of the law, the practice of discernment, and a love for the Church: "It is evident that, in the field of morality, one must proceed with scientific rigor and with love for the church and discernment."[124] In this way it may be possible to form consciences in the manner in which the Pope indicates in *Amoris Laetitia*,[125] with attentiveness to the search for truth and charity advocated by the gospel, the tradition of the Church, and the process of discernment. This is another way of considering mercy as a verb, an action to be undertaken always in the light of discernment, from a foundation of mercy received as a gift of divine grace.

The employment of this operative tool of discernment has meant that Pope Francis is open to the creative imagination that may, with a merciful gaze, rethink styles and methods of evangelization. As he wrote: "Pastoral ministry in a missionary key seeks to abandon the complacent attitude that says: 'We have always done it this way.' I invite everyone to be bold and creative in this task of rethinking the goals, structures, style and methods of evangelization in their respective communities. A proposal of goals without an adequate communal search for the means of achieving them will inevitably prove illusory."[126] The pope's stress on communal discernment is vital here: "The important thing is to not walk alone, but to rely on each other as brothers and sisters, and especially under the leadership of the bishops, in a wise and realistic pastoral discernment."[127]

This communal dimension of discernment for pastoral practice is one that Pope Francis has himself employed in the reform of the process of the Synod of Bishops. Introducing a more profound understanding of "synodality," his reform of the synodal process has meant the incorporation of free discussion among the bishops and therefore a fuller consultation. People could be afraid of voicing what is in their consciences, but this eviscerates discernment and was something that Pope Francis addressed directly at the beginning of the Extraordinary Synod on the Family in 2015.[128] This is all in accordance with his desire for a more discerning Church. Discernment is something that is understood more in practice than merely in terms of theoretical knowledge. Because it is a profound personal and spiritual form of insight, it necessitates a certain attentiveness, empathy, and disposition of charity. The maturity of discernment is a refined ability to perceive the action of the Holy Spirit in human experience. This is, however, a way of proceeding that must be learned; it is not automatically given with the grace of ordination.

Accordingly, just as Pope Francis urged his confrères in Poland to teach discernment to diocesan clergy and seminarians, here he is also introducing a path of discernment to the Vatican curia. He is well aware that a reform of structures and procedures—something generally seen under any new administration—will have little possibility of fecundity without the transforming of hearts and minds as well. While such a process resonates profoundly with those who are acquainted with Ignatian spirituality and/or are more contemplative by nature, for others the process can be very disconcerting.[129] The lure of the comfort of security, norms, and incisive rubrics is an ever-present temptation. Yet Pope Francis warns: "In order to receive the kingship of Jesus, we are called to struggle against this temptation, called to fix our gaze on the Crucified One, to become ever more faithful to him." He calls for an examination of conscience with these questions: "How many times, even among ourselves, do we seek out the comforts and certainties offered by the world? How many times are we tempted to come down from the Cross?" The way of the gospel, he asserts, is not the way of power and success; the kingdom comes to us by different means. He saw the Year of Mercy as an opportunity—an invitation to return to what is essential:

> This time of mercy calls us to look to the true face of our King, the one that shines out at Easter, and to rediscover the youthful, beautiful face of the Church, the face that is radiant when it is welcoming, free, faithful, poor in means but rich in love, on mission. Mercy, which takes us to the heart of the Gospel, urges us to give up habits and practices which may be obstacles to serving the Kingdom of God; mercy urges us to orient ourselves only in the perennial and humble kingship of Jesus, not in submission to the precarious regalities and changing powers of every age.[130]

It is to the service of the humble and poor Jesus Christ and under this standard that St. Ignatius of Loyola formed the Society of Jesus. It is to the Ignatian roots of Pope Francis's understanding of mercy that we turn in chapter 2.

CHAPTER 2

Ignatian Influence on Pope Francis

In the pontificate of Pope Francis it is possible to trace a clear influence of Ignatian spirituality, the result of his formation as a Jesuit and his experience as both a spiritual director and a professor of spiritual theology. Indeed, he once said of himself, "I feel like I'm still a Jesuit in terms of my spirituality, what I have in my heart. . . . Also, I think like a Jesuit."[1] Key to this spirituality is the making of the Spiritual Exercises of St. Ignatius of Loyola. Pope Francis clearly draws from this rich source in his homilies and written texts on the importance of mercy, receiving mercy, and giving mercy. So what are the Spiritual Exercises? There is a book of this name that is primarily a manual for the director, the one who gives the Spiritual Exercises, not for the retreatant who makes them. Yet across the centuries the making of these exercises has borne enormous fruit in the lives of individuals and of the Church.[2]

The Spiritual Exercises were developed out of St. Ignatius's own lived experience. A long period of convalescence following an injury sustained in battle led him to a pilgrimage that culminated in a cave at Manresa in the Basque country where he stayed for ten months. Here he began to note the different movements of consolation and desolation within his spirit. These notes formed the basis of the Spiritual Exercises and involved, for him, a process of transformation. The structure of the Exercises shows the movement of that transformation. The Exercises are divided into four "weeks" or periods that have specific themes and graces for which the retreatant prays. The scope of the Exercises moves from meditating on the purpose of one's life in the first week to praying to work in union with Christ at the end of the fourth week.

The Art of Discernment

The essence of Ignatian spirituality is growth in an interior freedom and holiness that leads to the service of Christ and his kingdom.[3] It involves a gradual learning of the art of discernment. Discernment, as we saw in the last chapter, is a constant effort to be open to the spirit of God that illuminates the concrete reality of everyday life. "Discernment . . . calls for something more than intelligence or common sense," the Holy Father stated. "It is a gift which we must implore. If we ask with confidence that the Holy Spirit grant us this gift, and then seek to develop it through prayer, reflection, reading and good counsel, then surely we will grow in this spiritual endowment."[4]

The Spiritual Exercises are essentially a process of—indeed, a school of—discernment and of reorientation of an individual's freedom so as to allow him or her to choose an option for the kingdom of Christ. This option will not be based on any inordinate attachment. It is a discernment made in the light of Christ's life in order to help a person know and put into practice God's will for that person. For Ignatius, discernment always involves an ongoing conversion—an option of love; it is the root of Christian commitment and praxis.[5] The Spiritual Exercises are meaningful only in the measure to which they help Christians grow in the freedom of love.[6] They help the person making them to attain true freedom in God through a process that is structured in weeks and days, preludes and points, *examens* and repetitions and rules—all with this one aim in view. The one who gives the Exercises accompanies the retreatant on this journey of growing freedom.

Accompaniment Revisited

Such accompaniment, as we saw in the previous chapter, and as Pope Francis has insisted, is a substantial contribution to the life of all people and especially those young people who are moving toward vocational choices of marriage or religious life. "The Church must accompany the young in their journey towards maturity, and it is only with discernment and not abstractions that young people can discover their path in life and live a life open to God and the world," the pope has said.[7] But it is also an accompaniment of each other within the Church, as Cardinal Vincent Nichols made clear: ". . . [an accompaniment of] bishops with the Pope in the Synod, priests in a council, pastoral reflection in a deanery or in a parish, the confessor in the confessional box—as we try to discern the working of God in each concrete circumstance."[8] The art of accompaniment and discernment, Cardinal Nichols asserted, "is the art of learning to recognize our limits and to embrace our desires."[9]

Magnanimity

Openness to such a process requires great magnanimity—a great generosity of heart. This is what St. Ignatius sought in the one who was to make the Spiritual Exercises, and this is what Pope Francis emphasized as central to learning discernment and spiritual maturity:

> Following what St. Ignatius teaches us, [we need to learn] to be magnanimous. . . . This means having a big heart, having a greatness of soul. It means having grand ideals, the desire to achieve great things in response to what God asks of us and, precisely because of this, doing everyday things—all our daily actions, commitments, and meetings with people—well. [It means] doing the little everyday things with a big heart that is open to God and to others.[10]

So we see how pragmatically discernment is linked to discipleship— the following of Christ—which involves both an understanding of the life of Christ and a receptivity to the action of the Holy Spirit in an individual's own life in interaction with the lives of others. In making the Spiritual Exercises, the path of discipleship is indicated by the analogical imagination, which is tutored by praying with the mysteries of the life of Christ and the dispositions of the heart prompted by the Holy Spirit.

The Presupposition

Central to Pope Francis's dialogical principle, as explored in the last chapter, was the disposition of giving true attention and respect to the "other" in any dialogue. This positive focusing of energy toward the other, rather than constructing negative responses during an exchange of dialogue, takes significant form in the Holy Father's own engagement with others. It is also a key insight within the Spiritual Exercises and one encapsulated in the Presupposition: "To assure better cooperation between the one who is giving the Exercises and the exercitant, and more beneficial results for both, it is necessary to suppose that every good Christian is more ready to put a good interpretation on another's statement than to condemn it as false."[11] It is clear that St. Ignatius desires that there will always be a positive disposition toward the other rather than a negative one. Ignatius goes beyond this by implying that the responsibility of the one who hears someone speaking is not just to believe the other is trying to say something good but to be energetically open to the good the other might be trying to convey.

Pope Francis raises this same principled point regarding dialogue in the encyclical *Laudato Si'*, where he states: "An open and respectful dialogue is also needed between the various ecological movements, among which ideological conflicts are not infrequently encountered. The gravity of the ecological crisis demands that we all look to the common good, embarking on a path of dialogue which demands patience, self-discipline and generosity, always keeping in mind that realities are greater than ideas."[12] It is clear that Pope Francis is concerned to alert his readers to the ever-present temptation to become trapped in ideological positions that can blind us to the concrete persons and realities we experience and can prompt us to be less free,[13] as well as less merciful in dispositions and actions.

Anyone who makes the Spiritual Exercises discovers a growing appreciation of the need for discernment as a life-long process; indeed, genuine docility to the spirit of God is an art that is learned only in a lifetime of experience.[14] Gradually there emerges a delicate sensitivity to the inner motions of grace that are able to distinguish and be moved by the spirit of God. This is a matter of harmony and disharmony and is an intuitive sense. It is a profound imbibing of the art of discernment. It is, in a very real way, to be drawn more deeply into the way of Christ, which becomes the touchstone for integrity and the place of meeting with Trinitarian life.[15]

In the actual practice of discernment, we experience considerable interior movements as we come to understand the alternations of consolation and desolation. Both affectivity and reason are involved; thus mature emotional dispositions are vital.[16] Ignatius himself sought to find the will of God primarily through docility to interior lights and the motions of grace, but without neglecting the use of reason enlightened by the truths of faith. As Pope Francis writes: "Certainly spiritual discernment does not exclude existential, psychological, sociological or moral insights drawn from the human sciences. At the same time it transcends them . . . discernment is a grace."[17] This process leads to the development of a well-attuned interior sense and a keenly attuned heart characterized by habitual discerning love. For this to be the case, it is vital that significant time be spent in silent prayer, which enables us to better "interpret the real meaning of the inspirations we believe we have received, to calm our anxieties and to see the whole of our existence afresh in [God's] own light."[18]

The Dynamic of the Spiritual Exercises

The dynamic at work within the Spiritual Exercises is the work of the divine initiative involving the free loving invitation of God to an intimate encounter and deepening relationship with him that draws forth a free and loving response from human persons. As I have written elsewhere, "Because this is not an abstract but a concrete reality, that individual human response is located within a community — the Church."[19] Pope Francis has stated that when we spend time prayerfully reflecting on mercy, the dynamic of the Spiritual Exercises takes on a more profound imperative: "Mercy helps us to see that the three ways of classical mysticism: the purgative, illuminative and the unitive are not successive stages that, once experienced, can then be put behind us. We never cease to be in need of renewed conversion, deeper contemplation and greater love."[20] These three inter-related phases are continually re-presented in our lives. The Holy Father continued by asserting: "Nothing unites us more to God than an act of mercy. . . . Mercy makes us pass from the recognition that we have received mercy to a desire to show mercy to others."[21]

Such an encounter with God and subsequent response presupposes that the human person acts in freedom. Yet pragmatically we know that though we can desire to be free, our desires are often ambiguous. It is only with the help of God that we can grow in freedom. Such insight lies at the heart of the Spiritual Exercises, and such insight is one that Pope Francis puts before his hearers. In an address to students from Jesuit institutions Pope Francis emphasized: "Before all else be free persons!" said the Pope. "Freedom means knowing how to reflect on what we do, knowing how to evaluate . . . which are the behaviours that make us grow. It means always choosing the good. . . . Being free to always choose the good is challenging."[22]

The First Week: Engagement with Sin — What Impedes Freedom to Choose the Good

The first week of the Spiritual Exercises focuses on this recognition of the need for freedom, and during this week there is a significant encounter and dialogue with Christ on the cross that helps to focus both the sorrow and the gratitude that true awareness of sin bring. Pope Francis mentioned this dialogue when speaking of the importance of prayer: "For me [prayer] is the memory of which St. Ignatius speaks in the First Week of the Exercises in the encounter with the merciful Christ crucified. And I ask myself: 'What have I done for Christ? What am I doing for Christ? What should I do for Christ?"[23] These questions form for Pope Francis a "colloquy of mercy," focused as they are on the Lord placed on the cross for the sin of the world: "The entire second exercise [of the Spiritual Exercises] is a colloquy full of sentiments of shame, confusion, pain, and grateful tears, seeing who I am — making myself less — and who God is — making Him more — 'has given me life till now' — who Jesus is, hanging on the cross for me [Ex. 61]."[24]

Pope Francis saw that the way in which Ignatius had both lived and formulated his understanding of his experience of the mercy of God was of very significant personal benefit and also of benefit for the fecundity of the mission: "Jesus has given me an important grace: the grace of shame. . . . The shame is positive. It makes you act, but it makes you understand what you, your place is, preventing any pride and vainglory."[25] Also, his experience always required pertinent discernment to ensure that he kept before his eyes the reality that all is a gift of God, without whom we can do nothing, and indeed that gift may even prove a stumbling block to others. So, he said: "Ignatius lived from the pure mercy of God even in the smallest details of his life and of his person. . . . Such was the mercy of the Lord, and such was the abundance of his tenderness and the sweetness of his grace with him."[26] Here it becomes ever more clear that "An essential condition for progress in discernment is a growing understanding of God's patience and his timetable which are never our own."[27]

Through the first week, this encounter with Christ in the memory of one's own life and in the reality of the sacrifice of Christ on the cross leads to a cry of wonder and amazement at the love of God made operative in the salvific work of Christ. These questions continue to focus attention on the centrality of Christ in a life lived, a life being lived, and a life that will be lived. Thus memory gives added stimulus for both the present and the future, an understanding that Pope Francis has been concerned to emphasize, not least by urging the interaction of the elderly, who carry the memory of the past, with the young, who embody the energy for the future. For the Holy Father, the elderly are also involved in the future. In a catechesis offered in 2015 he stated: "How I would like a Church that challenges the throw-away culture by the overflowing joy of a new embrace between young and old!"[28] For Pope Francis the elderly help all to appreciate the "continuity of the generations" because they have a special charism enabling them to bridge the gap of generations. They symbolize for us the divine initiative of mercy that encompasses all generations. They carry the memory of this mercy. "The lack of historical memory," Pope Francis wrote in *Amoris Laetitia*, "is a serious shortcoming in our society. . . . Memory is necessary for growth."[29]

The Second Week: The Centrality of Christ

In the second week of the Spiritual Exercises a growing freedom emerges along with a deepening desire for the exercitant to share in the redemptive work of Christ. But the time is not without temptation, as Pope Francis indicated when he spoke of the importance of

Jesus as the true door to the Kingdom of God: "The door is always Jesus and anyone who enters through that door isn't mistaken." Unfortunately, we still "want to have the key to interpret everything, the key and the power to make our own way, whatever it might be, to find our own door, wherever it might be."[30] We continue to need to learn that "discernment is not about discovering what more we can get out of life, but about recognizing how we can better accomplish the mission entrusted to us at our baptism."[31]

So Pope Francis has also emphasized the centrality of Christ for all members of the Society of Jesus. This is not just because the Jesuit coat of arms bears the inscription *Iesus Hominum Salvator*,[32] but precisely because Christ is the reference point for all members of the Society. "The question: 'is Christ the centre of my life?' For us, for any one of us, the question 'do I truly put Christ at the centre of my life?' should not be taken for granted. Because there is always a temptation to think that we are at the centre; and when a Jesuit puts himself and not Christ at the centre, he errs."[33] The content of this second week of the Exercises is a series of contemplations on the life of Christ interposed with certain key meditations. The aim in the contemplations is a certain configuring of the exercitant to Christ, and because of the intimate link between Christ and the Church, so also does the individual become, as it were, configured to the Church.[34] Thus the focus of attention becomes how the individual is called to enter into the mission of the Church, that is, to take the good news to all people and particularly, according to the pope, "to reach all the 'peripheries' in need of the light of the Gospel."[35]

The trajectory of the second week is toward participation in the redemptive mission of Christ, taking up the divine invitation that is extended in and through Christ to participate in his saving work. As Pope Francis wrote: "Each Christian and every community must discern the path that the Lord points out, but all of us are asked to obey his call to go forth from our own comfort zone."[36] The move to mission becomes also a more profound discernment of a particular call, having received the mercy of God, so also to share the fruit of this experience in a manner of living that will engage in risk rather than self-preservation.[37] What is most evident throughout this second week of the Exercises is the attractive nature of the salvific love of God made manifest in the life of Jesus Christ. This invites us to respond, "to see God in others and to go forth from ourselves to seek the good of others."[38]

Pope Francis continues to urge this going forth in the name of Christ to serve others even when it means taking risks. This is the way to be merciful. He insists that making mistakes is part of life and not to be considered an impediment to mission: "Go forward with courage and without fear of making mistakes! Someone who never makes mistakes is someone who does nothing. We must go forward! We err at times, yes, but there is always the mercy of God on our side!"[39] The Church must be actively involved in "mercifying" the cultures and environments in which her members live and work. In a most relevant passage from *Evangelii Gaudium* Pope Francis insisted it was better to have "a Church which is bruised, hurting and dirty because it has been out on the streets. . . . If something should rightly disturb us . . . it is the fact that many of our brothers and sisters are living without . . . the friendship of Jesus Christ"[40] Here discernment is vital to answer the question "What does God want me to do in this particular concrete situation?" As Pope Francis insists, we may all say of ourselves: "I am a mission on this earth; that is the reason why I am here in this world."[41]

Key meditations during the second week of the Spiritual Exercises bring into stark relief the nature of the struggle in which Christ and the Church are engaged against the one that St. Ignatius and Pope Francis call "the enemy of our human nature." The Spiritual Exercises understand the church as the community gathered around Christ engaged in this mysterious and fundamental struggle that lies at the heart of human history. This is the intractable conflict between the call of Christ and the influences of the antihuman. As I have written: "Against this subtext of a Church in struggle Ignatius proposes a crucial prayer for enlightenment, asking for the grace of knowledge of the deceptions of the enemy of our human nature in order to reject them and knowledge of the way Christ is calling in order to follow him more closely."[42] Pope Francis, in speaking to young people in Paraguay in July 2015, brought this Ignatian meditation on the Two Standards—that of Christ and that of the devil—into contemporary focus by using the image of two sports teams. He said that in today's terms, it would be like considering the soccer jerseys of two different teams and finding that we must choose "which team we want to play for."[43]

The pope invited his young audience to imagine what it would be like to belong to one or the other team. "In this life, which team do you want to play for?" he asked. The pope went on to describe the strategies of the two opposing teams. The devil, he said, "in order to recruit players, promises that those who play on his side will receive riches, honour, glory, and power. They will be famous. Everyone will worship them." Jesus, on the other hand, "doesn't tell us that we will be stars, celebrities, in this life. Instead, he tells us that playing with him is about humility, love, service to others. Jesus does not lie to us; He takes us seriously."[44] In our response, when we explore our life's journey in the presence of God, no areas can be off limits.[45]

Even though the devil's offer might sound better, the pope cautioned, there are other factors to consider. The devil promises happiness, but he doesn't deliver. "In the Bible," Francis said, "the devil is called the father of lies. What he promises, or better, what he makes you think, is that, if you do certain things, you will be happy. And later, when you think about it, you realize that you weren't happy at all. "Following the devil's advice," Francis said, far from giving you happiness, makes you "feel more empty, even sad."[46] The pope said that Satan is a 'con artist' "because everything he promises us is divisive; it is about comparing ourselves to others, about stepping over them in order to get what we want." He added that the devil is "a con artist because he tells us that we have to abandon our friends, and never to stand by anyone. Everything is based on appearances. He makes you think that your worth depends on how much you possess."[47]

Jesus is very different, Pope Francis said, and He plays by a different strategy based on honesty and truth. Jesus "doesn't con us, nor does He promise us the world. He doesn't tell us that we will find happiness in wealth, power, and pride,"[48] As a coach, the pope continued, Jesus tells His players, "Blessed, happy are the poor in spirit, those who mourn, the meek, those who hunger and thirst for righteousness, the merciful, the pure in heart, the peacemakers, those who are persecuted for righteousness' sake." Francis asked, "Why?" Then he gave the reason: "Because Jesus doesn't lie to us, he shows us a path which is life and truth. He is the great proof of this. His style, his way of living, is friendship, relationship with his Father. And that is what He offers us. He makes us realize that we are sons and daughters." Unlike the devil, Jesus "does not trick you,"[49] Pope Francis said. "Because He knows that happiness, true happiness, the happiness which can fill our hearts, is not found in designer clothing, or expensive brand-name shoes." The way of Jesus is utterly different: "Christ knows that real happiness is found in drawing near to others, learning how to weep with those who weep, being close to those who are feeling low or in trouble, giving them a shoulder to cry on, a hug." The key to true happiness, Pope Francis said, is "to join His team and play His game."[50] This game is one of mercy in action.

Key Virtues: Gentleness, Humility, and Simplicity

The mode of being involved in this game is with the virtues of gentleness, humility, and simplicity, which mark the way of proceeding for those who follow the poor and humble Christ. A significant meditation in the second week of the Spiritual Exercises and one central to the life and work of Pope Francis is titled Three Kinds of Humility.[51] This moves toward a prayer (the Triple Colloquy) that expresses the desire to be with Christ in the manner of his life and his Passion.[52] As I have written elsewhere: "The Triple Colloquy is a prayer that asks for the individual to be drawn, at an ever deeper level, into the experience of Christ. We are actually praying to enter into Christ's work and his way. This prayer is also expressing a willingness to enter into the consequences of walking in this way."[53] Pope Francis took up a similar theme in one of his homilies when he urged us to see gentleness, humility, kindness, and tenderness as virtues that help us to follow the road to which Christ points, the path of mercy. To receive them, he wrote, is "a grace. A grace which comes from contemplating Jesus. . . . Only by contemplating Christ's suffering humanity," the pope asserted, "can we become gentle, humble, and tender like him. There's no other way."[54] Only in this way can we both recognize the effect of mercy in our own lives and be empowered to engage in merciful action with others. "Seeing and acting with mercy," Pope Francis indicates, is the manifestation of holiness.[55]

These graces are also linked with the inheritance we receive "from the simplicity of mothers, of grandmothers, this is the cornerstone . . . we are simple people," Pope Francis maintained, in an address to the Marian Fathers of the Immaculate Conception. It is when we have "grown" in simplicity that we are able to "draw near with this simplicity to those who are simple, to those who suffer the most: the sick, children, the abandoned elderly, the poor, everyone."[56] Though we are always aware of our own inadequacies, we need to keep faith in the power of God to undertake all that is necessary. The Holy Father continued: "Our smallness is precisely the seed, the tiny seed that then sprouts and grows, the Lord waters it, and that is how it goes on."[57] By contrast, Pope Francis warns in *Laudato Si'*, when "we lose our humility and become enthralled with the possibility of limitless mastery over everything, we inevitably end up harming society and the environment."[58]

The Third Week: Configured to the Cross

The third week of the Spiritual Exercises draws attention to the Passion and death of Christ on the cross. During this time retreatants pray for a willingness to enter into the consequences of walking in the way of Christ, and praying on the Passion makes these consequences clearer. It is evident that Pope Francis is deeply touched by contemplating the crucified Lord, and he sees Jesus present in so many brothers and sisters who are suffering.[59] In one of his addresses, the pope made clear that letting ourselves be moved by the crucified Lord is at the heart of understanding the works of mercy: "I have deliberately used the plural, because mercy is not an abstract word, but a lifestyle that places concrete gestures before the word. These gestures touch the flesh of the neighbour and become institutionalized in works of mercy."[60] Pope Francis is ever conscious of his own experience of God's mercy as one whom the Lord looked upon with mercy and chose for his service.[61] "Only if we experience this healing power [of mercy] first-hand in our own wounds, as people and as a body," he said, "will we lose the fear of allowing ourselves to be moved by the immense suffering of our brothers and sisters, and will we hasten to walk patiently with our people, learning from them the best way of helping and serving them."[62]

The contemplations of this third week draw the retreatant to desire a life lived more in conformity with Christ and the experience of his merciful love. For some, this will involve the reality of a religious vocation. It is within religious life that Pope Francis desires to see once more the radical nature of prophecy and a renewed asceticism. In a meeting with the superior generals of men religious in Rome he urged a return to consideration of the Church Fathers: "They remind us that we are called to come out of our comfort zones, forsake all that is worldly: in our way of life, but also in thinking up new ways forward for our Institutes. New roads are to be found in the founding charism and initial prophecy. We have to acknowledge what our worldliness is personally and as a community.... True asceticism must make me freer."[63] This freedom allows the individual and the community to be more merciful not just in theory but also in terms of practical living. Inevitably such a manner of living will lead to persecution and the cross.[64]

The Fourth Week: The Way of Consolation

The way of Christ is always through death to resurrection, and the contemplations of the fourth week of the Spiritual Exercises focus on the resurrection appearances. Always the final hermeneutic is the cross, without which there can be no resurrection. The grace of this week is the joy of the risen Christ—the grace of consolation. This is the grace the retreatant prays for, to joy in Christ's joy in being fully alive—to opt to be open to joy. It is Christ himself who brings this joy. Pope Francis has consistently underlined the importance of joy. *Evangelii Gaudium* speaks of the joy of the gospel: "The joy of the gospel fills the hearts and lives of all who encounter Jesus.... With Christ joy is constantly born anew.... I wish to encourage a new chapter of evangelization marked by this joy."[65] In *Amoris Laetitia* he states, "The joy of love experienced by families is also the joy of the Church."[66] With regard to our ecological understanding and spirituality, Pope Francis maintains in *Laudato Si'* that "Christian Spirituality proposes an alternative understanding of the quality of life, and encourages a prophetic and contemplative lifestyle, one capable of deep enjoyment free of the obsession with consumption."[67] Joy is possible at all levels of our existence, in our relationships with one another and with the whole of created reality if it is profoundly rooted in the joy of our ongoing encounter with Christ.

In speaking to the Jesuit members of the General Congregation in October 2016, Pope Francis emphasized that "the true work of the Society [is] to console the faithful people of God and to help them through discernment so that the enemy of our human nature does not rob us of our joy: the joy of evangelizing, the joy of the family, the joy of the Church, the joy of creation."[68] For this work to be effective the Pope insisted on the necessity of prayer, a prayer which asks insistently for God's consolation. "To practice and teach this prayer of petition and supplication for consolation is the principal service we render to joy."[69] The Holy Father asserted that the reason for such persistence in the practice of prayer for consolation, whether people consider themselves worthy of it or not, is that "joy is constitutive of the Gospel message,"[70] and should be asked for, for oneself, for love of others, and for the world. Joy attracts others to the grace of the good news. Joy indicates that love is active in the life of the one who radiates such joy.

Interestingly, Pope Francis emphasizes that "time is the key to recognizing the action of the Spirit."[71] In this connection, the Pope drew attention to the fact that progress in the spiritual life, as the Spiritual Exercises gives evidence for, is brought about during a period of consolation.[72] In addition Pope Francis made explicit how important is the joy involved in announcing the good news "through preaching, faith and the practice of justice and mercy" as he understands it "that is what leads the Society to the peripheries" and in a statement of great consolation to the assembled members of the Congregation he stated:

> The Jesuit is a servant of the joy of the gospel, both when he is working as an artisan, conversing and giving the Spiritual Exercises to a single person, helping him or her to encounter "this interior forum whence comes the power of the Spirit, which guide, free and renew him" (Pierre Favre, *Memoriale*) and when he is working with structures organizing works of formation, of mercy, or of reflection which are institutional expansions of those turning points where the individual will is broken down and the Spirit enters to act.[73]

This is true in all aspects of the Jesuit apostolate but particularly when the Jesuit is involved in organizing works of mercy.

Ignatian Guidance and Governance

At the heart of Pope Francis's leadership style is a certain quality of mercy showing forth in a gentle and humble approach to all with whom he comes into contact. We can see the derivation here from the Spiritual Exercises. The pope clearly saw humility at the heart of what it means to be a good shepherd. In his own life he had learned that he needed to be humble. This humility is not just an intellectual stance but something that has been nurtured through prayer, and, according to a bishop who knew him well, "his humility and simplicity are actually an expression of his magisterium."[74] The way in which he exercised authority was through this humility conjoined with his service of the Church and the many individuals he encountered both there and in the wider world.[75]

Within the Spiritual Exercises, and enfleshed in the Jesuit Constitutions, is a certain understanding of the union of guidance and governance. At the heart of this union is the life-giving, consoling spirit of Christ mentioned in the fourth week of the Exercises as the one who is the source of consolation during contemplations on the resurrection. This gift of consolation also lies at the heart of the guidance and governance that the Sprit brings to the individual through the Church: through the various hierarchical authorities and through the sacraments, scripture, and tradition. In addition, the Spirit guides by the change effected in human subjectivity. In particular, through a deepening love of and friendship with Christ that transforms an individual's intellect, affectivity, existential experience, and even, over time, their ontological being. The effect on the human person is that the guiding presence of the greater love of the Spirit at work inside the person brings order to the lesser external loves.

The outworking of Pope Francis's principles here, derived as they are from the Exercises, produces a certain robust leadership style that is not dependent on overt dominance but springs from the sense of the importance of dialogue, framed according to the presupposition of the Spiritual Exercises such that he can both mercifully listen to and respect those who are actively hostile to his work of reforming the Roman Curia. Here, as Austen Ivereigh asserts, Pope Francis uses disagreement as a mechanism of ecclesial reform.[76] In accordance with his Ignatian heritage, he appears able to work with the different and sometimes conflicting wills of a group of people to "conduct" or direct them in such a way that they end up flowing in the same direction without the conductor's having had to issue a definitive order that this should be the case. His way of merciful working is to see his leadership role as being to bring those who disagree into a relationship and to hold them there, allowing the various tensions to be worked out such that something positive may emerge. A significant example of this is the way in which Pope Francis facilitated the two Synods of Bishops on the Family.[77] His vision of the way in which he would like the Church to operate is profoundly relational in its theology, anthropology, ethics, economics, and ecology. This stands in stark contrast to the un-relational, individualized postmodern context that he aims to redress.[78] The encounter we have with Jesus must affect all our interactions.[79]

Pope Francis's manner of achieving this kind of positive interaction, costly though it may be for all involved, avoids direct confrontation. This does not mean that he avoids tension—far from it. The Holy Father sets a positive premium on the importance of tension for the life of the Church. He sees it as integral to the practice of mercy. There appear to be four key principles that the pope espouses and that seem to work well in bringing participants together from across the spectrum of allegiances and with a wide divergence of opinions. First, that time is greater than space.[80] Therefore, the leader should be open to developing processes over time that allow room for the Holy Spirit rather than seeking to occupy the space of power. As the pope wrote: "This principle enables us to work slowly but surely, without being obsessed with immediate results. It helps us patiently to endure difficult and adverse situations, or inevitable changes in our plans. It invites us to accept the tension between fullness and limitation, and to give a priority to time."[81] Such a way of living is countercultural to a world moving at an ever more frenetic, stressful pace.

A second axiom is that unity prevails over conflict.[82] Here the pope's focus is on building relationships, not fleeing from conflict but attempting to reconcile differences if at all possible into some life-giving synthesis. It is based on the conviction that the Holy Spirit can speak through difference and division, leading to a new life-giving possibility: "The unity brought by the Spirit can harmonize every diversity. It overcomes every conflict by creating a new and promising synthesis."[83] Indeed, as Eamon Duffey has indicated, Pope Francis is the first pope of modern times who has believed in the fruitfulness of disagreement.[84]

St. Ignatius of Loyola spoke of this principle in relation to the dialogue between the superior and members of a community. In that open dialogue a new position may emerge that is where the spirit of God is leading. An example of this principle in practice was seen in the extraordinary and the ordinary synods on the family, where the dynamics of disagreement were clearly apparent. Pope Francis allowed the ferment of disagreement. He positively encouraged the bishops to speak honestly and listen carefully. He provided the contained environment in which they were freed to work together within the synods with "Peter" at the helm. As he said to the synod fathers:

> It is necessary to say all that, in the Lord, one feels the need to say: without polite deference, without hesitation. And at the same time, one must listen with humility and welcome, with an open heart, to what your brothers say. *Synodality* is exercised with these two approaches. For this reason I ask of you, please to employ these approaches as brothers in the Lord; speaking with *parrhesia* and listening with humility. And do so with great tranquility and peace, so that the Synod may always unfold *cum Petro et sub Petro*, and the presence of the Pope is a guarantee for all and a safeguard of the faith.[85]

The third principle is that realities are more important than ideas. "There also exists a constant tension between ideas and realities," the pope wrote.[86] Like his order's founder, St. Ignatius, Pope Francis has a keen appreciation for reason and the intellectual apostolate and, at the same time, in the dialogue between ideas and reality he sees an important incarnational principle of starting with the given reality: "What calls us to action are realities illuminated by reason," he wrote.[87] This brings us back to the importance of spiritual discernment, which for Pope Francis lies at the heart of all renewal of the individual or the Church. Discernment always attends first to the concrete reality, with all the goodness and limitations found there, always attentive to the "shades of progress." So the focus is not on a battle of ideas and ideologies but on a reverential encounter with the life and lives of others: "A battle of ideas, so beloved of the media, tends to take us away from the very place that should fill our hearts and minds . . . the reality of a person's life and how God is at work in it at any moment."[88] This principle of realities' being greater than ideas is also incarnational and gives us a rich tradition from which to draw and to which to make our own contribution.[89]

Finally, the fourth principle is that the whole is greater than the part. Pope Francis looks to the image of a polyhedron, which has many facets, but all are attached to one geometrical shape.[90] In like manner, the communal whole—the body of Christ to which all individual members of the Church belong—has primary significance.[91] As the pope wrote: "The whole is greater than the part, but is also greater than the sum of its parts. There is no need then to be overly obsessed with limited and particular questions. We constantly have to broaden our horizons and see the greater good which will benefit us all."[92] This brings a realization that in the mystery of the heart of God nothing is too great or too small. The radical demands of the gospel demand of us an attentiveness that challenges us on occasion to engage in great enterprises but also in the simple small gestures of daily living and loving with a merciful heart.

These four principles are highly significant in a more profound appropriation and activation of the reality of merciful living where there is clear evidence of a certain tension of being totally dependent upon God and fully and actively engaged in the mission. The harmonization of this and of the other tensions (contemplation and action, faith and justice, charism and institution, community and mission) is not expressed in abstract formulations but is achieved in the course of time through what Favre called "our way of proceeding."[93] This is a way in which, as the Formula of the Institute makes clear,[94] always kept in mind are the concrete times, places, and persons so that all rules are aids—*tantum quantum*—for concrete things.

Heart Speaking to Heart

Pope Francis has a liberating way of speaking from the heart. On a number of occasions through his pontificate he has decided not to proceed with an address prepared for a group—though he usually leaves it with participants for later reflection—but rather to speak simply from the heart, sometimes in responding to questions and at other times because he feels inspired to raise certain points for the particular gathering he is attending. In this way we might see in him a certain docility to the Spirit that he himself acclaimed in the Spiritual Exercises and emphasized as he quoted the words of Michel de Certeau: "The Spiritual Exercises are the apostolic method par excellence" that make possible "a return to the heart, the beginning of docility to the Spirit which awakens and propels the exercitant to personal fidelity to God."[95]

This focus on the heart, particularly the merciful heart, also raises the issue of popular devotion to the heart of Jesus.[96] This is a devotion that was encouraged by the Jesuit St. Claude de la Colombiere and thereafter firmly entrenched within the Ignatian tradition.[97] The Feast of the Sacred Heart of Jesus is celebrated in June—indeed, the whole month of June is traditionally dedicated to the Sacred Heart—and emphasizes the highest human expression of divine love. Over time, though, devotion to the Sacred Heart diminished to such an extent that Fr. Pedro Arrupe, SJ, then the superior general of the Society of Jesus, felt the need to remind his brother Jesuits of the importance of this devotion. In 1981, in his last address to the Society, "Rooted and Grounded in Love," he stated: "I have always been convinced that what we call 'Devotion to the Sacred Heart' is a symbolic expression of the very basis of the Ignatian spirit, and an extraordinary power— '*ultra quam speraverint*'—both for personal perfection and for apostolic fruitfulness. This conviction is still mine today."[98] He indicated that he had not spoken previously about the devotion because it had aroused certain "allergic reactions" in some quarters, not least due to certain traditional artistic representations of the Sacred Heart. Nevertheless, he had considered it important to share "my deep conviction that all of us, as the Society of Jesus, should reflect and discern before Christ crucified what this devotion has meant for the Society, and what it should mean even today. In today's circumstances, the world offers us challenges and opportunities that can be fully met only with the power of this love of the Heart of Christ."[99]

Fr. Arrupe had the firm conviction that "the Society needs the power (*dynamis*) contained in this symbol and in the reality that it proclaims: the love of the Heart of Christ." In addition he added:

"Perhaps what we need is an act of ecclesial humility, to accept what the Supreme Pontiffs, the General Congregations, and the Generals of the Society have incessantly repeated."[100] He was convinced that a re-appropriation of this devotion to the loving merciful heart of Jesus would lead to widespread spiritual renewal within the Society of Jesus: "Our apostolate would receive new strength and we would see its effects very soon, both in our personal lives and in our apostolic activities."[101] The devotion roots one in the dynamic merciful love of God made manifest in the heart of Jesus and sends one forth to share in the redemptive work of Christ. This work is made effective through the loving mercy and compassion of God.

Fr. Arrupe's conviction is one that Pope Francis seems to share, particularly in the way he extols the devotion as one most significant for popular piety and as having a profundity that contributes to the life of the wider Church. As he indicated in an Angelus address early in his pontificate: "Popular piety highly prizes symbols, and the Heart of Jesus is the ultimate symbol of God's mercy—but it is not an imaginary symbol, it is a real symbol, which represents the center, the source from which salvation for all humanity gushed forth."[102] The heart of Christ not only draws the hearts of believers in a particular practice of devotion but is itself the life-giving center of faith. In his homily for the Jubilee for Priests during the Year of Mercy, which was celebrated on the Feast of the Sacred Heart, Pope Francis spoke of the heart as "the deepest root and foundation of every person, the focus of our affective life and, in a word, his or her very core."[103]

In the heart of Christ, the pope emphasized, we see the most profound expression of the mercy of the Father. The heart of Christ "is not only the Heart that shows us mercy, but *is* itself mercy. There the Father's love shines forth; there I know I am welcomed and understood as I am; there, with all my sins and limitations, I know the certainty that I am chosen and loved."[104] The image of the Sacred Heart expresses the whole of Jesus's life and salvific mission, contained in the image of his heart alive with love. Though the depictions across generations have varied in artistic quality, they have aimed to convey the same central truth of the intimate love of Christ for each human person. The heart of Jesus is, as it were, a "space" for the profound personal exchange of heart speaking to heart that St. Ignatius advocated for retreatants in the Spiritual Exercises.[105] Devotion to the

Sacred Heart can give dynamic witness to the merciful heart of Jesus, a primordial truth integral to the mission of the Church.

In this chapter we have explored the Ignatian influence on Pope Francis's understanding of mercy through the contribution of the Spiritual Exercises. We have considered the operative tool of discernment and how this has affected the way in which the Holy Father leads the Church through a union of guidance and governance attentive to four key principles. Finally in emphasizing this devotion to the heart of Jesus we have seen how this involves participation in the redemptive love of God made real in the person of the Son, Jesus Christ. This focus on the Christology underpinning the reality of mercy is the subject matter of our next chapter.

CHAPTER 3

Specific Christological
Underpinnings of Mercy

Devotion to the Sacred Heart, as indicated in the previous chapter, might well be seen as a pedagogical summary of how the loving mercy of the Father is perfectly revealed in the passion and death of his incarnate Son on the cross for the salvation of humanity. It also reveals the way in which human persons may enter into that mercy through the grace of conversion and a subsequent desire to share with others the same loving mercy and compassion that we ourselves have received. Cardinal Joseph Ratzinger stated:

> In the heart of Jesus, the centre of Christianity is set before us. It expresses everything, all that is genuinely new and revolutionary in the new covenant. This heart calls to our heart.[1] It invites us to step forth out of the futile attempt of self-preservation and, by joining in the task of love by handing ourselves over to him and with him, "to discover the fullness of love which alone is eternity and which alone sustains the world."[2]

The acme of the expression of the Christian faith, Cardinal Ratzinger insisted, lies in the heart of Jesus, as it expresses in human form the divine love of the Trinity that desires the "fullness of love" for all human persons. This assertion resonates with Pope Francis's own identification of the centrality of the heart of Christ in understanding the divine initiative of love as evidenced in the last chapter.[3] It is apparent that once more we may perceive something of the way in which "Pope Benedict, with regard to many questions, theologically prepared the present pontificate to a greater extent than may appear at first glance," as Philip McCosker has said.[4] Also, references from the early fathers of the Church and popes across generations indicate the importance of the heart as the source of love and mercy.[5]

In this chapter I highlight key features of the Christology underpinning Pope Francis's elevation of the discourse on mercy. First there is an ongoing consideration of the importance of the heart of Christ as the revelation of mercy, and here we identify also the influence of Romano Guardini. In the latter's work we may perceive precursors to the concern of both Pope Francis and his predecessor to re-appropriate a culture of encounter with Christ. Then we consider the life of Christ as conveying the message of God's mercy, as well as the exemplarity of the corporal works of mercy. The second half of this chapter indicates the Christology latent within key papal documents, highlighting particularly the importance of mercy in *Evangelii Gaudium*, *Misericordiae Vultus*, and *Misericordia et Misera*.

The Influence of Romano Guardini

Pope Francis's attentiveness to the heart of Christ identifies the heart as the deepest level of interiority and the place of integration within the human person, a perception that owes much to the work of Romano Guardini.[6] The latter understood the heart of the incarnate Christ as both fully human and the perfect expression of God's own heart, such that the renewed heart out of which the believer encounters the world shares in Christ's own heart and is therefore capable of an authentic understanding of the world (*Christliche Weltanschauung*). This *sensus Christi*, which the path of discernment impels us toward, "requires a complete conversion, not only of the will and the deed, but also of the mind," Guardini wrote. "One must cease to judge the Lord from the worldly point of view and learn to accept his own measure of the genuine and the possible; to judge the world with his eyes."[7] It becomes clear that Christ himself is the establisher of all norms: "Once we meet him the only way he can be met, in faith; once we renounce all personal judgement . . . the Son of God and man (who) escapes all categories . . . steps out of eternity, the unknown, an immeasurable Being revealed to us bit by bit through the word of his messengers or through some personal trait."[8] Such a personal engagement with Christ impels us toward a union with the redemptive work of Christ.

It is evident how resonant these words of Guardini are with those at the beginning of the chapter by Cardinal Ratzinger, and there is an echo of the kerygmatic thrust of Pope Francis's words regarding the encounter with Christ. Indeed the idea of encounter appears central throughout *Evangelii Gaudium*. There is a clear intention to stimulate the Church to walk "a path of pastoral and missionary conversion."[9] This path involves a going forth from comfort zones and engaging in encounters, as we have already seen in the previous two chapters.[10] For Pope Francis, "every encounter is fruitful."[11] Thus he invites us to work to ensure a culture of encounter following the example of Jesus, whose actions "truly show the tenderness of an encounter, and not only the tenderness, but the fruitfulness of an encounter. . . . Each encounter returns people and things to their place."[12] This place that Pope Francis speaks of is the dignity of each person as a child of God, "the dignity of living."[13] For this fecundity to be realized it is necessary to move beyond the simple practice of observation to a more profound level of perception in order to build such a culture of encounter.[14] Pope Francis said: "If I do not look— seeing is not enough, no: look—if I do not stop, if I do not look, if I do not touch, if I do not speak, I cannot create an encounter and I cannot help to create a culture of encounter."[15] Indeed, as part of this message for World Communication Day 2017 Pope Francis clearly stated: "I would like to encourage everyone to engage in constructive forms of communication that reject prejudice towards others and foster a culture of encounter, helping all of us to view the world around us with realism and trust."

Such sentiments echo Guardini's understanding of what it means to see the world not in a passive mode of being but with an open readiness to what can be perceived as truth (*wahr-genommen*).[16] Indeed, Guardini understood such a disposition to be among the most original and natural of human attitudes, "the attitudes of being called and of revealing oneself, of listening and of immersing oneself,"[17] and of "encountering."[18] There is a gift dimension to the encounter, as Hans

Urs von Balthasar underlines: "The encounter reveals not only that which is essential and unique but also the mystery, that is, the mystery of 'being there' and 'being thus' (*Dasein* and *Sosein*) existence and essence."[19] This is concretized for Guardini in the unique person of Jesus Christ, who is the ultimate center of his worldview. A constant theme running through his work is that human life becomes meaningful in the encounter with the mystery and person of Jesus. Influenced significantly in his own work by the Franciscan Bonaventure,[20] Guardini brings together Christology and "opposition." He emphasizes how Christ for Bonaventure is "the mediator or *medium*." Because of sin, the distance between Creator and creature has become an opposition, "Gegensatz." God is merciful and so wills reconciliation with creation, and a mediator is needed, so Guardini highlights how for Bonaventure the *medium* "must be between two extremes, is differentiated from both, but is in relation with both and participates in the nature of both and is 'confected' out of both."[21] Christ, as mediator and *medium* between God and humanity, is one person of two natures—the Son and the eternal Father.

It is important to reassert that the differentiated unity of opposites in the two natures of Christ is possible only because of the profound transcendence of the Father, who begets and creates the one person of Christ. In the apostolic exhortation *Evangelii Gaudium*, it is possible to see a not dissimilar theological outworking as the interlocking reality of the form of mercy that is made known in Christ, gives a more profound insight into the loving relations of the Trinity through whom the incarnation was made known, and gives a dynamic impetus for life-giving love and joy to form essential ingredients of active encounters between human persons.[22]

Discipleship for Guardini, involved this personal relationship with Christ: "Individuals come to him, too, men desiring to associate their lives exclusively with his. . . . Thus a community of disciples closely attached to the Master and to his destiny springs up around him."[23] In a not dissimilar manner, Joseph Ratzinger wrote in his *Introduction to Christianity*, "It seems to me that this is the reason for what to other world religions and to the man of today is always completely incomprehensible, namely, that, in Christianity everything hangs in the last resort on one individual, on the man Jesus of Nazareth."[24]

Encountering Christ in Scripture

For Guardini, "the true Jesus is revealed through the apostle, only through him, indeed, through all of them jointly."[25] Therefore, he focuses on the importance of the scriptures and indeed of reading and praying the scriptures to understand the integral unity of the historical Jesus and the Christ of faith. In a not dissimilar manner, Pope Francis emphasized that the entire mission of Jesus Christ was to reveal the mystery of God's merciful love; this informed all his words and deeds. "Everything in him speaks of mercy," he wrote. "Nothing in him is devoid of compassion."[26]

Accordingly, Pope Francis emphasized the importance of reading the gospel because it is "the book of God's mercy to be read and reread, because everything that Jesus said and did is an expression of the Father's mercy."[27] Here we find a singular echo also in Pope Francis's concern to advocate the carrying of a Bible or New Testament to be able to read daily and therefore familiarize oneself with the scriptures. He invited the faithful to carry a pocket-sized gospel all the time. "What would happen if we read the message of God contained in the Bible in the same way we read messages on our cellphone?," he asked the crowd during an Angelus address.[28] He continued by asserting that carrying the gospel also provides a source of positive resistance to temptation: "If we always carried God's word in our hearts, no temptation would distance us from the Father and no obstacle would take us off the path towards good."[29] So convinced was Pope Francis of the importance of reading the scriptures that on occasion he has had copies of the New Testament distributed to pilgrims in St. Peter's Square who have come to participate in his Angelus addresses.[30]

In 2017, when a new youth Bible was published in Germany, Pope Francis wrote the prologue, saying to the young people: "The Bible is not meant to be placed on a shelf, but to be in your hands, to be read often—every day, both on your own and together with others."[31] He encouraged the young people to gather in small groups to read the Bible together, but he asserted that this must not be done in a superficial way: "Read with attention! Do not stay on the surface as if reading a comic book! Never just skim the Word of God!"[32] The pope added that the young people should ask what God says to them through the Bible: "Only in this way can the force of the Word of God unfold. Only in this way can it change our lives, making them great and beautiful."[33] In this manner of re-appropriating the scriptures, Pope Francis's words are reminiscent of Guardini's concern for attending to the Bible with the eyes and ears of faith: "In order to apprehend the Bible's subject matter, i.e., God's word, believers must be disposed to hear it," and they must "interpret the Bible within the church's living tradition."[34] Guardini considered it important to reiterate that although individually we are recipients of God's self-communication, this takes place within the believing community. Accordingly, it is important to give due importance to the Church's interpretation of texts and be guided by it.

ENCOUNTERING CHRIST IN THE EUCHARIST

In a not dissimilar manner, Pope Francis's predecessor, when a student, learned from Guardini that liturgy is the best context within which to understand the Bible as it is the product of the Church celebrating the Eucharist and proclaiming the gospel. As Joseph Ratzinger he wrote: "Church, scripture, and liturgy form one hermeneutic unit."[35] The liturgy is profoundly Christological. In 1918 Guardini published *The Spirit of the Liturgy*, a title that would be used many years later by Joseph Ratzinger in what may be seen as a sequel to Guardini's work. It was the intention of the latter, wrote Emery de Gaál, "to unlock for a large readership the concrete liturgical execution within an overarching anthropological, cultural and philosophical (*kulturphilosophisch*) context."[36] There is a common concern running across both books to emphasize that the acme of the liturgy is grounded in "the transcendent reality of God's free being."[37] The dynamic movement of the liturgy is toward an awareness of the timeless nature (or an encompassing of all time) of what is being celebrated in the free gift of the Being of God, in and through God's Trinitarian being, to the human persons who come to offer "the sacrifice of praise and thanksgiving." No one who has been present at a celebration of the Mass by Pope Francis, or indeed by his predecessor, Pope Benedict XVI, can doubt the integral transcendent awareness in their presiding at the Eucharist.[38] For the faithful privileged to have attended Mass with these two pontiffs, the timeless reality of the movement of the Eucharist, where the present is caught up into the past and oriented to the future in one seamless Trinitarian dynamic, is very evident.[39]

INCARNATION: THE UNVEILING OF DIVINE MERCY

Jesus is "the Incarnation of the mercy of the Father," Pope Francis maintains.[40] Indeed, in *Amoris Laetitia* he asserts: "The Incarnation of the Word in a human family, in Nazareth by its very newness changed the history of the world."[41] Cardinal Walter Kasper, in his book *Mercy*, enunciated a key principle regarding consideration of the incarnation as an epiphany of mercy.[42] "Whatever happens in a particular place and at a particular point of time in history," he wrote, "belongs simultaneously in the complete story of God's dealings with humankind."[43] This is most clearly evinced in the gospel account of the genealogy of Jesus in the Gospel of Matthew, which situates the historicity of the Son of God within the entire history of salvation.

The figure of Zechariah, dramatically silenced for his lack of faith and stunningly eloquent when released from his dumbness, announces "the tender mercy of our God (Luke 1:78),"[44] while Mary's Magnificat makes this poignantly evident when she exclaims: "He has helped his servant Israel, in remembrance of his mercy, as he spoke to our fathers, to Abraham and to his posterity for ever" (Luke 1:54–55). Alongside the joy of this communication and the nativity is the conscious prefiguration of the cross in the flight into Egypt to escape the terrorism of Herod and the massacre of the innocents. The eternal mercy of God irradiates all human categories with the fire of divine love.[45] The word becomes flesh, and there is a "trans-valuation" of human parameters. Two women, one a virgin and the other barren, become pregnant; divine omniscience and omnipotence are expressed in the desire for the salvation of humanity and become manifest in a newborn child; and both poor shepherds and foreign kings come to pay homage.

When Jesus begins his public ministry, he does so calling for repentance in the face of the reality of God's mercy, which extends to all. It is the loving mercy of God that he proclaims in his teaching and his actions, the compassion of God extended to all human persons: the leper (Mark 1:41); the widow who has lost her son (Luke

7:13); the sick (Matt. 14:14); the hungry (Matt. 15:32); the blind (Matt. 20:34); and even the dead (John 11:35, 38). In all of these encounters it is the mercy of the Father that is revealed in the words and actions of the Son. Pope Francis insisted: "The example of Jesus is a paradigm for the Church."[46] He then proceeded to indicate the details of this paradigm in Jesus's public ministry, starting with the first miracle at the wedding feast in Cana (John 2:1–11). He emphasized the importance of pragmatic living in the family and with friends.[47] Jesus was able to identify with grieving parents and even brought children back to life (Mark 5:4; Luke 7:14–15). "In this way," wrote Pope John Paul II, "he demonstrated the true meaning of mercy, which entails the restoration of the covenant."[48] This is clear from his conversations with the Samaritan woman (John 4:4–30) and with the woman found in adultery (John 8:1–11), "where the consciousness of sin is awakened by an encounter with Jesus' gratuitous love."[49]

The Impact of the Parables of Mercy

The mercy of God is pivotal in the message Jesus came to bring, and the parables of Jesus, particularly in the Gospel of Luke, give further evidence of the overwhelming nature of this loving mercy of God. Like all parables, those that deal with forgiveness and the tenderness of God have a certain chutzpah, a parabolic quality that transvalues contemporary culture. In this way, too, they reveal how radical a truth of revelation is mercy and what a challenge and demand Jesus puts before those who would follow him. The parables disconcert the listeners because the situations are resolved in surprising ways that are contrary to what would be expected. It is contrary to normal logic to think that a shepherd would leave a flock open to danger to search for one lost sheep (Luke 15:3–7). It is shocking that a recalcitrant son returning home should be feted (Luke 15:11–32) or that a hated Samaritan should be a compassionate hero (Luke 10:25–37).[50]

The parables of mercy disorient hearers because God's action in them reverses every kind of firm certainty people have and forces them to reconsider their way of thinking about God and of envisioning Jesus. Yet these parables, perhaps the best known, continue to orientate hearts and minds toward a more profound appreciation of the reality of the mercy of the Father that is operative toward human persons. It becomes clear that, as Kasper wrote, "divine mercy gives everyone a new chance and grants everyone a new beginning if he or she is eager for conversion and asks for it."[51] Indeed, Pope Francis wrote, divine mercy involves the lifting of burdens.[52]

It is apparent in the parables, which contain an implicit Christology, that the loving mercy of God supersedes all kin relationships, whether of immediate family, religious, friendship, or ethnic bonds. The loving expression of divine mercy is gauged only according to the reality of human need, and the deepest need is to restore the dignity of each son or daughter of God when it has been lost through sin. The redemptive work of Jesus is to bring us once more into that relationship with God that restores our dignity.[53] In this way Jesus is truly the one who is always for us (*pro nobis*). In this way also, Jesus enables a new beginning for human persons. As the first letter of St. Peter states, he gives us a new birth by his great mercy.[54] This lies at the heart of the mystery of Christ, who in himself inaugurates the kingdom that he proclaims.[55] "The deepest theme of Jesus's preaching was his own mystery, the mystery of the Son, in whom God is among us and keeps his word: he announces the Kingdom of God as coming and as having come in his person."[56]

The Fecundity of the Cross

The pro-existence (a "being for" others) of Jesus, namely that his whole existence is for us and indeed for all, is the meaning of the laying down of his life even unto death—death on a cross (cf. Phil. 2:1–11). It is the ultimate loving action of God's mercy that wills life, not death, and through which God reconciles human persons to Himself, renewing the covenantal relationship. The cost of such salvific action is what Guardini terms "the divine tragedy." He writes: "There are no words for the essence of the divine tragedy whose ultimate expression is Christ on the Cross."[57]

The cross forms the ultimate expression of Jesus's self-disclosure that was made evident in the incarnation. This is why the incarnation is always oriented toward the Passion of Christ.[58] His self-disclosure is the basis, writes de Gaál, for "all the subsequent unfolding moments in Christology."⁵⁹ It is in his dying and rising that we perceive that God's love "is never exhausted and it never gives up," as Pope Francis writes. "There we see his infinite and boundless self-giving."⁶⁰ The very fact of his living from a disposition of loving obedience to the Father reveals the unity of suffering and exaltation in his life. And it is the fact of the redemption that enables all Christians to be able to live in the face of God's mercy without fear. Pope Francis's consistent acknowledgment of this reality echoes that of Pope John Paul II when he stated: "The Redemption pervades all of human history, even before Christ, and prepares its eschatological future. It is the light that "shines in the darkness, and the darkness has not overcome it" (cf. John 1:5). The power of Christ's Cross and Resurrection is greater than any evil which man could or should fear."⁶¹

It is important to have a sense of how the union of our wills with Christ analogously relates to the union of wills between the Son and the Father.⁶² It was the will of the Father that guided the actions of Jesus as a living imperative, constantly enfolding him from moment to moment in each new situation that unfolded. It was also the will of the Father that guided Jesus in the darkness of the Passion, though Jesus's was not coercive obedience but a loving embracing of that common will. In the Garden of Gethsemane, when it seems as though the two wills are sharply distinguished, still there was a free, loving embrace of the agony of the passion, which was the seed ground of salvation.⁶³ We see at work here what Pope Francis calls "a love that bestows itself without limits,"⁶⁴ as well as "a mercy that accepts and forgives everything."⁶⁵ This kind of love is at the heart of the happiness that everyone desires, as the pope indicated in the same address: "It is always a matter of love; there is no other path. The true challenge is that of who loves the most? How many disabled and suffering persons open their hearts to life again as soon as they realize they are loved!"⁶⁶ He stressed the importance of recognizing both the small acts of love, such as even a smile, and also the reality of our own limitations, and he emphasized this: "The way we experience illness and disability is an index of the love we are ready to offer. The way we face suffering and limitation is the measure of our freedom to give meaning to life's experiences, even when they strike us as meaningless and unmerited."⁶⁷ A loving disposition enables a loving response both in the smallest of positive actions and in the face of grave suffering.

Mercy, Justice, and Atonement

This section could be a complete monograph in itself, yet it is important to reflect, even if only briefly, on terms that are so crucial to a more profound understanding of mercy and to indicate where there are deep ontological roots in common between justice and mercy. According to Aquinas, mercy is the presupposition of justice; "mercy is the primordial root (*prima* radix) and the prior reality, to which everything else is referred."[68] Although it is apparent that Pope Francis has made mercy a pastoral reality, this is not at the expense of doctrinal understanding. He is concerned to emphasize that there is not a contradiction between justice and mercy but that both are integrally related.[69] Another time he said: "Sacred Scripture presents God to us as infinite mercy and as perfect justice. How do we reconcile the two? How does one reconcile the reality of mercy with the demands of justice? It might appear that the two contradict each other; but in fact it is not so, for it is the very mercy of God that brings true justice to fulfilment."[70]

For Pope Francis, justice and mercy are not contradictory realities but rather two dimensions of a single reality, one that "unfolds progressively until it culminates in the fullness of love."[71] He sees mercy as the fundamental aspect of the mission of Jesus, which, of its nature, then challenges those who would limit themselves to the formal observance of the law. It is the willingness of Jesus to go beyond the law and to keep company with those considered sinners that reveals the depths of his mercy. Accordingly, Pope Francis reiterates that mercy is not opposed to justice but is the very way that God reaches out to sinners, calling them to conversion and belief. In doing so, God does not deny justice, but rather "envelops it and surpasses it with an even greater event in which we experience love as the foundation of true justice."[72] The pope reiterates that "mere justice is not enough. Experience shows that an appeal to justice alone will result in its destruction. This is why God goes beyond justice with his mercy and forgiveness. Yet this does not mean that justice should be devalued or rendered superfluous."[73] There is an enormous disproportion between the self-giving, merciful love of God by which we are redeemed and the reality of what we deserve as the result of our actions. Yet "God believes in us, infinitely beyond our merits any merits that we have."[74] Indeed, "no human efforts, however good they may be, can enable us to merit so great a gift as salvation given through God's mercy."[75] It is by the sheer grace of God that we are made one with him.

Pope Benedict was likewise concerned to emphasize that in exercising mercy God always wants to serve the cause of justice as well.[76] At the heart of the common understanding of Popes Benedict and Francis is the recognition that "only where there is mercy does cruelty end, only with mercy do evil and violence end."[77] Pope Benedict stated that "it is mercy that moves us towards God, while justice frightens us before him."[78] Yet, as the biblical writers assert, the wages of sin are death, underlining the depth and gravity of sin and its destructive effects at all levels of the human being; it also becomes clear that God alone can deliver us from such adversity. By the common will of the Father and the Son on the cross, Kasper writes: God "takes the life-destroying effects of sin upon himself in order to bestow upon us, life anew."[79] Here once more there is resonance with the thought of Romano Guardini, who was concerned to emphasize that "the justice of God means that He fulfills His promise to man, and the justice of man consists in placing himself within the covenant, seeking God's kingdom first, putting it before all else, and trusting God's holy guidance."[80] Accordingly, there is still a need for a human to freely respond to this gift of salvation through conversion, repentance, and openness to the guidance of the Holy Spirit.[81]

THE THEOLOGY OF THE CROSS AND JUSTIFICATION BY FAITH

It is St. Paul who issues the cri de coeur that he desired to know nothing except Christ crucified.[82] This theology of the cross is co-inherent with the doctrine of the resurrection. The latter underlines the glory and the victory of the former. It is the one movement of God's mercy, just as in liturgical terms we speak of the liturgy of the Easter Triduum as being part of a greater liturgy that extends from Holy Thursday through the Easter Vigil. This salvific action restores the freedom of the children of God, not a freedom that is mere arbitrariness. Rather, it is a freedom from the impossibility of fulfilling the law by our own efforts and from the weight of sin, from which we can never release ourselves. There is no way in which we can justify ourselves.[83] It is thus a threefold freedom: a freedom from all that would make us cling to any worldly thing or person as we seek to justify ourselves; a freedom to be open to God and others as we look way beyond the confines of individual ego; and a freedom to relate all things to God in the manner of discipleship and mission as we live out the paschal mystery in our own lives.

The gospel comes to its fullest fruition in and through the paschal mystery. It opens the possibility of a righteousness based on faith in Christ, since God's justice has been shown to be not a punitive justice for the reality of sin but a justice that, in and through the death and resurrection of Christ, justifies the sinner who believes and comes to conversion. As Pope Francis stated, "God's justice is his mercy given to everyone as a grace that flows from the death and resurrection of Jesus Christ. Thus the Cross of Christ is God's judgement on all of us and on the whole world, because through it he offers us the certitude of love and new life."[84] It is the work of divine grace. As the pope once said, "Contemplating the Crucified One with the eyes of faith, we can understand in depth what sin is, how tragic is its gravity, and at the same time, how immense is the Lord's power of forgiveness and mercy."[85]

Pope Emeritus Benedict has stated that he believes that in the theme of divine mercy is expressed in a new way what is meant by justification by faith: "Starting from the mercy of God, which everyone is looking for, it is possible even today to interpret anew the fundamental nucleus of the doctrine of justification and have it appear again in all its relevance."[86] He raised the difficulty that contemporary twenty-first-century human persons have with the expression of Anselm, who asserted the necessity of Christ's death "to repair the infinite offense that had been made to God, and in this way to restore the shattered order."[87] The pontiff emeritus understands that such an expression is in a language incomprehensible to contemporary ears. In addition, it can potentially project an image of a God of wrath who is violent and aggressive. The difficulty is how to speak of the justice of God without undermining the profound reality that the Christian God is compassionate and merciful—rich in mercy.

It is the task of contemporary theologians, Benedict believes, to try to understand the truth underlying "the conceptuality of St. Anselm [which] has now become for us incomprehensible."[88] The focus on a substitutionary atonement of earlier times—when the Church fathers spoke often of a sacred exchange (*sacrum commercium*)[89]—has been used in recent years as an argument against Christianity. In response to this, proponents of a certain liberal theology have tried to replace substitutionary atonement with the notion of the solidarity of Jesus with all human persons. This, however, does not appear to be congruent with the forcefulness of the biblical testimony to the gravity of sin and its death-dealing consequences.[90]

Pope Benedict offered three measures to assist us in this task of making more comprehensible the relationship of justice and mercy. The first was to clarify the false dichotomy of the Father who insists on an absolute standard of justice and the Son who obediently accepts the cruel demands of justice. The pope emeritus underlined that not only is this incomprehensible in our day but that it is also erroneous from the point of Trinitarian theology.[91] The wills of Father and Son are intrinsically one since they are united in one God. What might seem to be a struggle of wills, as indicated in the gospel accounts of the agony in the garden of Gethsemane, "is not a matter of [the Son's] accepting for himself a cruel disposition of God, but rather of attracting humanity into the very will of God."[92] Within Jesus Christ divinity and humanity are united in one person who, in the garden, commits himself anew to the redemptive work of God.

Realizing the oneness of will in God leads to the second consideration, namely, a consideration of why the cross and the atonement were necessary. Here twenty-first-century human beings realize only too vividly the proliferation of evil, violence, hatred, and arrogant cruelty in the world. Such a "mass of evil," to use Augustine's term,[93] cannot simply be ignored or declared non-existent; rather, it needs to be overcome and cleansed from human reality. The Israelites believed that their daily sacrifices for sins, in particular those on the Day of Atonement, were necessary as counterweights to the evil they perceived in the world and in themselves.

Christians understood that, as Pope Benedict said, "the temple destroyed was replaced by the resurrected body of the crucified Lord and in his radical and incommensurable love was created a counterweight to the immeasurable presence of evil."[94] Indeed, this was the only genuine counterweight, which had been prefigured in the cult of temple sacrifice, because in the face of "the excessive power of evil only an infinite love was enough, only an infinite atonement."[95] It is only the power of the crucified, risen Lord that can counter the power of evil and save humanity. In the strength of this understanding, Christians came also to understand their own sufferings as conjoined to the suffering of Christ and thereby, through the gracious invitation of God, part of the redemptive work of Christ and the redemptive power of divine love. It is only Christ, through his incarnation and passion, coming to share in the world's sufferings, who can redeem the world.

Having articulated these first two points, the relationship between Father and Son becomes more comprehensible and we move to the last consideration raised by Pope Emeritus Benedict. Here a meditation from the second week of the Spiritual Exercises may assist us. It is the meditation on the incarnation, at the start of which Ignatius asks the one praying to imagine the Trinity in dialogue, observing the many facets of humanity: joy, suffering, new life, death, violence— the whole gamut of human existence. The conversation of the Trinity is centered on the Son's incarnation, through which he came to share the reality of human life and the suffering involved. The dynamic impetus for the word becoming flesh was the passionate love of God for human persons. This is encapsulated in the wisdom corpus, where we find this: "When peaceful silence lay over all, and night had run the half of her swift course, down from the heavens, from the royal throne, leapt your all-powerful word" (Wis. 18:14–15). This passage contains a dynamism that reveals the divine word impelled by the passionate love of God to become one with human persons.

Henri de Lubac reflected on this reality and asserted in more moderate terms: "The Redeemer came into the world out of compassion for mankind. He took upon himself our passions even before being crucified, indeed even before descending to assume our flesh: if he had not experienced them beforehand, he would not have come to partake of our human life."[96] This raises the question as to what this suffering was that Christ endured in advance for us. De Lubac's response is to assert that it was the passion of love, which overflowed Jesus in mercy and compassion.[97]

The Father, as Father, shares inwardly in the sufferings of the Son. This indicates also a more profound perception of what the mercy of

God means, involving, as it does, the participation of God in human suffering. This is not to deny either the immutability or the omnipotence of God; rather, it is to say, as Kierkegaard asserts, that the omnipotence of love involves allowing oneself to be affected by suffering without being under its control.[98] A medieval image that visually portrays this is the depiction of the "throne of grace,"[99] where the Father supports the cross and Jesus crucified, lovingly bending over him, so that, as Pope Benedict stated, "the two are, as it were, together on the cross."[100] Ultimately such statements and images serve to illuminate what Benedict calls "the truth and the reality of creation: the true intimate overcoming of evil that ultimately can be realized only in the suffering of love."[101] This is an echo of a similar thought that Pope Benedict clarified in his encyclical *Spe Salvi*: "Man is worth so much to God that he himself became man in order to *suffer with* man. . . . Hence in all human suffering we are joined by one who experiences and carries that suffering *with* us; hence *consolatio* is present in all suffering, the consolation of God's compassionate love—and so the star of hope arises."[102] In divine freedom God allows himself to be affected by human pain and suffering.[103]

VICARIOUS SUBSTITUTION

It is that same divine-human love of Jesus Christ that is always greater than any possible power of evil. As Pope Benedict said: "Christ's mercy is not a grace that comes cheap, nor does it imply the trivialization of evil."[104] Recognition of this reality prompts us to reflect further on the concept of vicarious substitution, not in an abstract manner but as a compelling dynamic. In this way the manner of Christ's pro-existence (a "being for" others) is also an expression of what is fundamental for the Church and all Christian life. We are called to live in such a way that the orientation of our lives is a being for others in service, particularly to the poorest, who receive so little genuine loving and merciful service.

Pope Benedict indicated: "It is true that the problem [of being for others] is not fully resolved, but it seems to me that this, in fact, is the key insight that thus impacts the existence of the individual Christian."[105] Then the pope turned his attention to Christ: "Christ, as the unique One, was and is for all Christians, who in Paul's awesome imagery make up Christ's body in the world and thus participate in this 'being-for.'"[106] This understanding of Christ, then, impacts our understanding of the manner of our being in the world. Benedict continued: "Christians, so to speak, are not so for themselves, but are, with Christ, for others. This does not mean having some sort of special ticket for entering into eternal happiness, but rather the vocation to build the whole."[107]

Having indicated the wider horizon, the big picture of our calling, Pope Benedict indicated the means we might use for this purpose: "What the human person needs in order to be saved is a profound openness with regards to God, a profound expectation and acceptance of Him, and this correspondingly means that we, together with the Lord whom we have encountered, go towards others and seek to make visible to them the advent of God in Christ."[108] Accordingly, the Holy Father clarified the process whereby we are both made deeply aware of the mission of Christ in this world and the call to those who are his disciples and form his body to take their part, individually and collectively, in serving the world community. In this process the cross will always be the final hermeneutic that marks our living and our service, and here the profound hymn of Philippians 2:1–12 identifies the reality of divine *kenosis*, which will be the consideration of the next chapter.

Latent Christology and Christ-Centered Mercy in Papal Documents

It would be accurate to state that the Church's teachings and pastoral outreach have always been Christocentric, but in recent times this has become more prominent so that it is possible to detect the Christology latent in papal documents. Laurent Touze maintains that there is a common thread of Christ-centered mercy that unites

> the proclamation of the Heart of Jesus, fundamental to the papal magisterium of the late 19th century up to the 1950's; the proclamation of the kingdom of Christ, which Pope Pius XI particularly cherished; the proposals regarding the Christian mystery

that the two popes who presided over the Second Vatican Council sought to put forth in patience and in dialogue; the "civilization of love" that Blessed Paul VI preached; charity, which Pope Benedict XVI highlighted; and mercy, which Popes John Paul II and Francis have proclaimed in a very direct way.[109]

Space does not permit a comprehensive coverage of all such documents, and in chapter 1 I indicated significant areas of continuity between the pontificates of John Paul II, Benedict XVI, and Francis in this area of mercy.

Accordingly, we shall focus on the documents of the papacy of Pope Francis. Nevertheless, it is important to highlight certain insights from Pope Paul VI that are reflected in the writings of Pope Francis. In particular, the latter emphasizes that the history of salvation is that of the encounter of man's *misery* with God's *mercy*. The apostolic letter that Pope Francis wrote for the end of the Jubilee Year of Mercy got its name from this idea, *Misera et Misericordia*. This references an insight from St. Augustine when he was commenting on Jesus's meeting with the woman taken in adultery in John 8:1–11: *Ramansit misera et Misericordia*.[110] Pope Paul VI commented: "St. Augustine provides us with a formula, which is not only a formula in words, but a formula that is a human and theological reality encapsulated in two challenging words: misery and mercy. When we say misery, we are speaking about sin, the human tragedy that unfolds throughout the history of evil, that abyss of darkness that leads to horrendous ruin."[111] This state, however, is not the truth of human existence, the pontiff asserted. He continued: "Another truth emerges; another fate is reserved for man in order to attain the gratuitous, powerful, and mysterious plan of God's mercy. Divine mercy comes to rescue man from his misery."[112] In an earlier catechesis at a general audience, Pope Paul had emphasized that redemption presupposes, "or rather demands, a plan for divine mercy that is divinely restorative."[113]

It is time to turn to three significant documents of Pope Francis's papacy (*Evangelii Gaudium; Misericordiae Vultus*, and *Misericordia et misera*) that exemplify the Christological lynchpins that are consistently present in his witness to mercy in the written word, his homilies, and indeed his interventions on social media.

The Christology of Evangelii Gaudium

The very title of the apostolic exhortation—*Evangelii Gaudium: The Joy of the Gospel*—is clearly focused for Pope Francis on the person of Christ, who is our joy.[114] It is that encounter with Christ, so pertinently delineated in chapter 1, which is the impetus for Christian joy. The pope wrote: "Jesus Christ is the face of the Father's mercy. These words might well sum up the mystery of the Christian faith. . . . Jesus of Nazareth, by his words, his actions, and his entire person reveals the mercy of God."[115] In another encyclical he wrote: "It is this same Jesus who by his death and resurrection reveals and communicates to us the Father's infinite mercy."[116] Here, the pontiff makes a clear statement of the integral relationship between the person and the work of Christ. Thus we see once more that the incarnation and the passion are inextricably linked, that Christology and soteriology are inseparable in Pope Francis's understanding of Christ. This also enables us to understand more clearly his emphasis on "encounter," which we saw in earlier chapters. By becoming incarnate, God prioritizes the reality of encounter. It is the person-to-person or rather heart-to-heart encounter with Christ that affects all our encounters with other people. Indeed, it is to a renewal of relationships that the Pope looks,[117] a renewal that of its very nature enables persons to refrain from gossiping about others (conduct much deplored by Pope Francis) and instead inspires relationships that support and encourage others.

Here Pope Francis sees a valuable aid in popular piety, which is at one and the same time both incarnational and relational. He emphasizes the importance of the concrete encounter with Christ, which leads to transformation, not a theoretical encounter that remains both cerebral and vacuous. In this way, McCosker writes, "Christology is key for Christian witness and action."[118] It is not that Pope Francis desires to undermine the importance of the intellect. Reason has a part to play in understanding, but the encounter with Christ transforms the whole person, not only the mind. Since the whole human person—body, mind, and spirit—are subject to this transformation, then, the response is also one of the whole person in interaction with others. Such interaction is not superficial but calls for a more profound exchange, given significant stimulus through the original encounter with Christ. This is an endless dynamic rooted in the eternal grace of mercy.

So we return once more to the key principles that Pope Francis proposes toward the end of *Evangelii Gaudium*. The first, as indicated in the previous paragraph, is the importance of concrete reality rather than ideas.[119] To recall the others: "time is greater than space"; "unity prevails over conflict"; and "the whole is greater than the part."[120] McCosker sees these principles as "different ways of thinking through different aspects of differentiated unities."[121] He emphasizes holding together *both* difference *and* unity. My own sense is that it is a more profound tension that looks not at *both/and* or even—in my post–Vatican II preference—*together/with*, but rather at a fundamental co-inherence of difference and unity; thus unity in diversity emerges from this deeper platform of grounded integrity in Christ. In this light, Pope Francis links his interpretation of these principles to Christology.

Accordingly, the pope envisages time as being greater than space in the position of human persons held in the tension of the temporal specificity of space and oriented to the eternal infinity of realized eschatology. In other words, we live in a particular time and space, and yet we are oriented to something beyond ourselves, namely, the eternity of God.[122] Such a perspective, which has one eye on the present historicity and the other on the eternal beatitude, McCosker helpfully designates as stereoscopic. I would suggest, however, that this perspective is beyond a normal sight that is able to perceive three-dimensionally and therefore sees at greater depth. I would suggest that stereoscopic vision and perspective is again a more co-inherent relationship, and I would thus propose the graphic image of interrelating myopia and hyperopia such that relating to the immediacy of what is seen in the fullness of temporal short-sightedness is integral to the fullness of perception of long-sightedness. This image emphasizes the ongoing tension in a way that a stereoscopic perspective seems to resolve. The outcome of such tension and vision is that the ordinary becomes extraordinary as the epiphany of the eternal is perceived within the temporal. Such a perspective impels us toward further encounters both with Christ and then, from that fundamental encounter, to engage with the reconciling work of Christ in ongoing human encounters.

The penultimate principle that unity prevails over conflict underlines the unity of all things in Christ and the peace that he brings. Indeed it is the work of the Holy Spirit[123]—whom Christ promises in the Johannine last supper discourse (John 14–17)—who brings this depth of peace, who, Francis wrote, "overcomes every conflict by creating a new and promising synthesis."[124] This is not a superficial synthesis but rather an engaged dialogue facing the reality of tensions at the heart of human dialogue without a false resolution but rather seeing that "conflicts, tensions [and] oppositions can achieve a diversified and life-giving unity."[125] It is commitment to ensuring the engaged communication in listening and speaking that is at the heart of true encounter that enables the possibility of such unity.

Finally, the principle that the whole is greater than any part assists a perspective beyond the parochial to a larger vision.[126] Once more it is important for Pope Francis to maintain the tensions of these two different perspectives, as the narrowness of parochialism can foster a detachment from global affairs and the vast numbers of other members of the human family. By contrast, it is possible to become overwhelmed by the global perspective and lose sight of the fact that we are the providence of God where we are located, if we are open to daily encounter.[127] It is at this point that Pope Francis introduces his comparison between a sphere and a polyhedron.[128] The possibilities of the latter figure are innumerable, as they include not just surface recognition but the many-sided three-dimensional possibilities poised in the light reflected and refracted at many different levels. To concretize the image we might just consider the way in which light strikes the many different surfaces of a diamond, which make up the one precious jewel. Ultimately all this diversity is reconciled in Christ, not in a form of syncretism or absorption but rather in an inclusivity that can bear the weight of diversity and tension in a life-giving unity.[129] Such a recapitulation of all in Christ ensures a dynamic newness—a message of deep inner peace, joy, and hope—emerging from this infinite source of mercy, which is the Trinitarian life of Father, Son, and Spirit. This message stands in real contradistinction to a world that has lost both joy and hope and often appears self-constricted.

*The Resurrection of Christ as the Stimulus
for the Mission of Mercy*

In his homily for Easter Sunday 2017 Pope Francis emphasized how important the resurrection was for the Church both as a witness to the veracity of the person and work of Christ and as a stimulus for the mission of mercy that the risen Jesus transmitted to his Church as her first and primordial task. It was to ensure that all should hear "the concrete proclamation of forgiveness."[130] In the radiance that issues forth from the Easter proclamation, Pope Francis insisted, "mercy is perceived as a *true form of knowledge.*"[131] It was a novel proposition that the importance of asserting that mercy is not just a passive reality that is received by faith but is also itself a true form of knowledge.[132]

The pope indicated the many different forms of knowledge that are open to us through our senses, by the use of reason, and by recognizing a certain intuition. Clearly this was not an exhaustive list, but Pope Francis was also concerned to assert that "one can also know through the experience of mercy, because mercy opens the *door of the mind* to understand better the mystery of God and of our personal existence."[133] In other words, our experience of mercy is at the heart of our encounter with God and therefore enables our intellect to have a deeper sense of the profound mystery that is God. In addition, the pope continued, mercy gives us greater insight into the human condition, particularly those emotions and affections that are contrary to our deepest humanity: "Mercy makes us understand that violence, rancor, vengeance make no sense, and the first victim is the one who lives these sentiments, because he deprives himself of his dignity."[134] The dignity intrinsic to each human person is so profoundly at the heart of all human experience that in denigrating the dignity of another we have already undermined the very existence of that dignity within ourselves.

Not only does the experience of mercy draw us to a deeper encounter with God and a more perceptive understanding of what undermines the dignity of a human person; it also enables a compassionate reaching out to others, especially the poorest and those most in need: "Mercy also opens the *door of the heart* and enables us to express closeness especially to all those who are alone and marginalized, because it makes them feel brothers and children of one

Father. It fosters the recognition of all those in need of consolation and makes us find the appropriate words to give them comfort."[135] Finally, Pope Francis emphasized how the experience of mercy has a transformative effect on the human person, enabling a common sharing reminiscent of the early Christians, and promotes the mission of justice, peace, and reconciliation to which all Christians are invited. He continued: "Let us never forget that mercy is the turnkey in the life of faith, and the concrete way with which we give visibility to Jesus' resurrection."[136]

The Christology Embedded in Misericordiae Vultus

Pope Francis begins this document inaugurating the Jubilee of Mercy with the definitive statement that "Jesus Christ is the face of the Father's mercy . . . [who] by his words, his actions and his entire person reveals the mercy of God."[137] Indeed, the pope makes it explicit that he understands mercy as being the word that gives a deeper revelation of the life of the Trinity.[138] He entrusted the life of the Church, all humanity, and even the whole cosmos to the Lordship of Christ, "asking him to pour out his mercy upon us like the morning dew."[139] Pope Francis sees the very institution of the Eucharist and the passion and death of Jesus as irradiated by the light of God's mercy: "Everything in him speaks of mercy. Nothing in him is devoid of compassion."[140]

It is from this stance of mercy that the Pope understands Jesus to read the hearts of those who came to him; that he forgave sins; that he looked upon all people. In his reading of the gospels Pope Francis sees that "mercy is presented as a force that overcomes everything, filling the heart with love and bringing consolation through pardon."[141] He asserts that Jesus made mercy a criterion for the credibility of faith and recalls what he wrote in Evangelii Gaudium, that the Church "has an endless desire to show mercy" because it is "the fruit of its own experience of the power of the Father's infinite mercy."[142] He recalls Pope St. John Paul II's sense of obligation, which he expressed thus: "The mystery of Christ . . . obliges me to proclaim mercy as God's merciful love, revealed in that same mystery of Christ."[143] Such a proclamation is of even greater importance in the face of a culture that appears to have forgotten any understanding of the reality of mercy, as Pope John Paul II reminded us: "The present-day mentality, more perhaps than that of people in the past, seems opposed to a God of mercy, and in fact tends to exclude from life and to remove from the human heart the very idea of mercy."[144]

The Christology in Misericordia et Misera

Misericordia et Misera was the document that concluded the Extraordinary Jubilee of Mercy and inaugurated the ongoing mission of mercy. The Christological stage is set from the very beginning of this document, where Jesus is identified as mercy in the scene in John's gospel where he is facing the woman taken in adultery, who is designated as the face of misery, placed as she is before all those who condemn her (John 8:1–11). The setting has an epiphanic quality, as the person and work of Christ are revealed, Pope Francis says, in the "love of God which is capable of looking into the heart of each person and seeing the deepest desire hidden there."[145] It is God's love made manifest in Jesus that has primacy in the scene as the sinner stands in the presence of her Savior and "the misery of sin is clothed with the mercy of love."[146] The woman leaves with a sense of forgiveness and, as Pope Francis asserts, "Forgiveness is the most visible sign of the Father's love, which Jesus sought to reveal by his entire life."[147] The entire life of Christ evinces this dynamic love that manifests itself most particularly in the forgiveness of sin. Even on the cross, Jesus forgives, and asks the Father's forgiveness for, all involved in his passion and death.[148]

This reality of forgiveness is the gratuitous unmerited act of the Father's love made manifest in the Son.[149] It is the imperative of the incarnation and the salvific consequence of the cross. It has the power to transform human persons and radically change lives,[150] to bring a life-giving joy that radiates from the forgiven sinner to all with whom they come into contact, and thus to empower human persons to become themselves instruments of mercy and bearers of joy. "The joy of forgiveness is inexpressible,"[151] Pope Francis asserted, but it is a source of illumination; it is recognized when experienced and overflows to others who are attracted by it. This joy is something the Holy Father insists needs to be conserved in the light of the difficulties of life. On a number of occasions he has stated that it is important not to allow ourselves to be robbed of this joy.[152] It is the very experience of mercy that brings such joy and can enable a profound serenity of spirit when dealing with the pragmatic events of life.[153] Pope Francis emphasizes that this spirit of joy is accompanied by the virtue of hope, and hope and joy are important witnesses in a world where loneliness and emptiness appear to prevail for so many people. He writes: "We need to acknowledge the joy that rises up in a heart touched by mercy."[154]

It is in the references to the Eucharistic celebration that the Christology of *Misericordia et Misera* finds a pragmatic focus.[155] Within the Eucharist, the pope states, we are called to celebrate the mercy of God, and mercy is a theme throughout the celebration, from the penitential rite onward. Indeed, the term is repeatedly invoked. In the liturgy of the Eucharist we find explicitly Christological references as the priest proclaims: "For you so loved the world that in your mercy you sent us the Redeemer, to live like us in all things but sin."[156] The culmination of the liturgy is the offering of the Eucharistic sacrifice, the reality of the paschal mystery that is the essential source of salvation for all humanity. In its timelessness the celebration of the Eucharist embraces history, the present and the future in one infinite celebration in which each moment references the reality of God's mercy. Included in this trajectory of mercy is the liturgy of the word, the proclamation of Scripture, and the preaching of a homily. Pope Francis was concerned to emphasize that Christ continues to speak through the word of scripture that is broken open by the homilist and also in the sacramental life of the Church.

In particular, the sacrament of penance and reconciliation makes present for human persons the personal appropriation of Christ's salvific action in their lives.[157] In *Misericordia et Misera* Pope Francis explicitly calls for a renewed appreciation of the sacrament of reconciliation. Indeed, he states, "The Sacrament of Reconciliation must regain its central place in the Christian life."[158] The Holy Father has been consistent throughout his papacy in calling members of the Church to return to the practice of confession and calling priests to exercise this ministry more generously,[159] in the spirit of Christ himself, whom they represent in the administration of the sacrament.[160] Any true appreciation of the paschal mystery calls a person to conversion. Conversion is brought to fruition through a call from Jesus. It is not a monologue but a dialogue between the individual and Christ. This is what takes place in a fruitful engagement with the sacrament of reconciliation. As Balthasar writes, "Conversion is of necessity an individual process and yet it is also situated within the larger drama of redemption.[161] It is focused in a dialogue between God and human persons where the entire Trinity is involved, where infinite and finite freedom are engaged, and where the role of the Church is made manifest."[162] Such conversion deeply recognizes that Christ is "the radiant face of the Father's mercy" and leads to a participation in the redemptive work of Christ through a sharing of mercy and a cultivation of a culture of mercy.

Pope Francis insisted, "We are called to promote a *culture of mercy* based on the rediscovery of encounter with others, a culture in which no one looks at another with indifference or turns away from the suffering of our brothers and sisters." These encounters with others are all unique, and thus "*the works of mercy are 'handcrafted'*" in the sense that none of them are alike. Our hands can craft them in a thousand different ways, and even though the one God inspires them and they are all fashioned from the same "material," mercy itself, each one takes on a different form."[163] Yet each one is a sharing in the experience of the poorest; in this way it is a true imitation of Christ. The cross is the most profound revelation of how Jesus shared the experience of those who have been stripped of their dignity and who lack the necessities of life.[164] God in Christ allows himself in divine freedom to be affected by pain and suffering. This recognition is rooted in the love of God made visible in the incarnation, which involved the kenosis of the Son, which, as Hans Urs von Balthasar insisted, revealed the kenotic event at the heart of the Trinity and the self-gift of loving mercy that infuses Trinitarian relations and that our next chapter will explore.

CHAPTER 4

The Trinitarian Horizon

As Pope Francis writes, "With our eyes fixed on Jesus and his merciful gaze, we experience the love of the Most Holy Trinity."[1] Within the theme of mercy it is possible to see the profound co-inherence of distinct parts of theology—Christology, Trinity, and ecclesiology—into an organic whole. One way of undertaking this is to explore mercy in dialogue with Hans Urs von Balthasar's understanding of kenosis and the kenotic event within the Trinity.[2] We can consider Balthasar's thinking as a radicalization of the more traditional language of "self-gift" in the Trinity. The Father "has" nothing apart from what he "is," so his gift to the Son is an act of total "self-expropriation." The Son is the perfect image of the Father, who returns the Father's self-gift in an act of thanksgiving that likewise involves his whole self. And the Spirit is the fruitfulness of this mutual gift that always exceeds and overflows both, so much so that it is not only object but also its own subject vis-à-vis the others.

God is not merely another ontic being whose positive attributes exist only relative to their negations; we might think of Cusanus's notion of God as *non aliud* (not other) when Balthasar writes, after the manner of F. Ulrich, that "in God, poverty and wealth (that is, wealth of giving) are one and the same."[3] There is, then, a primal or *supra*-kenosis within the Trinity that encompasses God's various economic acts of kenosis, from creation itself to covenant to the incarnation, and above all to the cross of Christ. If the Trinitarian context of the cross is overlooked, we fail to see the deeper significance of divine mercy. In this case any analysis of the cross cannot help but degenerate into an interpretation of the individual existence of Jesus. In such a misinterpretation, the Christological and soteriological dimensions of the cross are misconstrued in an abstract transcendentalism. In such an interpretation, the absolute uniqueness of the kenosis of Christ is also lost.[4]

Christ is the love of the Triune God made manifest. It is Christ who reveals to us, in all its fullness, the inner workings of the Trinitarian mystery of mercy and calls us to participate in it. As the Bible tells us, "No one knows the Father except the Son and any one to whom the Son chooses to reveal him" (Matt. 11:27). It is he who speaks of the co-existence of the Holy Spirit with the Father, and who sends him to the Church to sanctify it by his loving mercy until the end of time; and he it is who reveals to us the perfect oneness of life of the three divine persons (cf. John 16:12–15). The Father eternally engenders the Son, and the Father and the Son together eternally breathe forth the Holy Spirit.[5]

Balthasar's *Theo-Logic* helps us to understand this dynamic when he emphasizes the gift of the Son, Christ's gift of Himself to the end, as a form of exposition—almost like a biblical exegesis—of the loving compassion of the Father for the world.[6] In this way it takes up the Johannine emphasis on "truth" that is so evident in the high priestly prayer in chapters 14 to 17 of John's gospel. As Juan Sara indicates, Christ himself is truth, "logical form as plenitude and, for the same reason, covenant: in him, the whole of the Father's love is exposited in the whole incarnate Son in and for the whole world by the Spirit."[7] Christ said of himself that to have seen him was to have seen the Father. Sara unpacks this in terms of the Spirit's being "the exegete of the Son's exegesis of the Father."[8] The Holy Spirit helps us to understand the profundity of Christ's words and witness, and in understanding this we are brought to glimpse something of the merciful reality of the Father.

The desire of the persons of the Trinity is, in loving mercy, to bring us into the life of God. In the utter fullness of his self-giving merciful love to the end, Christ is raised from the dead, from hell, and in that very moment, "the Spirit both seals Christ's exposition of the Father's love and unfolds its riches with creative fidelity as the *Spiritus Creator*. Only then is the Spirit made free to exegete Christ's exegesis of the Father in our hearts—the plenitude of truth is achieved and the New Covenant sealed."[9] If one may make an imaginative leap, to see the joy of the Spirit enables us to be drawn ever deeper into relationship with the Father. In the relationship with the Father, we re-realize our relationship with Son and Spirit, and so the life of the Trinity flows in and through us.

Balthasar, Sara writes, "highlights how the descent of the Son is an act of Trinitarian love that goes to the end, and in so doing reveals the absoluteness of divine love, whether in aesthetic, dramatic or logical form. Holy Saturday, the extreme point of the Son's descent is like a sealed center of the form of revelation."[10] From the reality of the divine mercy and love expressed in the events of Holy Saturday all other manifestations of divine love are enhanced. The full humanity of Christ is revealed in his self-giving, which gathers the whole of creation into the body of Christ. So the Son becomes the one mediator and reconciler in the Trinity's redemptive mission of mercy for the salvation of the world.[11]

It is in the kenosis of Christ, in his abasement and exaltation, the two-fold action as recounted in Philippians 2,[12] that we see the one mission evident in Christ that encompasses this two-fold movement. Karl Barth captured this in his statement that "[Christ's] single work which must not be parceled out into different stages or times in his existence, but which in this two-fold form, fills and constitutes, rather his *entire* existence."[13] A series of questions by Balthasar helps to clarify this point for us. He stresses the co-inherence of humiliation and exaltation in Christ in his mission of mercy: "Where and when is he not both the humiliated One and the exalted One: already exalted even in his humiliation, and still the humiliated One even in his exaltation?"[14]

THE KENOTIC EVENT IN THE TRINITY

For Balthasar, however, to understand kenosis only in Christological terms is insufficient. He calls us to see that the theological meaning of kenosis is more properly grounded in a Trinitarian understanding. "We spoke of a first kenosis of the Father, expropriating himself by 'generating' the consubstantial Son. Almost automatically, this first kenosis expands to a kenosis involving the whole Trinity." This is because "the Son could not be consubstantial with the Father except by self-expropriation; and their 'We' that is, the Spirit must also be God if he is to be the 'personal' seal of that self-expropriation that is identical in Father and Son." He continues "For the Spirit does not want anything 'for himself' but, as his revelation in the world shows, wants simply to be the pure manifestation and communication of the love between Father and Son. This primal *kenosis* makes possible all other kenotic movements of God in the world; they are simply its consequences."[15]

Balthasar understands the Trinity to be an event of kenotic love, as the divine persons are constituted in and through movements of kenotic self-giving and receiving. One might suggest that this is divine mercy operative *ad intra*. There is a self-emptying at the heart of the Trinity such that each person is self-gift to the other two persons. In explaining this, we come to see that kenosis is an ecstatic movement and that there cannot be a true kenosis without hiatus. At this point it is vital to stress that distance is not the same as separation. For there to be true distinction between the persons of Father, Son, and Spirit there needs to be "distance," but this is not to raise the specter of tritheism—the belief that there are three separate gods. Rather, it is to affirm that the distinction of persons is most clear in the relations that exist within the one God. There is within the Trinity the reality of "otherness"—the Son is not the Father, and the Spirit is neither the Son nor the Father. There is both communion in one God and otherness in terms of distinct persons.

Accordingly, we learn from the Trinity that kenosis and otherness are simultaneous events and expansive in the dimension of mercy. This Trinitarian kenosis not only speaks about God but also indicates what true human personhood means. Because of the revelation of the kenosis of Christ and his lived mission of humble obedience to the will of the Father, there is a clear indication that the fullness of humanity lies in the movement from eternal thanksgiving for the reality of divine mercy to humble obedience and back to eternal thanksgiving. This is also an indication of a way in which the distance within the Trinity is also an inclusive space into which God in mercy draws human persons. In this light it is possible to understand the "naturalness" of Christian gratitude and note the divine invitation to live from this disposition in obedience to the leading of the Spirit of God and with a merciful gaze toward others. This is what it means to be a fully alive human person.

In Balthasar's Trinitarian anthropology, personhood is not defined in terms of a quality possessed but as a gifted event. One is a person only in kenotic relations of freedom as merciful love. We realize ourselves only in an ability to freely give ourselves in self-emptying love. Human personhood, understood as formed in the *imago Dei*, truly finds its fulfilment in obedient response to the Father's call to a unique and personal mission, just as Jesus did. He was completely of one will with the Father in the living out of his redemptive mission — a proclamation of the mercy of God. Each person is uniquely called, and each one who responds to that call receives a personal mission, which is, by the gracious invitation of God, some small share in the outworking of divine mercy in the redemptive mission of Christ.

For Balthasar, however, there is not only a descending theodicy — the movement of God toward human beings — that speaks about the fulfilment of personhood. There is also an ascending theological anthropology — human persons, by the mercy of God, are drawn into the very life of the Trinity. In this context, Balthasar understands self-consciousness as inherently inter-subjective, a love drawing toward divine communion. There is a longing at the heart of human beings for a unique identity and for that infinite freedom that is God's alone. There is within us a yearning, in our finite freedom, for divine infinite freedom. In the kenotic descent of God in Christ there was a transformation of the negative distance between God and human beings into a distance of merciful communion. As indicated in the previous chapter, the time of the greatest distance between the divine persons, as revealed on the cross, was in reality the time when the relationship between Father, Son, and Spirit was closest. The distance was not a division but the space for difference constituted in merciful love and freedom. Accordingly, we come to see that personhood is defined not in terms of a quality possessed by human beings but as a merciful dynamic event initiated by God within us.

In this way, then, the reality of kenosis is more than self-sacrifice. This self-emptying is a precondition for relations of mercy, love, and freedom. It is the only context in which the self is truly given. Here there is always a tension between intimacy and distance, likeness and unlikeness, profound love and the fear of the Lord, which is rooted in reverence and awe. This tension is integral to the relationship between God and human beings. It is not something to be resolved. It is to be lived out in fullness in the drama of our lives.[16]

The Scriptural corpus clearly indicates that the reality of the cross can be interpreted only in the context of the Trinity and through faith. Likewise the full doctrine of the Trinity can be explored only on the basis of a theology of the cross. The doctrine of the Trinity is, in the words of Balthasar, "the ever-present, inner presupposition of the Cross."[17] In this drama the divine soteriological initiative infused with merciful love both invites and initiates human beings into the life of the Trinity. Here we may glimpse something of the mystery of all mysteries. At the heart of the divine dynamic is a kenotic event, Balthasar writes: "The Father's self-utterance in the *Word*, the *Son*, is an initial kenosis within the Godhead that underpins all subsequent kenosis,"[18] and it is the most profound revelation of mercy.

It is important to recall that the Father, in surrendering himself unreservedly and uttering forth the Word as Son, does not lose himself as Father. He is not extinguished in this self-giving. Rather, in this very self-surrender of himself he *is* the whole divine essence. Balthasar clearly asserts that "he cannot be God in any other way but in this kenosis within the Godhead itself."[19] This self-gift, this self-emptying reality, is at the heart of God's way of being. It is the very "manner" of mercy understood as a verb. In the consubstantial reality of the Son there is a divine reciprocity that includes the self-given nature of the Son. It also includes the reality of filial thanksgiving in a reciprocity of self-gift to the Father. Here we enter the profound mystery of faith. "Spanning the gulf of the Divine persons' total distinctness," Balthasar writes, "we have a correspondence between the Father's self-giving expressed in generation, and the Son's thanksgiving and readiness . . . to the limits of forgiveness. . . . This is maintained and bridged by the [self-gift] of the Holy Spirit."[20] It is the perichoretic action of the eternal grace of mercy.

It is evident, therefore, that Balthasar appropriates the classic doctrine of kenosis associated with the second person of the Trinity and extends its application to all persons of the Trinity "in the differentiated unity of their immanent life. The total kenosis of each and the thankful ['eucharistic'] return to each of himself by the others becomes the ground of Trinitarian unity, being and love."[21] In the fourth gospel, the high priestly prayer of Jesus makes clear that in the relationship between the Father and the Son there is a reciprocity of loving self-gift and self-surrender.[22] I would suggest that this is a manifestation of divine mercy. In a similar manner, Balthasar argues that since the wealth of both is a received wealth from the other, this coinheres to a oneness: "For both, the event of this oneness is a gift: the *bonum* of a mutual love is a *donum* for the lovers. Thus both, the loving Father and the loving Son receive this mutuality as a gift."[23] When it comes to the Holy Spirit, the very being of the Spirit is a gift from the Father to the Son and from the Son to the Father.[24]

Self-Surrender and Blessedness

This extraordinary claim is made by Balthasar: "God's blessedness consists in his *being* self-surrender."[25] Yet after our previous exploration it comes as no surprise and with a certain resonance, as it is consonant with all we have considered so far and the very way in which we have explored God's gracious gift of self leads to this conclusion. It is the way in which God pours forth his merciful love. Within the being of God, that state of blessedness is the mutual self-gift of the three persons. The Father and the Son are so rich in divine being that they give away their being to one another. And in this gift of being to one another—in not retaining hold on divinity for themselves—they become analogously "poor," but this poverty is actually an expression of their overflowing merciful love—rich in mercy—and the fruit of this love is the Spirit.

Thus, it may be said not just that the being of God is inclined to self-surrender and mercy but that self-surrender and mercy form a constituent part of who God is, the way God is within Godself, and the way God is consistently with human beings. As Balthasar writes: "Right from the outset, the eternal life that the Son brings into this life explodes the self-reference of an egotistic 'I'; it *is* perfect self-surrender in merciful love, manifesting itself ultimately in suffering and death."[26] It is the expression of divine mercy that correlates the Trinity *ad intra* and *ad extra*. If this is so, then also, in the most extreme suffering of the Son "dying in the agony of God-forsakenness, it is for him [and the other divine persons] not only an external work undertaken out of absolute [mercy,] love and joy but also the expression of his very own, his very specific life."[27] From the moment of the incarnation the Son expresses the reality of this self-surrender in his relationship to the Father and through the guidance of the Holy Spirit. It is above all an expression of love from the "unfathomable depths" of God's mercy and love. This merciful love is both the guiding dynamic within the Trinity and also the principle of engagement that guides all divine interaction with human beings.

"All authentic being in love," Bernard Lonergan maintains, "is a total self-surrender ... something in itself, something personal, intimate, and profoundly attuned to the deepest yearnings of the human heart. It constitutes a basic fulfilment of man's being."[28] The very possibility of such self-surrender, and the intrinsic nature of this to authentic being in love, lies at the heart of the mystery of God and therefore is reflected in human beings created after the image of God. Accordingly, it is not surprising that for Balthasar, self-surrender is a characteristic of relations within the Trinity and is thus part of the prevenient grace and intimacy that God mercifully offers to human beings. Christ reveals the reality that the Trinity is involved in the world as Father, Son, and Spirit for the salvation of the world. "But it is as *God* that he is thus involved," writes Balthasar. "He does not *become* 'love' by having the world as his 'thou' and his 'partner': in himself, in lofty transcendence far above the world, he 'is [merciful] love' already."[29]

Balthasar believed that the essence of mercy and love is a mystery of self-giving that reveals itself in self-surrender. In Christ this was seen in "the sublimity" of the humiliated Lord in terms of glory.[30] Both giving and receiving are for merciful love a form of self-giving. So the love at the heart of the Trinity becomes an exchange of the gift of self and the riches within the distinction of persons. This spills over into a divine fecundity that embraces human beings, drawing them into the reality of merciful divine love and intimacy.[31]

Balthasar maintains that human beings can make no progress in love until there is a degree of self-surrender and this becomes, then, a source of energy that further impels the progress of love.[32] Self-surrender is a reflection of God's ongoing mercy, love, and desire for each person and the consequent blessedness for a human respondent. So Balthasar states, in words resonant of Lonergan: "In seeking and hearing God [the human being] experiences the highest joy, that of being fulfilled in itself, but fulfilled in something infinitely greater than itself and, for that very reason, completely fulfilled and made blessed."[33] In this mystery of personal love there is already, by the divine initiative, this willingness to be in love with God "without limits, qualifications or conditions or reservations," as Lonergan puts it.[34] Such whole-hearted loving of God leads to an obedience that is determinative of life's choices and courses.

OBEDIENCE AS AN OUTWORKING OF MERCY

Twenty-first-century culture gives little positive value to the term "obedience." Certainly, in North America and Western Europe there is a resistance to authority and a deep distrust of any commitment that calls for an attitude of obedience. Indeed, for many the term evokes the specter of fundamentalism with the twin threat of terrorism. Obedience, however, has an honorable Christian heritage, and it is in this vein, and focused on the obedience of Christ, that we see something of the disposition of obedience as an outworking of mercy at the heart of the Trinity. Applying the term "obedience" to the Trinity is, of course, an anthropomorphism.[35] It is, however, the manner in which humans articulate what we have glimpsed concerning divine life; although, at the same time, we continue to remind ourselves of the necessary caution of the Fourth Lateran Council, namely, that we must remember that the dissimilarity between God and creatures is always greater than any similarity.

We can indicate the reality of Trinitarian obedience from the time of the incarnation when, in response to Mary's *fiat*, the Spirit comes upon her. At this point, Balthasar writes, "the Son is already obedient, insofar as he entrusts himself to the activity of the Spirit in accord with the Father's will."[36] This is crucially an active endeavor and not the result of passivity, and this self-surrendering action forms a leitmotif of his life. Balthasar states: "Jesus' obedience to his mission, the embodiment of his existence, was the presentation and the exposition of God [John 1:18], of the eternal unity of merciful love between God [the Father] and his eternal Word." Following from this: "The total exposition of this love in the world that is not divine and is opposed to God demanded that Jesus take the path into the uttermost darkness, because otherwise there would always have been some matter that would not let itself be used for the exposition of God; but it is an act of unsurpassable, blind obedience to have to seek God in that which is absolutely non-divine, in order to portray him where it is impossible to find him—to portray eternal light in eternal darkness."[37] It is an action of eternal merciful love.

Since Jesus was obedient to his own mission, it is clear that human beings are also called to such obedience. Indeed, the individual who is truly obedient to the call and mission of Christ is thus drawn into the work of mercy, which is God's redemptive work, and finds the true fulfillment of his or her being.[38] In the gospels, the prologue, as it were, of Jesus's obedience is seen in his encounter with the doctors of the law in the temple as an adolescent. Then in the baptism we have a dramatic indication of the nature of how, through his obedience, the magnitude of the incarnation is revealed in its transformative dynamic, and this is the precursor of the events of his life that follow along the way to his passion and death.

Jesus's act of obedience in submitting to the baptism of John is a response to the prophetic word of God that John proclaims.[39] Yet it is at the same time an "incomprehensible" act; it appears back to front or upside down for Jesus to be baptized by John. John himself protests, but eventually lets it happen.[40] Jesus emphasizes that his baptism is a fulfillment of God's ways and "obedience incarnated in history." Balthasar writes: "Jesus' descent into the river is at one and the same time solidarity with all who confess their guilt and dive into the waters of judgment and salvation, and—as solidarity—obedience to the voice of God which sounds forth from the prophet's voice, and thus obedience incarnated in history."[41]

Accordingly, in Jesus's baptism we encounter the way in which the incarnation has a transformative effect on our understanding of the nature of obedience. In the incarnation, God out of his merciful love imposed upon himself boundaries of space and temporality. The dissolution of these boundaries took place from within the incarnate Word in the outworking of his life, passion, death, and resurrection, but this took place in such a way that the very humanity of Christ was not negated but rather brought to fulfillment in God. Thus, in the resurrection the incarnation was not disincarnated but was brought to spiritual fulfillment and abolished the alienation of human beings from God.[42] Accordingly, the response of faith is not an act that inaugurates a new truth but rather the acceptance of a truth made available to us from the beginning of time.[43] It is to be conscious that we were eternally conceived in the mind of God, and thus the word of grace that is addressed to us is a deep interior word of mercy that being eternal is more a part of ourselves through grace since it was addressed to us before our birth. If this is so, then the call to faith, Balthasar writes, is "more reasonable than my own reason, so that the act of obedience in faith is more truly reasonable than the most reasonable act could be."[44]

It is in the fulfillment of Jesus's mission that we once more encounter the dramatic dimension of divine mercy. Here it is important to make clear that this dramatic reality belongs to the whole person of Christ and is not confined only to his human reality; according to Balthasar, "its ultimate presuppositions lie in the divine life itself."[45] The outworking of this drama, which is ultimately a drama of merciful love, is through the twin realities of self-surrender and obedience. Through Jesus's absolute obedience he totally identified himself with the Father's will and the mission he had come to accomplish.

In accordance with his redemptive work and the ongoing nature of his mission, Jesus called disciples of his time and across generations to a principle of merciful loving and to an obedience that is an acceptance of a creative collaboration in his absolute salvific obedience. Balthasar elaborates the nature of this drama of divine obedience by indicating that it is in the God-forsakenness of the cross that Jesus still maintains his identity — "as the matrix of all possible dramas, he embodies the absolute drama in his own person, in his personal mission."[46] In this way he is enabled to be steadfast in the preservation of his identity because of the Trinitarian nature of God.[47] "In order to be himself, he needs the Father and the Spirit."[48]

The life of Jesus was focused toward the cross, because the outworking of divine love that was determined to reconcile human beings with God was open to this ultimate sacrifice. Thus, his teaching, his proclamation of the kingdom, and his works of healing were all acts of self-disclosure that were finally authenticated in the reality of the Passion.[49] The core of the public life and teaching of Jesus pointed to that self-surrender that formed the heart of the Passion, a self-surrender that was a laying down of his life not just for his friends but indeed for all people.

This self-surrender is also revealed as the culmination of a life lived in obedience to the mission given by the Father, a mission of selfless merciful loving service.[50] In this way he becomes the witness of God's infinite irrevocable love for the world. "Obediently identifying himself with his mission," Balthasar writes, "he himself is his mission in person, and therefore, in his kenosis as the "servant of God," he becomes the manifestation of God's eternal love for the world."[51] Thus it is revealed that Christ's obedience and self-surrender are essentially the expressions of divine merciful love, and in this way the kenosis of Christ is also revelatory of the mystery of merciful love at the heart of the Trinity.[52]

In focusing upon the life of Christ it becomes clear that the outworking of divine love in his person and mission had a pedagogical dimension. He was—as it were—forming the disciples in the way of divine merciful love, in a way that challenged them to move beyond their own boundaries into the risky dimension of faith. "In the course of his introducing them into the Spirit," Balthasar writes, "Jesus withdraws his bodily, earthly presence, so that his and the Father's Spirit may come, who, as the fullness of [merciful] love, simultaneously fulfills and testifies to this kenotic self-effacement in [merciful] love."[53]

Balthasar links obedience with self-surrender in a way that focuses the dynamic of self-abandonment into a moment of attunement to the Ignatian "magis"—the ever-greater, the ever-deeper, movement toward the greater glory of God. In a manner like the way of St. Ignatius in the Spiritual Exercises—where the sections titled "Three Classes of Person" and "The Three Degrees of Humility" flesh out what is required of those who desire a deeper following of Christ— Balthasar tests the reality of any deepening self-surrender in terms of a person's real commitment to the leading of God and the outworking of God's mercy by attending to the needs of "neighbors," which is central to any concrete mission.

Accordingly, Balthasar emphasizes that both self-surrender and obedience are crucial to the mission. Without the latter, the former runs the risk of being a deceptively self-transcending asceticism. So self-surrender is a prelude and a prerequisite to the active co-operation of human beings in the divine enterprise of mercy. Indeed, the very fundamental "work" of contemplation can be translated into concrete acts of service to one's neighbor that reveal this active co-operation. Here we acknowledge the notion of "indifference," for the one who wishes to co-operate with the Lord practices the disposition of indifference in order to be ready to be disposed according to the will of the Lord and to follow the leading of the Spirit. Such an individual remains distinctly his or her own person but at the same time with a certain transparency to the leading of the Lord toward an outworking of the mission of mercy.[54]

As Christopher Hadley has observed, Walter Kasper's outline for a systematic theology of mercy in his book *Mercy: The Essence of the Gospel and the Key to a Christian Life* already bears substantial similarities to Balthasar's paschal Trinitarianism.[55] Both theologians outline a theology of the cross that envisages Christ's relationship to the Father and to humanity. With the distance that is experienced between Father and Son at Calvary—one that is never separation— the hymn of Philippians 2 can be seen as a kind of aesthetic measure of the space that God makes for suffering and indeed for sinners. In this way the depths of the kenosis of the Son referenced in the hymn of Philippians 2 may be contemplatively glimpsed as revealing something of the mystery of the kenotic event in the immanent Trinity, where the divine persons in an ever-dynamic merciful love seek to draw human persons toward the fullness of Trinitarian life.

Accordingly, kenosis is for both thinkers a major interpretive key to God's triune act of being, and at the heart of this kenosis, I would suggest, is the imperative of merciful love. Both Kasper and Balthasar also speculate about the eschatological truth of the world as a graced communion with God—a sharing in God's world by the very fact of being creatures of a Creator God who are continually maintained in existence by a merciful God. Within the vast space that exists between God and the world, where the operative principle that the dissimilarity is greater than the similarity is ever present,[56] still it is possible to glimpse signs of the inter-personal love shared between Father, Son, and Spirit.

The possibility of a Trinitarian ontology of mercy arises, as Kasper sees mercy (as do I) as a defining attribute of God, and this serves to refocus our soteriological perspectives. From the fulcrum of the cross, where we see Balthasar's more aesthetic focus on glory,[57] the imperative of mercy infuses all aspects of both Christ's sacramental presence in the world (in all the sacraments, but particularly baptism and Eucharist) and also the determinative action of the Church in the world (in the corporal and spiritual works of mercy), through a hermeneutic of mercy. It appears that Kasper is calling for something like a divine ontology based on the biblical witness to the God of mercy, according to which the world's communion with God, in the space that God has made, would not only give expression to the mystery of the economic Trinity but would also shape the presence of the Church in the world. Just as, according to Balthasar, the kenosis of Christ reveals the kenotic event in the Trinity, so also Jesus makes known the reality of mercy at the heart of the economic Trinity: "In mercy, God's Trinitarian essence is admittedly not actualized, but it does become reality for us and in us in a concrete way."[58] The mercy we receive from God and perceive as fundamental to the life of the Trinity both infuses the Church and prompts her members to endeavor to express their gratitude for so great a gift of loving mercy by being merciful to others, particularly the most vulnerable in society.

Consequently, a refraction of this merciful love of the Trinity is always present for human persons in the Church's actions of compassion for the suffering; forgiveness for sinners (a group to whom we all belong, as Pope Francis continues to remind us); and a passionate engagement in expressing mercy and justice for the poorest and most vulnerable. These elements of mercy are inseparable and mutually condition each other, fueled by the sustaining energy of prayer. At the center of the command to be merciful as God is merciful (Matt. 5:7), we now see a call to make space for others in our lives. The operative nature of mercy is not just about doing something for another to relieve a current situation of suffering or vulnerability; it is also about the prior attending to and making space in one's life for the other, which has to do with valuing and reverencing the intrinsic worth of another.

Such a way of proceeding mirrors the way in which God attends to, reverences, and profoundly values the worth of human persons made in his image and desires to bring them into the fullness of

Trinitarian life. It also enables a more profound glimpsed apprehension of the mystery of the Trinitarian way of proceeding; the relating enables a real mutuality in reverence, in giving and receiving, in a kenotic activity inclined by merciful love. True love respects the difference of otherness and allows the other to be other, in the wild glory of Trinitarian life. The paradox of Trinitarian love, according to Kasper, is that "it is a unity that includes otherness and difference."[59] What Kasper appears to be asking for here is a new theological dramatics—in contradistinction to the *Theo-Drama* of Balthasar, now construed in terms of divine love, indeed, merciful love—as inclusion and exaltation of those who are poor and suffering.[60]

In Balthasar's *Glory of the Lord VII*, his New Testament theology, the kenosis of Jesus on the cross is "materially identical" with the process by which the Father and the Son glorify each other in the world. The coming of the Spirit, according to *Theo-Drama*, volume 4, as the "we" of Father and Son reveals God's hospitality, which offers an inclusive "space" in divine life even for sinners. It also reveals the wild glory of God's fidelity to God's own self, God's justice as the rightness of relationship. Mercy is an invitation to dwell in the land of justice in forms of right relationship, and forgiveness makes dwelling in justice possible for the sinner. This is why God's mercy is, in a sense, wider than God's justice, but also completely inseparable from it.

Kasper invokes Jesus's taking our place as an expression of divine mercy, which of course is also the manifestation of divine justice. Jesus takes our place so that we can be included with him in the place where he always is, with the Father and the Spirit, and be made righteous by him in that place.[61] He has become for us the place where life breaks in, because he cannot be conquered by death. With our covenantal relationship to God thus restored at Jesus's side, we can actively participate in our own restoration because "Jesus' substitutionary atonement liberates us for a new life and makes us a new creation."[62] The cross creates a space for suffering and for sinners, a "life and living space."[63] The divine self-communication in love through the cross of Christ, because it is also a divine kenosis, a making of space, contains all possibilities for mercy. It holds the infinite space in which all of creation can be contained, along with all of the deeds and acts of mercy done in the world in faith, and we can participate in the incarnate Son's love for the Father and for the world.

BORNE ON THE BREATH OF THE SPIRIT

A pneumatology follows from this understanding, because it is actually the Spirit who perfects this reality in us. Reflection on the cross alone does not enable us to comprehend the whole Triune mystery, but it points us toward it and provides a sure way to approach it. However, we must face the world at the same time in all its messiness and know ourselves to be empowered by mercy to hand on mercy in its concrete form. God has already made mercy concrete for us, and the Spirit enables us to remember the work of God's mercy within us.[64] The Holy Spirit, equal in divinity to the Father and the Son, receives something from them both: his divine nature and mission.

Pope Benedict XVI, in Sydney for World Youth Day in 2008, spoke of the Holy Spirit as "the bond of unity within the Blessed Trinity . . . unity as communion, unity as abiding love, and unity as giving and gift."[65] The Holy Spirit is shared by the Father and the Son and gives unity to Father and Son. Indeed, He is the very unity or merciful love of those two persons eternally giving themselves in a kenotic action with merciful love to each other. If the Holy Spirit is the force who unites the divine persons eternally in love; if he is the one who proceeds from them into our world and back to them from our world; if he is "the Lord, the giver of life" to the world since creation and to the Church since the first Pentecost, as our faith proclaims; then he it is who unites human persons when they might be inclined to fall apart; he it is who brings the wisdom of the Father and the Son to us and draws us back with Him to them in eternity; and he it is who breathes mortal life into our material flesh, eternal life into our mortal natures, and divine grace into our dreams and projects. As St. Augustine taught, it is the Holy Spirit who allows us to be and to remain in God and God to be and remain in us. If Christ is "God as flesh," God in the flesh, the Holy Spirit is God as merciful Love or God in merciful love.[66]

Kasper says that Balthasar emphasizes that the full understanding of truth is given only by an inspiration from the Spirit within the realm of cognitive understanding. Human beings, of their own volition, commitment, and determination, cannot plumb the fullness of truth. Any deeper understanding is always an inspiration of the spirit of God.[67] The spirit of God, however, is quintessentially free, "blowing where it will."[68] It is this mercy and freedom of the spirit that introduce human persons into the deep levels of the mystery of mercy and freedom that is rooted at the heart of God. Accordingly, we come to see that our growth in freedom and our cognizance of mercy are in proportion to our growth in relationship with God, since both freedom and mercy are gratuitous gifts of God.

The Son is the way to the Father, and the Spirit promotes our understanding both of the way in which self-surrender and loving merciful obedience are key to the dynamic relations of the Trinity and also to the way in which we are invited into this dynamic way of being. It is the Spirit, who was poured out upon the disciples at Pentecost after the Lord had ascended into heaven, who both draws us into the way of imitation of the Son and opens to us the wonders of Trinitarian merciful love. This is particularly made known in the reality of the Eucharist.[69] Here the self-giving that formed the imperative of Christ's life and that was a self-surrender even to death, in the outworking of divine merciful love for the world, continues in the self-giving of his body and blood under the form of the Eucharistic species.

The dynamic of self-surrendering obedient merciful divine love thereby ensures that human beings continue to be nourished and sustained by the very life of Christ in the outpouring of that life in a sacrifice that is a Trinitarian reality, continually made present to the believer at every Eucharist. It is the Spirit who enables the individual to perceive the reality of Christ's body and blood and to understand the mysteries of the Word.[70] It is the Spirit who teaches the truth concerning the Son and helps the believer to glimpse something of the reality of Trinitarian mercy and love. It is the Spirit who opens the riches of the knowledge of God, leading the individual deeper into the truth of God and assisting him or her in understanding Sacred Scripture.[71] It is a paradox of growth in the spiritual life that the more the Spirit leads a person to a deeper understanding of these depths and riches, the more the one who contemplates them is drawn to an attitude of humble wonder, which in turn enables a greater understanding. The Spirit continues to lead through finite existence into eternity, empowering the person with the eternal grace of mercy.[72]

Accordingly, self-surrender and merciful loving obedience, seen as characteristics of the dynamic relations of the Trinity, indicate a contemplative stance of mercy within the Trinity, such that we might, with Adrienne von Speyr, speak of prayer in the Trinity.[73] Here she asserts: "Prayer has no beginning because Father, Son and Spirit have been in conversation from all eternity, united in an eternal expectation and an eternal decision."[74] The overflow of this self-surrender, obedience, and prayer into relations with human beings involves the ongoing invitation of the Spirit to a greater depth of faith and wonder at the overwhelming grace of mercy and contemplation. There is also a growing imperative in the lives of believers to respond in an imitative way by living lives that are characterized by a self-surrender and merciful loving obedience to God through the leading of the Spirit. This leading gives believers a primary appreciation of the wonder of the Eucharist and a keen sense of the need for such food for the living of a Christian life.[75]

CONTEMPLATION AND ACTION

The Spirit also draws a person to a deepened appreciation of the importance of the contribution of the surrendered and mercifully loving, obedient individual in the life of the community of the Church. Here merciful action becomes the fruit of inspired contemplation. Contemplative prayer is truly the fruit of the Spirit who indwells, informs, and inflames the believer who is disposed to be open to receive and whose heart is truly set in humility on the work of God. The action of mercy that flows from such contemplative prayer in its many and varied forms is a multiplicity that is gathered together by the Spirit into one unity of praise that is returned to the Father through the Son.[76]

There can be no true Christian contemplation except in and through the working of the Trinity. It is the indwelling of its three persons that enables the possibility of an indwelling within a believer. It continues to be part of the Trinitarian dynamic of loving mercy that God desires in self-surrender to enter into the most intimate form of communication with the individual through the indwelling of the Spirit and the sustenance of the Eucharist. Thus, the believer senses a more fervent prayer due to the working of the Spirit, which powerfully affects the soul. As Balthasar observes: "The action of the Spirit in pointing the way, stirring the heart, thinking, willing and praying in unison with the soul, springs from the inmost core of the soul's life; and, by this action, which as a general rule is not directed to the Spirit himself [whose primary aim is the glorification of the Father and the Son], the contemplative is placed in the closest intimacy with divine truth."[77]

MERCY AS A DEFINITIVE DIVINE ATTRIBUTE

St. Thomas Aquinas emphasized that mercy is the greatest of all the virtues: "In itself mercy is the greatest of the virtues, since all the others revolve around it and, more than this, it makes up for their deficiencies. This is particular to the superior virtue, and as such it is proper to God to have mercy, through which his omnipotence is manifested to the greatest degree."[78] Since God is love, as we read in 1 John 4:8, and faithful to himself, God is also merciful. His mercy is an aspect of his very essence and in this way is revelatory of the ongoing fidelity of God to himself as he expresses the priority of his merciful love. Thus, mercy is seen as a fundamental attribute of God, and indeed Kasper asserts that it is "the most fundamental of all the divine attributes."[79] The corollary to such an understanding is that, in highlighting the importance of divine mercy in this way, we implicitly indicate a foundational hermeneutical principle. Since mercy, then, becomes the externally visible and active reality of the loving essence of God, Aquinas writes, "Mercy expresses God's own goodness and love. It is God's *caritas operative et effectiva*."[80] If mercy is fundamental in the way proposed, then all other attributes of God stand in an indissoluble relationship to it and, more than this, mercy itself may be the organizing principle of all divine attributes. Thus, Kasper believes it could be stated as a key hermeneutical principle "not to replace or to undermine doctrine and the commandments, but rather to understand and to actualize them in the right way, according to the gospel."[81] The repercussions of asserting mercy as the determining attribute of God also affect the ongoing question, referenced earlier in this work, of the relationship of mercy to God's justice and omnipotence. Kasper states the possibility as follows: "If mercy is the fundamental attribute of God then it cannot be understood as an instance of justice; on the contrary, divine justice must be understood from the perspective of divine mercy. Mercy then is the justice that is idiosyncratic to God."[82] And for Kasper the triunity of God is "the inner presupposition of God's mercy, just as conversely, his mercy is the revelation and mirror of his essence. In God's mercy, the eternal, self-communicating love of the Father, Son, and Holy Spirit is mirrored and revealed."[83]

FREEDOM AND MERCY

What is true freedom? This is a question raised across all generations and is not one commonly associated with the reality of mercy. Yet for people of faith, the answer to the question of freedom lies at the heart of the mystery of the relationship of human persons with God. At its most profound, the answer lies within the very depths of the Trinity. Here it is possible to glimpse that it is the merciful loving dynamic of the freedom of God that underlies and preserves human freedom. In particular, it is this same merciful divine freedom that sustains human freedom within the divine human encounter. And it is this same divine freedom that calls forth the free human response of individuals and the communal response of the Church to live out this merciful freedom in co-operation with the redemptive mission of Christ to bring the good news of God's mercy to the world.

We have seen throughout this chapter, in conversation with Balthasar and Kasper, that the dimension of mercy is integral to the reality of kenosis, that the kenosis of Christ reveals the kenotic event at the heart of the Trinity, that the outworking of kenosis is found in self-surrender and merciful loving obedience, and that all of these factors lead toward the positing of an ontology of mercy understood as an eternal grace. Now we turn our attention to the impact of divine freedom, which extends this attribute of mercy to humanity in a gratuitous generosity beyond all comprehension through divine self-sacrificing love.[84] In our contemporary cultural context, the question of freedom is often tied to certain ideological presuppositions that can imprison the humane tendencies that are embodied within our very creation. The imprint of the *imago Dei* involves a spirit of compassion and hope, a spirit of merciful loving self-sacrifice. This is the profound truth made known to us in the paschal mystery, which reveals the loving mercy of God.

The "sovereign" freedom of God, far from being an oppressive reality that coerces our freedom, is rather a merciful, reverential, and enticing dynamic within God that holds human freedom most precious.[85] God places a high value on human freedom. It is not something to be coerced or negated. Rather, the sovereign freedom of the Trinity guarantees human freedom—even unto the commission of sin. There is, as it were, a certain creative tension that God establishes that is a presupposition of the "dramatic action" that takes place between God and human beings. This divine creative tension rests on the truth that human persons are quintessentially dependent beings: created, nurtured, and sustained by the loving mercy of God. In this gratuitous, generous grace, human beings receive abundant blessings. It is the wonder of merciful grace that such blessings are freely bestowed by divine design with no regard for merit. "This is the paradox of a being which knows that it can only fulfill itself through grateful dependence on a grace on which it has no claim," writes Balthasar.[86] This ultimate and eternal grace is mercy.

The Trinity, having in merciful love created human beings, desired to enter into a more profound relationship with them such that there would be a concrete shared, redemptive history. The fruition of this desire occurred in the incarnation, life, passion, death, and resurrection of Christ. In him, as true God and true man, we may also perceive the sacramental dimension of the creative tension at the heart of human life—life that is always sustained by the merciful love of God.[87] The union of Jesus with the Father such that they were also "of one merciful will" is the union to which all human persons are called, and the fecundity of this movement toward union is a deeper participation in the work of mercy in the redemptive mission of Christ.

This way of being in God guarantees the free action of the human agent—even to the possibility of committing sin. Indeed, the way God guarantees human freedom bespeaks the fundamental generosity and forbearance of God toward human persons. As Balthasar writes: "In forbearance he not only allows him to continue on his erring path but actually accompanies him, supporting him with his *providence*, so that all man's errors take place within the realm of divine love."[88] This is not to suggest that there is a divine condoning of sin but rather that even sin is not outside the encompassing love and mercy of God. In this way it is always possible for the human person to turn to God for mercy and forgiveness. For what is most paradoxical, and yet also most clear, is that the human being is most free and most expresses the fullness of human personhood when open to relationship with the Triune God. In our very creation we were made for such relationship, and it is only in this relationship that we become the persons we were created by the God of mercy to be.[89]

As we have established earlier, there is no incompatibility between the oneness of God and the distinctness of persons in the Trinity. There is both merciful communion and otherness within the Godhead.[90] Accordingly, there is no incompatibility between the Trinity and the otherness that is found in human beings created in the divine image. Within the divine *perichoresis* there is a constancy of mercy in reciprocal self-giving and receiving between the three persons. It is, however, the gratuitous gift of the divine persons to have freely chosen to share their love. It is part of the mystery of divine mercy that human beings are invited into the space of the life of the Trinity through the loving mercy of God as realized in the redemptive work of Christ. Such a process of growing intimacy with God encompasses the entire life span of a human person who desires to respond ever more profoundly to this invitation to experience divine mercy.

John O'Donnell indicates that a key feature of Balthasar's work is the contemplation and analysis of the interplay between divine and human freedom grounded in God's unconditional merciful love for human beings.[91] Due to the very act of the creation of human beings, human freedom is an integral truth of the human reality guaranteed by God. We have already noted that this freedom is a gratuitous outworking of divine mercy. Since freedom is of the very nature of God and therefore a "truth" inherent in God, some analogous freedom would be imperative for human beings made in the image of God.

Here we return to the reality of kenosis at the heart of the Trinity. It is the self-gift of the three persons that enables the possibility of human freedom. It is the merciful kenotic action of Father and Son that enables the Spirit's freedom to blow where it will, giving gifts. As Balthasar writes, "[Father and Son] refuse to be understood except in terms of self-emptying. Their bestowal of freedom presupposes this self-emptying, this kenosis."[92] It is the gracious generosity of the Trinity to enable and to guarantee human freedom. The full force of this gift of freedom is given by a merciful kenotic dynamic at the heart of

God that refuses to determine or proscribe human freedom. When we conceive of the life of the Trinity as one of infinite mercy and self-giving, it becomes clearer how the possibility of a free creation might exist. It also illuminates how a relationship of the Trinity with human beings and with the world might be possible.

It becomes apparent, therefore, that mercy is part of the reality of the sphere of divine freedom. It follows, then, that the actualization of mercy, the truth of this, is an event that brings together in a dramatic encounter the Trinity and human persons.[93] In this encounter the luminous form of the Trinity—specifically God in Christ—informs or illuminates Christians if we are disposed to listen and are open to receive. Indeed, it is only by our participation in the life of Christ, which involves the loving response of the Son to the Father in the dynamic of the Spirit, that our freedom can come to perfection in us,[94] and also that mercy can be the operative force of our lives. We cannot by our own efforts come to that perfect human freedom that the Trinity desires for us. It is true, however, that if we dispose ourselves to be drawn ever more deeply into relationship with Christ, then we shall come to a more profound freedom over time, as we are drawn by the Spirit of God into the life of the Trinity. It is—as it were—the seal of the Spirit upon us, and the less resistance there is within us, the more clearly is this seen.

The clearest instance of this transparency to the Spirit at work is Mary's fiat. Indeed, the moment of the incarnation indicates the supreme graciousness of the mercy at the heart of the Father, Son, and Spirit, who wait upon the response of Mary from her freedom. St. Bernard, in contemplating the scene, spoke of the urgent necessity of Mary's response thus: "Answer, O Virgin, answer the angel speedily; rather through the angel, answer your Lord. Speak the word and receive the Word; offer what is yours and conceive what is of God; give what is temporal and embrace what is eternal."[95] In Mary's openness to receive and willingness to co-operate with God's designs, we see the perfect response of the human creature—a response that is truly free. And consequent upon this is the great proclamation of the Magnificat, which extols the mercy of God and indicates the preferential work of the Trinity with the lowly, the humble, the poor, and the persecuted.[96] Within Mary we see the radiance of Christ shining forth within her. We are not speaking of self-luminosity here. For this radiance to be revealed, there needed to be space within Mary that was open to the interior dynamism of the Spirit at work within her. There is an imperative need for interior clarity, in order for the radiance that is a reflection of Trinitarian life to be revealed. This interior clarity involves a simplicity and humility that is so other-focused that the ego ceases to obstruct the work of the divine spirit within. This is evident in the person of Mary, in whom the radiance of Trinitarian goodness, beauty, and truth in-form her very being.

THE MYSTERY OF TRINITARIAN MERCY AND FREEDOM

From all we have considered so far in this chapter we may conclude that the mystery of divine freedom and mercy is co-inherent in the mystery of the Trinity. Here there is no rigid, static absolute but a dynamic divine reality that of itself encompasses an infinite vitality. Within the Trinity there is creativity, beauty, truth, and goodness beyond all comprehension and rooted in a Trinitarian ontology of mercy. From the abundance of divine life, God desired by merciful loving free design to forge a creation within which human beings would be invited into relationship with God. Human beings are the creation of an utterly gratuitous divine generosity. God does not need relationship with human persons but desires such relationship solely from his mercy and for the good of human beings.

We are aware that our language is limited in its capacity to indicate the mystery of God. Our verbal skills do not provide the necessary linguistic framework. Therefore, we find that we often resort to using poetic and symbolic language to express more adequately what we strive to say. In this way we may say of God that the Trinity is — at one and the same time — infinite self-possession and total self-gift. Within the Godhead there is complete self-possession in mercy with regard to the distinction of persons. The Father is the Father and not the Son; the Son is neither the Father nor the Spirit; and the Spirit is neither the Father nor the Son. There is within the Trinity, as we have already seen, the self-gift of each person to the others in the dynamic of mercy. In this way we can speak of a merciful kenotic event, or a self-emptying of each person of the Trinity in regard to the others. One might even postulate a *perichoresis* of mercy.

In the eternal inner vitality of the Trinity, Balthasar suggests, there is space for ongoing inventiveness in the expression of merciful love that flows between the three persons. In that inventiveness there is also an ongoing extension of divine life to human beings. In the relationship between finite and infinite, Balthasar asserts, "ultimately [this] must involve self-disclosure on the part of infinite freedom."[97] It is God's self-disclosure of his loving mercy that energizes human persons and enables them to move from a condition of estrangement to one of "free mutual openness graciously granted to us by God."[98] Thus we may see how it is the self-disclosure of the Trinity in mercy to human beings that enables the human possibility of merciful self-disclosure. Such a human response is both in relation to God and in interaction with other human persons with whom we share the gift of mercy. We are enabled through the grace of mercy to have an open disposition toward God that further enables the possibility of receiving this grace. At the same time, we are granted an open disposition toward other human persons that enables a depth of merciful interaction that is life-giving for others and for ourselves.

In the mercy and freedom that exists within the Trinity, there is a mercy and freedom unique to each of its persons. For this to be operative, the self-giving of each person to the others requires its own area of freedom. Therefore, we have further insight into the kenotic event within the Trinity in terms of the consequences with regard to divine mercy and freedom. In the self-gift of each person to the others there is a guarantee of the distance (*absend*) necessary to accommodate these distinct areas of mercy and freedom and for the exercise of each person's individual freedom and mercy within the one reality, without in any way diminishing the intimate reciprocal merciful love operative between the Father, the Son, and the Spirit that maintains the oneness of God. Integral to this intimacy is the reality of a distinction that, by its very nature, involves distance. As Balthasar writes: "Something like infinite 'duration' and infinite 'space' must be attributed to the acts of reciprocal love so that the life of the *communio*, of fellowship, can develop."[99] In this way, each of the divine persons is free, with the sovereign freedom and mercy proper to God, although each is oriented to the Trinitarian unity. In this way God is, as it were, always "greater" in and through the freedom and mercy that lie at the heart of the Trinity. It is this freedom that guarantees the intimacy within the Trinity. Indeed, in this mercy we can speak of the divine persons as interpenetrating one another, as they are open to one another in the absolute freedom of the divine relationship.[100] The most profound mystery of the eternal grace of mercy lies at the heart of the kenotic event within the Trinity. This loving mercy is not a "static" event but rather the dynamic operative within the life of God and an irradiating principle of all divine relating to human persons. Thus, the grace of mercy is revealed not just as a gift, but as a gift of the very life of God, and thus a dynamic life-giving reality enabling consonance with the will of God—a life lived for God. This life is lived within the community of those who desire to follow the Lord—the ecclesial community.

CHAPTER 5

Engaging Ecclesiological Ramifications

Mercy has been the leitmotif of the papacy of Pope Francis and the
hermeneutical lens through which he has appeared to reference all
the concerns of his papacy. In previous chapters we have explored
the theological underpinning of this focus on mercy. By identifying
key theological anthropological considerations, specific Christological lynchpins, and a Trinitarian horizon—which has led us to suggest the possibility of a Trinitarian ontology of mercy clearly rooted
in Balthasar's understanding of the kenotic event in the Trinity—we
have indicated the theological gravitas of *misericordia* within Church
teaching. It is time now to consider the impact of mercy on ecclesial
practice. What are the ecclesiological ramifications of mercy in the
life of the Church?

In order to respond to this question, I was particularly concerned to listen to individuals in the Vatican Curia who had experienced the Year of Mercy at first hand but who were also well aware
that for Pope Francis the trajectory of mercy neither began nor
ended within that one year. In a series of meetings across different
congregations, councils, pontifical academies, and embassies,[1] I was
most grateful for the time individuals gave to meeting with me and
for their thoughtful and reflective engagement in conversations. In
all cases I made it clear that I was not looking for attributable quota-
tions but rather to gain a sense of further insight into the impact of
this elevation of the discourse on mercy on the life of the Church as

seen in Rome, which is both a hub and conflux of the international entity of the Church.

Accordingly, the most basic question I asked of the individuals with whom I met was "What effect has this elevation of the discourse of mercy, the principle of dialogue, and the operative tool of discernment had on the work of the respective congregation, council, pontifical academy, or embassy to which you belong?" The response to this question was far reaching, as individuals took the opportunity to reflect on their work and to share insights. At times there was a clear mutuality in the exchange that I could attribute only to the presence of the Holy Spirit, ever active in the life of the Church and the lives of those who strive to serve both the person of the pope and the wider Church throughout the world.

What became apparent was that the language of mercy was not confined either to the sacraments or to outreach on behalf of the most vulnerable. It clearly did imbue these areas with and call the attention of members of the Church to a deeper understanding of faith in a real encounter with Christ and a more profound reception of the sacraments. There was also a definite link established between faith and the need for all members of the Church to be involved in outreach to the poorest and most marginalized members of society. In addition, Pope Francis brought the discourse of mercy into all areas of life: the family, the school, the workplace, and even the sphere of the language of international relations and diplomatic exchange. Here, the Holy Father emphasized the need for all matters of politics and diplomacy to be inspired by the hermeneutic of mercy since mercy is God's way of acting in history.

In this chapter I shall start by indicating the way in which Pope Francis has moved the parameters of mercy to include all facets of human life. As the Holy Father asserted in a quotation already cited in this work but is so important that it bears repeating: "Mercy cannot become a mere parenthesis in the life of the Church; it constitutes her very existence, through which the profound truths of the Gospel are made manifest and tangible. Everything is revealed in mercy; everything is resolved in the merciful love of the Father."[2] Thereafter I raise a series of ecclesiological ramifications both *ad extra* and *ad intra* that emerged from reading many of the addresses of Pope Francis, considering the apostolic constitution *Predicate Evangelium*,[3] and observing and having conversations with Curia personnel.

THE EXPANDING PARAMETERS OF MERCY—*AD EXTRA*

Pope Francis appears to believe that there is both an expansive and a profoundly integrative process of mercy. He has often emphasized that receiving mercy makes people more merciful. The grace of mercy, once recognized and received, overflows in a greater openness to grace and a deeper sensitivity to the needs of others and to the concomitant merciful actions. "The 'glory' of God shines in . . . the form of mercy," writes Massimo Borghesi,[4] because it is a revelation of the closeness of God and of his tenderness and compassion. In this way mercy is—as it were—an epiphany of the truth of God.

By contrast, in so many parts of the world there is a state of existential loneliness among people with no connections or relationships with others. This loneliness appears to be a consequence of the diminishment in those ties of family, friendship, and kinship that promote closeness and real affection. Pope Francis identified this state as a world of spiritual orphan-hood.[5] His perception is very akin to that of Romano Guardini, who wrote in his prophetic work *The End of the Modern World*: "Loneliness in faith will be terrible. Love will disappear from the face of the public world." And yet this is not the total picture that he paints; rather, there is a sense of hope that emerges when he states: "but the more precious will that love be which flows from one lonely person to another, involving a courage of the heart born from the immediacy of the love of God as it was made known in Christ." This sense of a perceived encounter with Christ then allows him to consider a renewed sense of love. "Perhaps man will come to experience this sense of love anew, to taste the sovereignty of its origin, to know its independence of the world, to sense the mystery of its final why? Perhaps love will achieve an intimacy and harmony never known to this day."[6] There is a resonance here with Hans Urs von Balthasar when the latter states: "There arises in the consciousness of the Church a tremendous hope and love; so that the deepest source of love springs up from the chasm of the darkest tragedy of world history. . . . The Church more closely bound to the cross, can thereby obtain a deeper view into the King-dom of resurrected love."[7]

It is the joyful hope of this intimacy and harmony, which Guar-dini speaks of and Balthasar infers, that informs the serenity with which Pope Francis proclaims the importance of mercy. His own en-counter with Christ is the source of his discernment, a practice that he also espouses for all members of the Church. According to Austen Ivereigh, "The struggle Francis was asking Catholics to attempt . . . was to embrace the call to mercy, but ever ready to ask for God's help in attending to the human weaknesses the devil was ready to exploit."[8] Here discernment was a vital imperative, particularly in the face of an existential insecurity that obstructs an encounter with oth-ers and thus impedes the action of merciful living.

In a world increasingly volatile with, so many threats to the peace and the security of people and nations, Pope Francis stated that such insecurity is "first and foremost an existential insecurity that makes us afraid of the other, as if it were our antagonist who takes away our living space and goes beyond the boundaries that we have built."[9] Such fears can easily lead to isolationism, individualism, and ideologi-cal colonization. This clearly has specific connotations regarding the issue of migration, immigration, and identity, an issue that has come to dominate the political situations of many countries of the West. It seemed that Pope Francis felt that the world is faced with a critical situation not experienced before. In response to this, the Holy Father asserted the prominence of mercy as God's method of acting in history.

Accordingly, the primordial consideration must be to recall that we are all members of the one human family. Thus, there are clear priorities that need to be established, as Pope Francis insisted in his message to the Davos gathering in January 2020:

> The moral obligation to care for one another flows from this fact, as does the correlative principle of placing the human per-son, rather than the mere pursuit of power or profit, at the very centre of public policy. This duty, moreover, is incumbent upon business sectors and governments alike, and is indispensable in the search for equitable solutions to the challenges we face. As a result it is necessary to move beyond short-term technological or economic approaches and to give full consideration to the ethical

dimension in seeking resolutions to present problems or propos-
ing initiatives for the future.[10]

Such considerations led Pope Francis to propose an "integral
ecology" that takes into account the complexity and interconnectedness of living today in the world, which he likes to designate as "our
common home." The implications of this proposal involve a renewed
and interconnected ethical approach, "a humanism capable of bringing together the different fields of knowledge, including economics,
in the service of a more integral and integrating vision."[11] What is vital
is that this vision should form the basis of a concern that is universally upheld and should not degenerate into a source of ideological
conflict between factions espousing different views of reality. As the
pope said: "The protection of the home given to us by the Creator
cannot be neglected or reduced to an elitist concern."[12]

A further consequence of such a stance of inclusion must be that
even the language of politics and diplomacy needs to be inspired by
mercy. It is this belief that mercy must be the operating dynamic in all
areas, including political affairs and the workings of diplomacy, which
also informs Pope Francis's relations with the Vatican Diplomatic Corps.

In January 2016 Pope Francis met with the Diplomatic Corps
partway through the Year of Mercy, which had begun the previous
November. This annual post-Christmas papal gathering inevitably
stands within the radiance of the celebration of Christmas just past
and the beginning of a new year, and as such recalls the importance
of the Incarnation, when God revealed himself as a vulnerable infant
in the person of Jesus. Accordingly, on this occasion Pope Francis
stated: "The mystery of the Incarnation shows us the real face of God
for whom power does not mean force or destruction but love and for
whom justice is not vengeance but mercy."[13]

MERCY AS THE RESPONSE TO FUNDAMENTALISM AND VIOLENCE

Indeed, in his 2016 meeting with the Diplomatic Corps, Pope Francis
mentioned mercy eight times and indicated that it was, for him, a dynamic imperative in a political, diplomatic, and geopolitical context.

It had been central to his apostolic journeys of the previous year, not least when he opened the first Holy Door for the Year of Mercy—not the door of the Basilica of St. Peter in Rome, but rather the door of Bangui Cathedral in the Central African Republic on his apostolic journey to that country as well as Kenya and Uganda. The symbolism of this precedent was not lost on the peoples of Africa. In an area in which violence and conflict had left deep wounds, the opening of the first Holy Door for the Year of Mercy in Africa encouraged moves toward dialogue and hope for the future. Pope Francis asserted that he had chosen this place because there, where "God's name has been misused to perpetrate injustice, I wanted to reaffirm, together with the Muslim community of the Central African Republic, that 'those who claim to believe in God must also be men and women of peace,'[14] and consequently of mercy, 'for one may never kill in the name of God.'"[15]

It was a source of joy to Pope Francis that he was able to see "signs of peace and reconciliation" during his visit to Africa in 2019. He said: "I experienced concrete hope in the form of many encouraging events, starting with the further progress achieved in Mozambique by the 1st August 2019 signing of the agreement on the definitive cessation of hostilities."[16] By contrast, other parts of Africa caused Pope Francis to grieve. As he said: "It is painful to witness, particularly in Burkina Faso, Mali, Niger and Nigeria, continuing episodes of violence against innocent people, including many Christians persecuted and killed for their fidelity to the Gospel."[17]

Pope Francis's assertion of the prohibition of killing in the name of God was reiterated in 2019 with the signing of the Document on Human Fraternity for World Peace and Living Together by Pope Francis and the Grand Imam of Al-Azhar, Ahmad Al-Tayyeb.[18] Pope Francis stated that this is an important text "aimed at fostering mutual understanding between Christians and Muslims, and peaceful co-existence in increasingly multi-ethnic and multi-cultural societies. In forcefully condemning the use of 'the name of God to justify acts of murder, exile, terrorism and oppression.'"[19]

Such a clear assertion underlines the Holy Father's understanding of religious fundamentalism. In his address to the Diplomatic Corps in 2015 he stated: "This phenomenon [of violent fundamentalism] is a consequence of the throwaway culture being applied to God.

Religious fundamentalism, even before it eliminates human beings by perpetrating horrendous killings, eliminates God himself, turning him into a mere ideological pretext."[20] In the following year Pope Francis reiterated the same point when he stated: "Only a distorted ideological form of religion can think that justice is done in the name of the Almighty by deliberately slaughtering defenceless persons."[21]

In a similar manner, in his Address to Participants in the International Conference on Violence Committed in the Name of Religion on February 2, 2018, Pope Francis talked about the importance of political authorities and religious leaders meeting to discuss how to respond to acts of violence committed in the name of religion.[22] He began by reiterating something he had often stated, particularly during his visit to Egypt in 2018: "God, the lover of life, never ceases to love man, and so he exhorts us to reject the way of violence. Above all and especially in our day, the religions are called to respect this imperative, since, for all our need of the Absolute, it is essential that we reject any 'absolutizing' that would justify violence."[23] He continued: "For violence is the negation of every authentic religious expression."

In response to such violence, at the International Peace Conference held in Cairo in 2017, Pope Francis emphasized the responsibility of religious leaders: "We have an obligation to denounce violations of human dignity and human rights, to expose attempts to justify every form of hatred in the name of religion, and to condemn these attempts as idolatrous caricatures of God."[24] In addition, during the February 2018 conference on violence he insisted that any violence that was promoted and initiated by reference to religion serves only to discredit religion: "Consequently, such violence must be condemned by all, and especially by genuinely religious persons, who know that God is always goodness, love and compassion, and that in him there is no room for hatred, resentment or vengeance."[25] Indeed, the Holy Father asserted the heinous nature of any attempt to justify such crimes in the name of God: "The religious person knows that among the greatest blasphemies is to invoke God as the justification for one's own sins and crimes, to invoke him in order to justify killing, mass murder, enslavement, exploitation in whatever form, oppression and persecution of individuals and entire populations."[26] The God of mercy does not deal in the weapons of destruction and the denigration of human persons but is rather the inspirer of those who seek for peace and mutual growth among the community of nations.

A DIPLOMACY OF MERCY

For Pope Francis, the most profound form of political or diplomatic action is the one that is imbued with mercy, such that we might even speak of a diplomacy of mercy; some of the traits of this process we have explored in previous chapters. A consistent feature is that spirit of a patient and trusting dialogue, "which is capable of embracing the values of each culture and accepting the good which comes from the experience of others."[27] An example of this way of dialogue, which he cited from his apostolic journeys in 2015, was used in the visit he made to Sarajevo, the capital of Bosnia and Herzegovina and a city that had been badly damaged by the war in the Balkans, on June 7, 2015.

In a country that had known the ravages of a war with ethnic cleansing and religious genocide, Pope Francis emphasized that the city of Sarajevo was symbolically placed to be "uniquely significant for Europe and the entire world. As a crossroads of cultures, nations and religions, it is working successfully to build new bridges, to encourage those things which unite, and to see differences as opportunities for growth in respect for all."[28] Accordingly, we see that not only does Pope Francis give no political or theological legitimacy to terrorists, but he clearly works positively for the peaceful alternative of dialogue.

Challenges to Europe

The Holy Father adamantly rejects the threats of a holy war and insists that the only way to move forward against so many piecemeal wars in different areas of the world is through the use of mercy as a key diplomatic stance. Using this approach, there is the possibility of avoiding fundamentalist and apocalyptic narratives. In a not dissimilar manner, the pope rejects the idea of the implementation of the kingdom of God on earth, which had been the basis of the Holy Roman Empire in past ages of Europe. In his address to the parliament of Europe in 2014 he called for Europeans to look beyond a parochial focus to consider the needs of the poor, the lonely, the vulnerable, the elderly, the unemployed [and] to look upon those in need with a merciful gaze.[29] In this address he recalled the Christian roots of Europe: "An anonymous second-century author wrote that: 'Christians are to the world what the soul is to the body.'[30] The function of the soul is to support the body, to be its conscience and its historical memory. A two-thousand-year-old history links Europe and Christianity. It is a history not free of conflicts and errors, and sins, but one constantly driven by the desire to work for the good of all."[31]

Fundamental to the vibrancy of life in Europe and indeed throughout societies of differing cultures is the centrality of the family, which Pope Francis has been concerned to reaffirm.[32] He sees the family as the first and most important school of mercy

> in which we learn to see God's loving face and to mature and develop as human beings. . . . Out of the family's experience of fraternity is born solidarity in society, which instills in us a sense of responsibility for others. This is possible only if, in our homes and our societies, we refuse to allow weariness and resentment to take root, but instead make way for dialogue, which is the best antidote to the widespread individualism of today's culture.[33]

To follow this prescription is to enact that engagement with others from the stance of mercy, to look at others with a merciful gaze and with a profound commitment to the dignity of each human person.

Polyhedronic Possibilities of Mercy

Already, perhaps, we have perceived that mercy is—as it were—a multi-faceted geometric divine action in history. This is reminiscent of the image of the polyhedron, a figure close to the heart of the Holy Father. Pope Francis appears to see mercy as a divine dramatic and therapeutic process. He has asserted: "God manifests himself in historical revelation, in history. Time initiates processes, and space crystallizes them. God is in history, in the processes."[34] Since the divine manifestation of mercy is not dependent on human or geopolitical determinations of what might be considered a favorable moment, inevitably there is no equation between the time of mercy and a time of peace. Rather, the time of mercy is present in all times, even in the midst of the most turbulent times, manifesting the drama of God's salvific revelation.

This can be seen in the scriptural account of the birth of Christ. It was in the fullness of God's time that "God sent his Son, born of a woman, born a subject of the Law, to redeem the subjects of the Law" (Gal. 4:4–5). It can also be seen, Pope Francis argues, in the reality of our contemporary times. The fullness of time is the divine presence in history in our days, not a construction of time based on geopolitical realities. We find it so hard to remember that this is God's world, lovingly created and sustained by the Trinity. The world is not a human-made construct.

The consequences of this are that we are called—all of us—to seek to recognize the presence of God through an increased sensitivity to the movement of the spirit of God in the world. This is why discernment is so important in the life of each person and community.[35] We need to recognize where the divine initiative is leading us forward, for God is always first in any encounter, and also God is at work in world affairs.

A Field-Hospital Church

In response to the presence of God in the world, Pope Francis sees the importance of the Church as a field hospital, as we saw so evidently in previous chapters. The Pope stated:

> I see clearly that the thing the church needs most today is the ability to heal wounds and to warm the hearts of the faithful; it needs nearness, proximity. I see the church as a field hospital after battle. It is useless to ask a seriously injured person if he has high cholesterol and about the level of his blood sugars! You have to heal his wounds. Then we can talk about everything else. Heal the wounds, heal the wounds.[36]

It is fundamental to note that the Holy Father uses the present tense; he says that the Church *is* a field hospital.

The emphasis of the pope here is almost an ecclesiological definition. In the face of what he seems to see as a river of misery, violence, and destruction whose trajectory appears at times apocalyptic in its proportions, Pope Francis is deeply aware that all of this misery, violence, and destruction is mysteriously engulfed in the vast ocean of God's mercy, which flows throughout the world. Therefore, the merciful presence of God at work in the world can transform a time of "geopolitical misery." It is here that there is a political dimension to mercy that can change the meaning of historical processes.

As Antonio Spadaro and Marcelo Figueroa write: "An evident aspect of Pope Francis' geopolitics rests in not giving theological room to the power to impose oneself or to find an internal or external enemy to fight." The way of mercy is different, and it is very important to discern carefully and not give in to the temptation "to project divinity onto a political power that then uses it for its own ends."[37] Again we are confronted with the need for wisdom and humility in discernment, as an abuse of power can exist both at the level of geopolitics and at the more domestic and communal levels of local and national groups, communities, institutions, and organizations. When the focus of their attention becomes narrowly parochial, and the need for maintenance of an existing status quo becomes more important than the call to look beyond the present parameters and discern where God is calling them to mission, in a world beyond current boundaries, there can be a foreclosing on discernment. Discernment is always an ongoing process that we need to continue to practice in faith and humility, thereby growing in an ever more profound listening both to the spirit of God and to the signs of the times.

The Call to Peace

On Sunday, January 27, 2018, Pope Francis made one of his many appeals for peace, this time in Afghanistan, after an atrocity in which a stolen ambulance was used by a suicide bomber to kill over a hundred people and injure many more. "How long will the Afghan people have to endure this inhuman violence?" the pope asked in his Angelus address the next day. "Let us pray for all the victims and for their families; and let us pray for all those, in that country, who continue to work to build peace."[38] Syria has been another country that has weighed heavily on the heart of Pope Francis. In 2019 he sent a letter to President Bashar al-Assad urging further moves for peace in

Syria.[39] The letter was delivered by Cardinal Mario Zenari, the apostolic nuncio to Syria. In September of that year he called for a day of fasting and prayer on the seventh of the month for peace in Syria, the Middle East, and the whole world.[40]

In June 2014 Pope Francis had underscored his desire for Middle East peace by inviting the Palestinian Authority president, Mahmoud Abbas, and Israel's president, Shimon Peres, to the Vatican for an evening of prayer for peace, just weeks after the collapse of another round of US-sponsored peace negotiations. From February 3 to 5, 2019, Pope Francis visited the United Arab Emirates. This was the first time a Pope had visited the Arabian peninsula, which is often cited as "the heartland of the Muslim world." Although, as Archbishop Michael Fitzgerald commented in an interview, "At the same time one could also say that [Pope Francis] is visiting the periphery of this world, since the Gulf States are a periphery, they are not Saudi Arabia."[41]

For his monthly prayer intention in November 2019 Pope Francis focused on his hope for dialogue among the religious communities of the Middle East, praying that "a spirit of dialogue, encounter and reconciliation may emerge in the Middle East."[42] It would be accurate to say that in every area of world conflict Pope Francis has sought to identify himself with those who work for the transformative effects of peace, and here, also, there is a great congruence with his predecessor, Pope Benedict XVI. An example of this is the opening paragraph of Pope Francis's message for the World Day of Peace, January 1, 2020, when he stated:

> Peace is a great and precious value, the object of our hope and the aspiration of the entire human family. As a human attitude, our hope for peace is marked by an existential tension that makes it possible for the present, with all its difficulties, to be "lived and accepted if it leads towards a goal, if we can be sure of this goal, and if this goal is great enough to justify the effort of the journey."[43] Hope is thus the virtue that inspires us and keeps us moving forward, even when obstacles seem insurmountable.[44]

Transforming the meaning of history, however, overcoming the debris and murky depths of violence, hatred, and war is the dynamic movement of mercy, which alone may lead to a sustaining peace.

Peace in the abstract does not exist. If we consider generations of history, human beings have never lived totally at peace. It appears that conflict is almost intrinsic to human nature, so humanity is always faced with conflict as an integral characteristic of human relations and therefore of international relations. And yet Pope Francis is convinced that mercy can change international relations and therefore can change the course of world affairs.[45] At the beginning of May 2018 he issued a request for the universal church to pray the rosary for peace in this month traditionally devoted to Mary. One of the many titles of Mary is Our Lady of Peace.[46]

Pope Francis's Travels to Areas of Particular Vulnerability

Many of the places to which Pope Francis has traveled have populations that are particularly vulnerable and have what might be termed "open wounds" caused often by walls or barricades or natural barriers. It is as though the Holy Father desires to bring the presence of Christ to that vulnerability to touch it and bring a sense of healing. This is an action of mercy. When he visited the Holy Land in May 2014 he alighted from his car and prayed at the wall that separates Bethlehem and Jerusalem, touching it with his hand and his head.[47] In his address in Bethlehem, he stated: "For decades the Middle East has known the tragic consequences of a protracted conflict which has inflicted many wounds so difficult to heal. Even in the absence of violence, the climate of instability and a lack of mutual understanding have produced insecurity, the violation of rights, isolation and the flight of entire communities, conflicts, shortages and sufferings of every sort."[48]

On his visit to Mexico from February 12 to 18, 2016, Pope Francis celebrated his final Mass at the border between Mexico and the US border. Here people gathered behind the barriers on both sides of the border to listen to the Mass. In his homily Pope Francis stated:

> Here in Ciudad Juárez, as in other border areas, there are thousands of immigrants from Central America and other countries, not forgetting the many Mexicans who also seek to pass over "to the other side." Each step, a journey laden with grave injustices: the enslaved, the imprisoned and extorted; so many of

these brothers and sisters of ours are the consequence of a trade in human trafficking, the trafficking of persons.[49]

These merciful gestures and words give encouragement to the vulnerable people caught in the circumstances of migration, who are escaping from violence as well as political, social, and economic instability and the inability to envisage a life that would provide necessities for their families. As the Holy Father makes these merciful gestures, traveling to places where people are most vulnerable, it is as though walls and barriers of one form and another become potential bridges that can lead persons back to a real participation in the affairs of mainstream society.

For a similar purpose, Pope Francis has traveled to places that have key contemporary significance. He visited Lampedusa on a number of occasions.[50] The island is the gateway to Europe for many migrants fleeing the violence and unrest in their home countries. The pope donated to the parish church of Lampedusa a great crucifix that had been given him by President Raoul Castro when he visited Cuba in 2015.[51] When he went to Cuba the following year, on February 12, 2016, to meet with the Patriarch of Moscow, it was again a meeting that appeared to bring together East and West, North and South.[52] In effect the Pope was helping to bridge long-held divides. For a similar purpose he visited Bangui, the capital and largest city of the Central African Republic,[53] where the reports from the country were of great concern and many of his advisers were concerned about the security hazards of such a visit. The Holy Father, though, was determined to make the visit even if he had to arrive by parachute, as he informed one of the journalists.

The pope's manner of enacting mercy, by going to places where people are most vulnerable and where he can, as it were, touch the open wounds that need healing, is a form of political mercy. It is a way of never considering anybody or anything definitively lost, but always being willing to reach out to try for dialogue and reconciliation. This may be a true feature of personal relationships, but Pope Francis desires to extend such an approach to include relations between nations, peoples, and states. He refuses to consider situations lost or irreconcilable. For him, mercy prevents such closure. Mercy he sees as able to redirect the course of history and, on occasion, to break through barriers that seemed determinedly closed.

This approach seems to bring the meaning of the Holy Door of mercy to the entire world.[54] The dynamic imperative of mercy pushes against doors, barriers, and blocks to enable what Pope Francis has defined as "incomplete thought," a form of open-ended thinking that is oriented toward inclusion and is always discerning the way forward. For the Holy Father such open-ended thinking is of particular importance in the political and geopolitical realms, where such thinking can facilitate a certain fluidity and lack of determinist closure that might enable the possibility of ongoing dialogue.

An example of this approach might be the letter that Pope Francis sent to Russian President Vladimir Putin in September 2013 on the occasion of the G20 meeting in St. Petersburg, in which he stated: "It should be noted that too many party interests have prevailed since the Syrian conflict began preventing a solution that would avoid the useless massacre we are witnessing." At the same time, it is important to note that, in accordance with his desire for ongoing dialogue, Pope Francis has received President Putin at the Vatican, on November 25, 2013, and June 10, 2015. The Iranian leader, President Hassan Rouhani, was also received, on January 26, 2016. At a time when other countries had shunned both Russia and Iran, Pope Francis was clear that for there to be any permanent solution to the situation in Syria and the wider Middle East, both Russia and Iran were necessary participants in the dialogue.

Another aspect of the diplomacy of mercy is the way in which Pope Francis continues to send telegrams to the heads of state of the territories over which the papal plane flies as it moves into their air space.[55] Of particular note is the number of times, three at least in 2018, that the papal plane has flown through Chinese air space.[56] Pope Francis is the first pope to have been allowed to pass through Chinese air space. It appears as though the Holy See is concerned to establish direct relations with the superpowers but without entering into networks of pre-established alliances and influences.

In his understanding of history Pope Francis sees the two world wars of the twentieth century as having been about a redistribution of power. In current world conflicts the Holy Father's assessment is that at the root of these confrontations is a similar power struggle for regional supremacy, which he sees as unjustifiable. He does not consider the world as divided into those countries that are right and those that are wrong. This is too simplistic. For him, it is important to immerse any conflict in the reality of God through prayer so that it takes on a spiritual form. His inspiration for this way of proceeding he draws from the life and work of St. Pierre Favre, SJ, one of the first Jesuit companions of St. Ignatius of Loyola, whom Francis canonized during the first year of his pontificate. Knowing that conflict is inevitable in the dynamics of human relations, still Pierre Favre, like Pope Francis, embodied openness to the love of God encompassing all persons.[57]

The Plight of the Most Vulnerable

For Pope Francis, the struggle for peace amid the complexities of international politics is an action undertaken in the name of those who are the weakest and most vulnerable. Accordingly, the papal peace efforts always focus on two major issues: social peace and the social inclusion of the poor. Because there is a profound link between geopolitics and economics in our contemporary world, so also is there a link between economics and war, so much so that war can be said to have become an economic tool.

During the Holy Father's apostolic visit to Poland, the murder of the French priest Fr. Jacques Hamel occurred.[58] While in Krakow, in speaking with journalists he reflected on the nature of so much violence: "The world is in a state of war in bits and pieces. . . . Now there is this one [war]. It is perhaps not organic but it is organized and it is war. We should not be afraid to speak this truth. The world is at war because it has lost peace . . . it is a war of conflict of interests."[59] In such circumstances Pope Francis saw the operation of mercy as a process of great realism and a real sign of hope, in the face of conflicts that seem to arise not from significant moral questions but from conflicts of economic or political interest.

As the pope wrote:

These conflicting interests are often economic in a world of vast inequalities where the scandal of poverty means that millions of human persons appear to be regarded as disposable, excluded and shackled by the designation of "trash" or "garbage." There is a process of exclusion within society which is fundamentally opposed to our understanding of mercy. Exclusion ultimately has to do with what it means to be a part of the society In which we live. Those who are excluded have no connection with society, they are no longer those who live on society's underside or its fringes. They are not even the disenfranchised—they are no longer even a part of society. The excluded are not worthy of being the "exploited" rather they are the outcasts, the "leftovers."[60]

In order to sustain such a societal lifestyle that excludes others, Pope Francis indicates that "a globalization of indifference has developed."[61] Yet this is both a selfish and a self-destructive reality, as "we end up being incapable of feeling compassion at the outcry of the poor."[62]

A fundamental feature of this situation, Pope Francis asserts, is our relationship with money, which we see as an authority at work in society and one that undermines the value of the human person and elevates the importance of consumerism and consumption.[63] This also is opposed to the way of mercy, grounded as that is in the essential worth and dignity of the human person. This is why for the Church the option for the poor is primarily "a theological category, rather than a cultural, sociological, political or philosophical one. God shows the poor 'his first mercy.'"[64] Pope Francis is convinced that the Church can learn a great deal from the poor, which is why he wants a Church that is poor and for the poor. "They have much to teach us," he writes. "Not only do they share in the *sensus fidei* but in their difficulties they know the suffering Christ."[65] Indeed he asserts that we need to let ourselves be evangelized by the poor in order to combat the cultural hunger for power and possessions that appears relentless. The pope goes on: "To all this we can add widespread corruption and self-serving tax evasion, which have taken on worldwide dimensions."[66] The Holy Father continues by asserting that behind these attitudes and actions "lurks a rejection of ethics and a rejection of God."[67] Such behavior fuels the drive in society toward manipulation, violence, and conflicts both at home and abroad.

The manner in which Pope Francis responds to these conflicts and what appears to be an escalating situation of violence and increasingly barbaric terrorism is to steadfastly adopt an anti-apocalyptic stance. In view of the atrocities that are committed, his first reaction is one of dismay, not of aggression. He does not argue according to the binary logic of victims and perpetrators but is convinced that all people stand in need of prayer. An example of this was seen when he visited the Auschwitz concentration camp,[68] where he spent time alone and in silence praying as he moved between different parts of the camp. At the end of his visit he wrote in the guest book: "Lord, have mercy on your people! Lord, forgiveness for so much cruelty!"[69]

He offers this plea for mercy for all, and in May 2014 he offered a prayer for terrorists, calling them "poor criminal people." His practice is a living out of the gospel injunction to love one's enemy, and Pope Francis is very clear that he can do this not by his own power but only by grace. Nevertheless, it is this love of the enemy that changes everything and empowers the outworking of mercy. This is clearly counter to the practice of terrorist organizations that desire to provoke a war of religion. In response, Pope Francis looks at their atrocities and the outpouring of such hatred with pity. It is at this point that the gospel prevails and the truth of mercy is revealed. By this very attitude and practice of mercy the Holy Father undermines the narrative of the terrorist propaganda machine that proposes an apocalyptic holy war founded on sectarian millenarianism and fundamentalism.[70]

The Peripheries and the Center

Pope Francis has been consistent in his call to members of the Church to move beyond their comfort zones and any narrow parochial focus to go to the peripheries. In this way, he stresses, the universal nature of the service of the Church becomes operative. This practice is particularly noteworthy in the priority that Pope Francis has given in his apostolic visits to the peripheral areas of the world. His trips in Europe have been to these peripheries: Lampedusa (visited on July 8, 2013),as noted earlier, the gateway to Europe, where many refugees have been received; Tirana (September 21, 2014) in Albania, a country that suffered much from a dictatorship during the period of the Cold War[71]; Turkey (November 27–30, 2014), notably the ancient city of Istanbul, the bridge between Europe and Asia; Sarajevo (June 7, 2015) in Bosnia and Herzegovina, a city that suffered considerably during the Bosnian War[72]; then, geographically speaking, a move eastward to

Armenia (June 24, 2015); Poland (July 27–31, 2016) and Auschwitz; and Georgia and Azerbaijan (September 30–October 2, 2016). In this latter visit, the complex situation of the Caucasus and their troubled geopolitical history was of particular importance to the pope. Azerbaijan has a Moslem Shiite majority in a country that has strong ties to Turkey, which has a Sunni Moslem majority.[73] In the Middle East there has been considerable animosity and violent exchange between these two opposing Moslem populations. It is clear that Pope Francis seemed to delight in visiting those places that are on the border between Asia and Europe. In all these countries what was most important to him was his encounters with the people he met, not the signing of official documents, although this also generally took place.

In many ways the pope, in his apostolic visits and journeys, appeared to circumnavigate the countries of Europe. It seemed as though, in making these journeys to the different peripheries and touching the reality of the suffering of the people in those places, Pope Francis returned to Rome with a better understanding of the center. To use a medical analogy, it was as though he could take the pulse of Europe not by going to the supposed central countries and major cities of Western Europe but rather by going to the peripheries, those places that were entry points or bridging points between East and West or places with long-suffering populations who had been forgotten by those who considered themselves the central foci of Europe.

In a similar manner, it was not to any major international journal that Pope Francis explained his understanding of his use of the term "the periphery." Rather, he spoke to *La Carcova News*, a small home-based newspaper circulated in the slum community of Gran Buenos Aires, a parish on the outskirts of Buenos Aries. The Holy Father explained that when he spoke about the periphery, he was talking about it in relation to the way we commonly set borders around ourselves as human persons. We believe that we have our personal spaces, to which we allow entry to a privileged few. Normally it is the spaces that we inhabit that we consider to be, in one way or another, the centers of our lives, which become the reference points for our involvement with others. For us, then, the center is a space we control. Insofar as we go out from this center and move away from it, we discover more things, and when we look at the centers of these new things we discover from these new places, these suburbs, that reality is different than we have seen it before. It is one thing to look at reality from the center, a place we control, and another to look at it from the last place we arrived at.[74]

Mercy as a Constant Process of Integration

"Integration" is another dynamic word for Pope Francis. When he looks at the continent of Europe he sees it not as a jaded dysfunctional entity but as countries involved in an ongoing process of integration within a developing world. Thus Europe is not just a space on a map of the world, but in itself a process of integration. The Holy Father is interested to ask if the process has an active, proactive, and dynamic attitude or if it is focused on the defensive; in like manner he looks at the reaction of many countries to the migrant crisis, in which countries closed their borders as a defensive measure. The Holy Father speaks of enlarging the soul of Europe through this process of integration.

For Pope Francis, integration means absorbing into this process differences of ages, countries, ethnic origins, and visions, and thus integrating them. In this way the identity of Europe widens. Identity, as the Pope understands it, is not only formed from data that need to be preserved from the past or from a concentration on the immediate present; identity also has a dynamic trajectory into the future. Identity, then, reveals not only who we are but what we hope for and who we might become. This is the real question for Pope Francis in relation to Europe: "What is Europe hoping for, and what might it become?" Inevitably this is an open-ended question, but it does shift attention from merely focusing on the problems and limitations of the immediate present, which of themselves may be also partially the result of decisions of the past. Instead, the Holy Father focuses on awakening the possibility of a hopeful future toward which all countries can work with renewed inspiration.

Speaking to ambassadors and diplomats accredited to the Holy See in January 2017,[75] Pope Francis urged Europe to rediscover its founding ideals as it marked the sixtieth anniversary of the Treaty of Rome, one of the most significant agreements that had led to the formation of the European Union. "Europe as a whole is experiencing a decisive moment in its history, one in which it is called to rediscover its proper identity," Pope Francis said. "This requires recovering its roots in order to shape its future."[76] He called for the creation of a new European humanism to update the very concept of Europe as a unified community of shared common values that was born from the experience of the destruction during the Second World War and the common desire for peace and the recovery and progress of peoples that prevailed thereafter. "In response to currents of divisiveness," he said, "it is all the more urgent to update 'the idea of Europe' so as to give birth to a new humanism based on the capacity to integrate, dialogue and generate that which made the Old Continent great."[77]

In an encounter with students at Roma Tre University in Rome later that year, Pope Francis set aside his prepared address and spoke to the students from his heart.[78] Many of their questions concerned matters of immigration. He assured them that the real threat to European Christian culture did not come from migrants; rather, welcoming such migrants to a country was an opportunity for the country to grow through the encounter with those of diverse cultures and languages. He indicated that in his own home country of Argentina 80 percent of the population had roots in other countries.

According to Pope Francis, there is a need to think about the many questions migration poses. He warned that simply denouncing people fleeing war and hunger is not responsible politics. Of course the ideal solution, he indicated, would be for there to be a cessation in wars and no more hunger across the world. For this to happen, he said "we need to build peace."[79] For there to be no hunger, "we need to make investments so [potential migrants] have the resources to live [in their home countries]." Migrants, he continued, "are hungry because they have no jobs, and they have no jobs because they have been exploited. They flee to Europe thinking they will find a better status, but even there they are exploited."[80] They are exploited, Francis added, even on their journey to Europe, in the boats allegedly carrying them to a better life,[81] but that have instead turned the Mediterranean Sea into a cemetery.[82]

In talking about welcoming migrants, the pope urged migrants themselves to be willing to be integrated into the local cultures that receive them, with organizations that could help them to learn the language of their new country and to find jobs and places to stay. Integration, he stated, should also involve a dialogue between cultures:

those who are welcomed into Europe have to keep their traditions alive but also have to share them with the home country while at the same time accepting new ones. "When there is this welcoming accompaniment, and integration," he said, "there is no danger. With immigration a culture is received and another offered. This is my response to fear."[83] Indeed, Pope Francis is consistently suggesting a counter-narrative to fear.

Throughout all the above, I hope it is has become clear that there is in Pope Francis's words and actions, as Antonio Spadaro has indicated, a certain diplomacy and geopolitics of mercy,[84] and this follows a logic and a rationale that is not limited to mathematical calculations and formulas. This is a theme that was espoused by Pope Benedict as well as Pope Francis, as Fr. Spadaro made clear in a presentation at the University of Notre Dame. As he stated: Pope Benedict XVI in 2006 talking with young people said: "God is not just mathematical reason but that this original Reason is also Love," and Pope Francis said in a homily at Santa Marta in 2015 that "God is greater than our human calculations. The theological pastoral logic and the geopolitical vision don't match with any kind of rigidity and needs an open way of thinking. We are not numbers. We are people.[85]

There is a certain numerical formulation in Pope Francis's approach, he likes to make three clear points in his homilies and often in his addresses. It may be in deference to this that Fr. Spadaro raises the importance of the diplomacy of the peripheries, the diplomacy of the field hospital, and the diplomacy of solidarity, which I have endeavored to explicate throughout this section.

RAMIFICATIONS *AD INTRA*

In the first part of this chapter I have focused attention on the ecclesiological ramifications of the dynamic of mercy *ad extra*. In this second part I lead us into a consideration of the ramifications *ad intra*, within the Vatican Curia itself. Clearly the two are inter-related and when functioning well give renewed support, energy, and reciprocity to the work of the Holy See and the local churches worldwide, while at the same time marking the concern of the Holy See for issues affecting human persons both within and outside of the Catholic

118 Pope Francis and Mercy

Church. The foci in this section will be on the need for reform; the document *Predicate Evangelium* and various reflections from Curia personnel; Pope Francis's concern for a poor Church for the poor; peace-building in Rome; and ecumenism and inter-faith dialogue as encouraged by the Curia offices in Rome.

The major reforms of the Vatican Curia that Pope Francis initiated with the Council of Cardinals were all designed to this end.[86] The apostolic constitution *Predicate Evangelium* was published on March 19, 2022.[87] It was the culmination of nine years' work involving forty meetings of the Council of Cardinals and the pope to consolidate reforms that had been requested in the pre-conclave meetings of cardinals in February 2013. The Council of Cardinals includes members from all parts of the world who brought the diversity of their experience to the radical revision of the Vatican bureaucracy. The initial focus for the work of the Cardinals was on financial reform. Here Cardinal Pell took a leading role, and a thorough overhaul of the bodies dealing with finance and economic affairs gradually resulted. A clear standard of transparency and accountability was established such that merciful action not only could be undertaken but could be clearly seen to be in action.

In addition, the practical measures taken by the Vatican in March 2020 with regard to preventing the spread of Covid-19, and in accord with measures issued by the Italian government, all served to indicate the compassionate care of the Holy See both for members of the Catholic Church and for all Italians and others who lived in Rome and were subject to the exigencies of the virus and the regulations issued by the Italian government.[88] In addition, the televising of the pope's Mass from Casa Santa Marta each weekday provided a source of comfort and hope for millions throughout the world.

In meetings with various members of the Vatican Curia during 2016–2017, my broader question concerning the elevation of the discourse on mercy, the vital dialogical principle and the operative tool of discernment, was supplemented by other developing reflections. I was conscious that the subjective, dialogical, and personal have to be embraced, understood, and articulated. I was particularly interested in how the injunction of Pope Francis that we look on others with a merciful gaze might be more dynamically undertaken using the tool of discernment. Clearly Pope Francis's own actions—including the televising of his daily Masses—were one example of such discerned action.

Increasingly, in reflecting on the resonance of the papacies of Benedict XVI and Francis, it appeared that the characteristics of love and mercy were a potential governing hermeneutic for theology in the twenty-first century. Certainly it seemed that Pope Benedict prepared the way for Pope Francis with his noble humility and courage, so clearly evinced in his resignation and, since that time, in the limit of silence that he has voluntarily placed on himself.[89]

The Need for Reform

In the whole process that preceded the election of Pope Francis it was evident that people were looking for some reforms in the Church.[90] The meetings of the Cardinals leading up to the Conclave seemed to make this clear. Accordingly, Pope Francis feels he has a mandate for his reforms. He appears to see the reformation of the Curia as his mission. Certainly, updating and restructuring would be normal for a new papacy. What appears novel is the way in which Pope Francis linked this reform and restructuring with the Jubilee of Mercy. He clearly realized that the first thing that needed to be reformed is the human heart—hence the Jubilee of Mercy.

Such an appeal to mercy is a deep and profound call to transformation. This transformation was to include the whole Church and, perhaps especially, the central organs of the Church in Rome. Within the Vatican Curia,[91] Pope Francis has demanded a movement from an intellectual understanding of reform to an affective embracing of such reform and the concrete outworking of that reform in terms of clear, simple, and transparent actions. He is well aware that until hearts are changed any reformation is a matter of the timed shifting of superficial structures and a lack of concrete action. The Holy Father, however, personalized the reform and challenged the leadership of the Church, as well as the whole Church—all the faithful—to take possession of their faith and religious identity. It was clear to him that reform needed to be the fruit of interior conversion with its deepest roots in the passionate love of God, which is always calling us to fullness of life.

The reason for such reform is that we are all, like the Pope, both impelled and compelled, by a dynamic of merciful love, to express our ongoing conversion through genuinely Christian action on behalf of the most vulnerable in the world. This lens of mercy through which Pope Francis views all his activity is refined through his regular practice of discernment, which is the filter for his decisions. In this way his Ignatian formation continues to inform his life and work, and central to this formation, of course, are the Spiritual Exercises of St. Ignatius of Loyola.

It has sometimes been with very strong words that Pope Francis has castigated those with a particular form of spiritual worldliness that he has identified within the Church, especially among the clergy in the Curia. It is a form of worldliness, according to Walter Kasper, that "relies on possessions, influence, privileges, or on organization, planning, doctrinal and disciplinary security, authoritarian elite consciousness, or a socially glamorous life-style."[92] In addressing bishops, Pope Francis stated how important it is that, like St. Paul, a bishop be one who is able to discern spirits so that he will know "when it is the Spirit of God speaking to him and who (also) knows how to defend himself when spoken to by the spirit of the world."[93] The challenge of spiritual worldliness is not just one that touches the clergy. It also pertains to the lifestyles of laypeople and religious. As Kasper writes: "What is required from everyone is simplicity, plainness, and frugality in one's personal lifestyle, as in institutional self-preservation."[94] In particular, these are seen as necessary pre-requisites for those who serve in the Vatican Curia.

Predicate Evangelium

Predicate Evangelium asserts that the task that the Lord entrusted to the Church is the preaching of the gospel: "The Church carries out this command above all when, in all that she says and does, she bears witness to the mercy that she herself has graciously received."[95] Thus, from the first paragraph of the document it is clear that the mercy of God is the driving imperative for the reform of the Curia that is envisaged. That reform is meant to be reviewed in the context of the call to evangelization, which illustrates the Church's missionary nature.

Accordingly, the Curia reform is designed to attune the Curia more effectively to this mission of evangelization.[96] Such reform also, by the nature of the Church's mission, leads to a greater sense of communion, and "the life of communion makes the Church *synodal*, a Church marked by reciprocal listening, whereby everyone has something to learn."[97] The great protagonist of such a synodal process is the Holy Spirit, who espouses ecclesial communion around "the Roman Pontiff as guarantee of unity of faith and of communion."[98] Accordingly, "We must first of all entrust ourselves to the Holy Spirit, who is the true guide of the Church and implore in prayer the gift of authentic discernment."[99] Finally, it is important to reassert, as the document does on a number of occasions, that "evangelization takes place especially by the proclamation of divine mercy, in a variety of forms and expressions."[100]

Predicate Evangelium also emphasizes that every Christian is called to be a missionary disciple, a witness to and bearer of mercy to others. A novel assertion is that, by reason of baptism, provision needs to be made for "involvement of lay women and men in roles of government and responsibility. [Indeed] their presence and their participation is essential, since they contribute to the well-being of the entire Church."[101]

It is significant that Pope Francis has moved ahead with his plan to include more women in Vatican structures. In 2019 he appointed Sr. Nathalie Becquart, XMCJ, as a consultor to the Synod of Bishops (not technically part of the Vatican Curia) and, in 2021, named her as one of the under-secretaries. Sr. Raffaella Petrini, FSE, was named in 2021 as secretary general of Vatican City State. In April 2022 Alessandra Smerilli, FMA, was named secretary of the Dicastery for Integral Human Development. In July 2022 Pope Francis named three women to the Dicastery for Bishops: Sr. Raffaella Petrini, FSE; Sr. Yvonne Reungalat, FMA; and Maria Lia Zervino, president of the World Union of Catholic Women's Organizations.

In the reorganization of the Curia, congregations and commissions have been replaced by dicasteries, and these have been reduced by unifying complementary ones and streamlining their functions, much as would be done in the secular professional sphere. The major difference, however, is that the aim of the reform has been to enkindle the imperative of divine merciful love in the Curia and the entire Church, and encourage a return to "the principles, teachings and resolves set forth by the Council, so that, fanned into flame by charity, they might truly bring about, in the Church and in the world, the renewal of mind, action, conduct, moral conviction, hope and joy which was the ultimate purpose of the Council."[102]

Reflections of Curia Personnel

A number of Curia personnel shared their own personal experience of the elevation of the discourse of mercy by Pope Francis and the challenge that this has confronted them with in their own lives and the execution of their duties. Assignments in the Vatican Curia can be sterile, as in it, as in any bureaucracy, there can be a temptation to a superficial engagement and a form of aloofness in dealing with others.[103] With this imperative for mercy, however, there is a disturbance of this superficiality and the "comfortable" such that what has emerged for many is a deeper awareness of the ability to engage in more human contacts, impelled by the example of Pope Francis.

A major concern for Pope Francis has been what he identifies as a spirit of worldliness that is manifested in a number of different attitudes—"ostentatious preoccupation for the liturgy, for doctrine and for the Church's prestige"—but not necessarily a concern with the needs of the time.[104] The pope writes: "It can also lead to a business mentality, caught up with management statistics, plans, and evaluations whose principal beneficiary is not God's people but the Church as an institution. . . . Evangelical fervor is replaced by the empty pleasure of complacency and self-indulgence."[105]

These are all temptations that can threaten not just the individual but the entire Church. Clearly such words have been provocative and a deep challenge to many. Pope Francis espouses a simplicity, plainness, and frugality both in personal lifestyles and in the way the institution of the Church presents herself. As Kasper writes: "The Church is not supposed to depend on political and social influence and glamor; it is not to rely only on programs, planning and organizations, but rather to rely on spiritual radiance."[106] The path toward such a disposition is being a poor Church for the poor and in that way reclaiming the joy of the gospel as we set our hope on God and on his providence.

A Poor Church for the Poor

Pope Francis's statements are profound, simple, and direct.[107] There is gospel simplicity about them, and they are often passionate in their articulation. He also makes many gestures that are direct and parabolic in their significance. His gestures border on political statements; we have already seen that above in his emphasis on touching places of vulnerability during his apostolic journeys. Only time will tell the lasting significance of these gestures. Nearer to home, Pope Francis called for the construction of showers for the homeless near St. Peter's Basilica. Regular medical care is offered, and even facilities for hairdressers to give regular cuts to people who would not be able to afford such attention to their own personal well-being.

In addition, a certain refocusing has occurred. Under previous pontificates there were many concerts and events for visiting bishops, dignitaries, and the Vatican Curia during the course of a year. During Pope Francis's papacy, the only concerts have been for the homeless, for whom also a tour of the Sistine Chapel was organized, and there have been a series of pizza lunches after major Eucharistic celebrations for them.

The very name Pope Francis chose indicates his desire for a poor Church that will be for the poor.[108] The focus of his attention is not so much on the material goods of the Church but on how the Church uses the goods that have been entrusted to it. What are priority purposes? Are they for the poor or to safeguard the Church's own interests? With the financial reforms of the Roman Curia, already certain procedures have been put in place—begun under Benedict XVI—that endeavor to guarantee transparency about the use of money and goods. It is obvious that decisions are now being made according to transparent procedures. Clearly there is a gospel imperative to care for the poor, and the dangers of wealth are starkly stated in the gospels. The call to a poverty of spirit that places all hope and dependency on God and not on material goods resounds loudly both in the gospel and in the words and practices of Pope Francis himself.[109]

A predecessor of Pope Francis whom he canonized, Pope John XXIII, had spoken of a Church for the poor, and the Vatican document *Lumen Gentium* makes specific mention of such a Church when it states:

Just as Christ carried out the work of redemption in poverty and persecution, so the Church is called to follow the same route. . . . Thus, the Church . . . is not set up to seek earthly glory, but to proclaim, even by its own example, humility and self-sacrifice. . . . The Church encompasses with love all who are afflicted with human suffering and in the poor and afflicted sees the image of its poor and suffering Founder. It does all it can to relieve their need and in them it strives to serve Christ.[110]

Pope Francis has gone out of his way in his travels to meet refugees and those suffering from violence and forced migration—for example, in the Philippines, where he travelled in 2014; on the Italian island of Lampedusa in 2013; and in a meeting with the Rohingya refugees while visiting Bangladesh in 2017. People see in Pope Francis someone who puts into action what he says, and that speaks volumes. It is impossible not to respect him. In many ways Pope Francis can appear to be a contemporary John the Baptist figure calling the Church to a more profound and radical living of the gospel; at the same time, he reaches beyond the parameters of the Church to call the world to a deeper appreciation of the essential dignity and value of the human person and the life-giving, not death-dealing, nature of any true religion. In this effort he has won the respect of religious leaders around the world and advanced the cause of both ecumenism and inter-faith dialogue.

Peace-Building in Rome

The Holy Father's call to work together for peace is one that is addressed to all people of good will and thus touches the essential and universal desire for peace ingrained in the heart of humanity.[111] This emphasis on peace is one that has been taken up most sincerely in Rome itself. The Sant' Egidio community, which celebrated the fiftieth anniversary of its foundation in 2018, is an example of a community that began as a group of Roman Catholics in Rome and now has around sixty thousand members scattered across seventy countries.[112] It is a community that espouses prayer, care for the poor, and peace-building, and these three foci are both integral to mercy and dear to the heart of Pope Francis. Care for migrants and refugees is also one of the cornerstones of Sant' Egidio's partnership with Pope Francis, as reflected, among other things, in the fact that the group was asked by the pontiff to care for the Syrian migrants he brought with him back to Rome aboard the papal plane after his 2016 visit to the Greek island of Lesbos.

There is also a commitment that the community has embraced since the earliest days of its existence, namely, the commitment to ecumenism and dialogue among cultures, peoples, and religions. Every year the community convokes in a different European city (with the exception of Jerusalem in 1995) a great meeting of prayer for peace, in continuity with the historic Day of Prayer for Peace held by Pope St. John Paul II in 1986 at Assisi, where he met with the religious leaders of the whole planet.

Ecumenism and Inter-Faith Dialogue

Alongside this major work for peace that is so closely linked to the practice of mercy, Pope Francis has also issued a request that members of the Church work together on common tasks to promote both the work of ecumenism and that of inter-faith dialogue. In the activity of encountering one another in a common activity he sees the outworking of the prayer for respect, compassion, and solidarity. Indeed, advocates for ecumenical work have also picked up the language of mercy. The Anglican Church has particularly appreciated the emphasis on mercy and, together with Roman Catholics in different parts of the world, has endeavored to bring this merciful stance to those most in need, taking the gospel to the ends of the earth, in particular to the peripheries. So there has come about a greater sharing in the mission of outreach to the world. This echoes the desire of Pope Francis that Protestants and Roman Catholics should walk together, pray together, and work together, not in a competitive manner.[113]

This joint activity, from an impetus of mercy, also stimulates deeper dialogue across denominational lines. Although there are significant blocks to ecumenism, still Pope Francis continues to urge us to take the path of accompaniment of one another in a form of Receptive Ecumenism.[114] In a not dissimilar manner, the focus on mercy has been significantly influential in moving toward inter-faith dialogue. Mercy is universally present in attentiveness to the poor and in being ready for joint action on behalf of the poorest from those of different religious faiths. One might suggest that this is how the poor contribute to inter-faith dialogue, by being recipients of such action. Since compassion is an expression of mercy and also a criterion for humanity, mercy also shows itself in a preferential option for those who suffer.[115] This is a concern that extends across the faith traditions. Pope Francis has issued invitations to other religions to align themselves with the Roman Catholic Church around the understanding and practice of mercy in the tradition, the life and action, and the theological and the spiritual dimensions of different faiths. These invitations have brought together members of different religions and even secularists. Pope Francis is himself a credible witness to mercy put into action, and this attracts those from other faith traditions and from none. It also helps others to see that in the fight for justice it is possible to discover faith.

Pope Francis is also clear that the corporal works of mercy are works of witness to faith in Christ.[116] During the Year of Mercy, he regularly made "mercy Friday" surprise visits to different marginalized groups, which he continued to make after the official Year of Mercy concluded.[117] In particular, the Holy Father evinces his concern for migrants, a concern that seems to be almost part of his DNA. The simplicity of his message and the correspondence between his words and his actions convey a strong teaching and witness to the dignity of all human persons, particularly those who are most in need. In a time that appears to reveal a lacunae in moral authority, his message has great credibility. It is apparent that when moral authority, such as that exemplified by the Holy Father, is present, people are ready to follow that message in all its simplicity, reawakening the spiritual dimension of their lives.

The Pontifical Council for Interfaith Dialogue is well aware that non-believers are very attracted to Pope Francis and that when he is with these people his dialogue with them becomes a form of evangelization. Also, in his references to the anniversary of *Nostrae Aetate*,[118] Pope Francis clearly has an open approach to Judaism, Islam, and other faiths.[119] Approaching other faiths from a position of discernment, he is concerned to heal historical wounds in relationships, particularly with Judaism, and to recognize members of other faiths as true brothers and sisters in our humanity. From the evidence of the

Holy Father's interactions, it seems that the Roman Catholic Church has a significant part to play in promoting dialogue with other faiths, and there appears to be a reciprocal openness to respond on the part of these faiths.

Mercy can bring people together across the inter-faith divide in the works of mercy: looking after the homeless, feeding the poor, and so on. In these actions, there is a coming together to strive toward a common goal, and in this process there can be growth in friendship and the broadening of a relational identity. What maintains the coherence of such a group is the frequency of contact between parties and a commitment to building on the initial foundation laid. Indeed, friendship has a common goal of mercy, as it can lead to both complementarity and convergent possibilities where there is space and room for differences and thus a deeper level of freedom and engagement. Here it becomes apparent that there are different levels of dialogue, formal dialogue and other, more informal, engagements. What is common to these different levels is the need to allow time for relationships to grow and become enriching such that bonds of attention, respect, and ultimately, love, pervade.

Pope Francis calls consistently *ad extra* and *ad intra* for a recognition of fragilities and vulnerabilities and before these his stance is one of tenderness, compassion, and mercy. This mercy has the form of solidarity and support in the way it is exercised for the poor and migrants. There is an attempt to overcome exclusion by fashioning inclusion. This way of being pope, this way of seeing the papal ministry, is what has shaped the pontificate of Pope Francis. There is a renewed presentation of the life of discipleship, one marked by attentiveness to relationships and the willingness to enter into a process of accompaniment. In this life of discipleship, relationships with God, one another, and creation have to find their proper balance in and through the application of the principle of justice. For Pope Francis, justice is first and foremost a form of kindness and mercy.

Conclusion

Let us then with confidence draw near to the throne of grace, that we may receive mercy, and find grace to help in time of need.

—Hebrews 4:15–16

The throne of grace is a Christian image that has been perpetuated throughout the centuries. Derived from the above verses in the letter to the Hebrews, the throne of grace has been the focal point as the place where mercy is received and grace in difficult circumstances is found. Images of the throne of grace have tended to show the Eternal Father holding the Crucified Son, with the Holy Spirit in the form of a dove hovering over the figures. One representation familiar to me is that portrayed in the the English College in Rome.[1] In 1580 Durante Alberti (1538–1616) painted what is commonly referred to as the Martyrs' Picture, which hangs in the college chapel (and also appears on the cover of this book).[2]

The painting depicts the Holy Trinity of the throne of grace in the traditional way but in a somewhat dramatic representation. The Father holds the broken and bleeding body of Christ, and the Spirit in the traditional form of a dove hovers over the head of Jesus. There are two English martyrs, St. Edmund of East Anglia and St. Thomas à Becket of Canterbury, below the Trinity and on either side, who beckon to those gathered before the altar to contemplate the scene.[3]

A map of the British Isles lies below the crucified Christ, and blood from his side drips onto the map. Fire springs from the droplets of blood. This echoes the motto of the college, held by a cherub: *IG-NEM VENI MITTERE IN TERRAM*, "I have come to bring fire to the earth." Clearly the aim of these representations was to indicate that mercy and grace—or, as I would prefer to say, the eternal grace of mercy—is a Trinitarian gift.

Throughout this book I have endeavored to highlight the wide-ranging nature of mercy as understood by Pope Francis and the determinative effect that mercy has had on so many facets of his engagement with the Church and the world. In himself, he embodies a rich co-inherence of theology, spirituality, philosophy, theological anthropology, political and economic insight, and a passion for the proclamation of the good news of the mercy of God, particularly to the poorest and most oppressed in our contemporary world. I have argued that mercy is the hermeneutical lens with which he approaches all, whether it be in prayer, the workplace, curial reform, marriage and family life, education, even the language of politics and diplomacy. Mercy, for Pope Francis, lies at the very core of the human person, for we are created out of the mercy of God.

The imperative of mercy is not relegated to pragmatic pastoral action. Clearly there is a trajectory toward such effective outreach, but this arises from a secure theological basis. As Pope Benedict emphasized in a letter to Msgr. Dario Edoardo Viganò on the publication in Italian of eleven volumes on Pope Francis's theology.[4] Benedict wrote: "Pope Francis is a man with profound philosophical and theological formation," and he emphasized "the interior continuity between the two pontificates even with all the differences in style and temperament."[5] At the heart of this interior continuity is the dynamic of mercy.

The omnipotence of God, said St. Thomas Aquinas, is shown, above all, "in the act of his forgiveness and the use of his mercy, for the way He has of showing his supreme power is to pardon freely."[6] We are most accustomed to considering mercy as confined to our experience of forgiveness and the mercy of God as revealed most fully in the Passion, death, and resurrection of Christ. This sacramental character of mercy is clearly one that Pope Francis also embraces, and indeed he has spoken many times of the importance of members of the Church reclaiming a life-giving understanding of the nature of the sacrament of reconciliation and the necessity of confession for the health of both the individual and the Church.

The pontiff has, however, elevated the discourse of mercy to a level far beyond merely a focus on the sacraments. For him, such mercy arises from the divine initiative of a radical love that draws human persons to an intimate encounter with God, an encounter that can become a communion of will affecting even the feelings of a person. From this perspective, in God it is possible both to love others—even those we do not like or even know—and to act mercifully toward them. This is possible only because it is divine love that unites us both to God and one another.[7] Pope Francis also includes within the purview of mercy a key dialogical principle: he has emphasized the need for a culture of dialogue and the importance of training young people in a grammar of dialogue in order that there may always be a reaching out to others, whether the others are friendly or hostile.

Alongside dialogue we have explored what has become for Pope Francis the operative tool of discernment. Indeed, his intention was that all sectors of the Church be involved in formation in the practice of spiritual discernment, and even made this desire the focus of his prayer intention for the month of March 2018. He has seen discernment as of quintessential importance throughout his papacy, since the heart of discernment is that constant disposition of openness to the movement of the spirit of God at work throughout the concrete reality of everyday life. This is why an interior awareness and understanding of the spirits at work within the heart is vital, as a preliminary to action.

The foci of dialogue and discernment owe much to the Jesuit formation that Pope Francis received and his own experience as both a receiver and a giver of the Spiritual Exercises. Indeed, it is impossible to exaggerate this important Ignatian influence on his understanding of mercy. In particular, the understanding of colloquy, in which heart speaks to heart in the context of encounter with God in prayer, is a significant characteristic of Pope Francis's way of proceeding. He has a liberating way of speaking from the heart, and on numerous occasions in audiences with different groups of people he has decided not to proceed with a prepared address but rather to speak simply from the heart, sometimes in responding to questions, at other times because he feels inspired to raise certain points for the particular audience he is engaged with.

This deeper engagement of the heart acknowledges the heart as "the deepest root and foundation of every person, the focus of our affective life and, in a word, his or her very core."[8] In the heart of Christ, Pope Francis has emphasized, we see the most profound expression of the mercy of the Father.[9] Such a personal engagement with Christ, then, impels a person toward a union with the redemptive work of Christ and results in a real fecundity in apostolic encounter. At the Mass that closed the Jubilee Year of Mercy, Pope Francis invited all present to "entrust the life of the Church, all humanity and the entire cosmos to the Lordship of Christ, asking him to pour out his mercy upon us like the morning dew, so that everyone may work together to build a brighter future."[10]

Pope Francis believes that in and through our encounters with Christ we are drawn to a more profound engagement with the life of the Trinity. It is by the indwelling of the Holy Spirit that we are initiated into that indwelling of the Father and the Son in the believer that was promised in the great high-priestly prayer of the Gospel of John.[11] The dynamic that impels this ever more profound movement is rooted in the Trinitarian ontology of mercy. Mercy is intrinsic to the divine essence and overflowing in and through the kenosis of Christ, which reveals the kenotic event at the heart of the Trinity. The fruitfulness of this for human persons involves that revolution of tenderness that is so beloved by Pope Francis and is made known in, and through, his gestures and inclusive engagements.

The loving merciful desire of the persons of the Trinity is to bring human persons into the very life of God. The love at the heart of the Trinity involves a constant exchange of self-gift within the distinction of persons. This dynamic self-giving overflows into a divine fecundity that embraces human beings, drawing them into the reality of divine love and intimacy. It is at this point that we raised earlier (in chapter 4), the question "Is mercy the organizing principle of the attributes of God?" It is clear that it is in and through the mercy of God that the love of Father, Son, and Spirit are revealed. If indeed mercy is an eternal grace, then it is also both a channel and a trajectory of the loving action of God revealed in the free divine initiative. Further, the creativity, beauty, truth, and goodness that are integral to divine life may also be considered inherent characteristics of the grace of mercy. Within the eternal inner vitality of the Trinity there is room for ongoing inventiveness in the expression of merciful love that flows between the persons and overflows into human life and the created order.

The glimpsing of something of the profound depths of divine mercy at the heart of the Trinity necessitates also the recognition that mercy is God's method of acting in history. Pope Francis appears to see mercy as a divine dramatic and therapeutic process within history. A most immediate consequence of this for the Holy Father is that even the language of politics and diplomacy needs to be inspired by the reality of mercy, since the most profound form of political or diplomatic action is that imbued with mercy, such that we can speak of a diplomacy of mercy. Always the spirit of a patient, trusting dialogue is paramount, a dialogue that rejects all attempts to give political or theological legitimacy to violence or terrorism. Rather, mercy is a multi-faceted geometric action in history, not dependent on human or geopolitical determinations of a favorable time but rather present in the most turbulent of times, manifesting the drama of God's salvific revelation.

The consequence of such an understanding of mercy is to underline that we are all called to recognize the presence of God in an increased sensitivity to the movement of the spirit of God. This recalls the importance of discernment in the life of the individual and the community. Discernment enables human beings to avoid the lure of abusing power at any level of engagement, from the most personal to the realm of geopolitics. Mercy involves a refusal to see anyone or any situation as definitively lost and a refusal to argue according to the binary logic of victims and perpetrators.

Understanding the primacy of mercy in the life of the Church is a central truth and wisdom that is necessary to be conveyed to future generations. In this context it is vital that ongoing consideration of the care of young people, an attentiveness to their concerns and a willingness to incorporate their energy and vision into the life of the Church, should also involve a sharing of the wisdom surrounding this eternal grace. Mercy, realized as a verb of action, a disposition, and a critical way of perceiving others and the world in which we live, requires a profound encounter with Christ in prayer and an openness to the kind of dialogue and discernment that we have already indicated is crucial in Pope Francis's proclamation of mercy. Accordingly, helping young people to pray is a primary imperative, and assisting them in the practice of discernment is vital. The provision of such opportunities in local communities could assist young people to feel more of an integral part of the Church. In addition, the inclusion of such young people, who could, in turn, draw others from among their peers, is a sign of hope both for the young people themselves and for the congregations in which they live and work.

All people wish for a full and authentic life, and this is particularly the case for young people, as well as the challenge of human existence. Pope Francis insisted that it is not concrete problems or difficulties, however serious or dramatic they may be, that form the greatest threat to human flourishing. "The greatest challenge in life," he said, "is to avoid being mediocre and fainthearted. If a young person settles for a life of bland mediocrity, even if he or she follows the rules, he will not live a full and authentic existence."[12] The pope asserted that it is vital for the Church to pray for young people. "We must ask the Lord to give today's youth the gift of healthy restlessness,"[13] he said, stressing that young people must hunger for a life of fulfilment and beauty.[14] Such a life has at its core the key dynamic of mercy, which enables a person both to be open to encountering the mercy of God and to a fruitful acceptance of limitations, and also to be able to look at others with a merciful, loving gaze that also accepts their limitations.

The mercy of God is beyond any human calculations. It bears the weight of divine love, ever seeking to embrace and encourage the truth of human fragility. It is the mercy of God that illuminates the depths of human sinfulness and offers life-giving forgiveness. Day by day it is the eternal mercy of God, revealed in the Eucharist, that enables the human person to be fed from the life of God and to be inspired and enabled to live in this way of mercy, holding fast to the action of divine grace and being an open conduit for that grace to encounter others.

Not only is the quality of mercy not "strained,"[15] but rather, in hearts and minds purified by this grace, it becomes a life-giving stream flowing at an ever increasing pace from the throne of grace to encompass all with whom the person and the community of the Church may engage. Mercy is not merely twice blessed but rather eternally blessed, an eternal grace, a divine hermeneutical lens through which to glimpse the loving, prayerful interaction within the persons of the Trinity and the merciful gaze of divine love upon all humanity and the whole of the created world.

Postscript

"His mercy endures forever," according to the psalmist (Psalm 136:12). This is what both the faith and the experience of Pope Francis have told him is true and which he desires to share with all people. Amid the darkness of a worldwide pandemic of Covid-19, that faith was sorely tried. Yet in the rain-soaked St. Peter's Square on March 27, 2020, the Holy Father presided over an extraordinary moment of prayer from the *sagrato* of St. Peter's Basilica. Walking through the rain without an umbrella, the figure of Pope Francis was seen by millions, exposed to the elements of that day but purposefully focused on his mission, to convey that loving mercy of God, to all who watched his message broadcast through the many forms of media connection.

He took for his text the storm on the Sea of Galilee, when Jesus is asleep in the boat and the disciples awake him, fearful that they will all drown (Mark 4: 35–41). Pope Francis said of the storm that it "exposes our vulnerability and uncovers those false and superfluous certainties around which we have constructed our daily schedules, our projects, our habits and priorities."[1] The pope drew to the attention of his listeners the fact that the pandemic, like the storm at sea, had uncovered our belonging as brothers and sisters of the one Father. In this light, he used as a constant refrain the words of Jesus: "Why are you afraid? Have you no faith?" He saw this as a calling, and indeed a recalling to faith in our times: "In this world, that you love more than we do, we have gone ahead at breakneck speed, feeling powerful and able to do anything."[2] Yet the truth is that this time is a call to faith: "Faith begins when we realize we are in need of salvation. We are not self-sufficient; by ourselves we founder; we need the Lord. Let us hand over our fears to him so that he can conquer them." Then we come to know the reality of the cross and to experience in our soul's depths his loving mercy and know that "nothing and no one can separate us from his redeeming love." And indeed "This is God's strength: turning to the good everything that happens to us, even the bad things."[3] So we can move forward with hope beyond the pandemic, for indeed God's mercy endures forever!

In addition to the gift of prayer that Pope Francis offered, he continually asked the papal almoner to offer practical assistance by means of financial contributions and also the donation of much-needed medical equipment. As a result, in June 2020 ventilators were sent to Haiti, Venezuela, Brazil, and Ecuador; in August 2020 ventilators and ultrasound scanners were sent to Brazil and Malawi. The attention that Pope Francis gives to the physical and material as well as the spiritual needs of people further serve to exemplify the dynamic hermeneutic of mercy that informs his life and actions.

APPENDIX

Mary, Mother of Mercy

From the beginning of his pontificate Pope Francis demonstrated a profound veneration for the person of Mary, Mother of God. It was less than twenty-four hours after his election to the papacy that Cardinal Jorge Mario Bergoglio asked for a car and journeyed across Rome to the Basilica of Santa Maria Maggiore. It is the first church in the Western world dedicated to Mary, Mother of God.[1] Pope Francis wished to venerate the image of Mary under the title Salus Populi Romani (Salvation of the Roman People, or Health of the Roman People), patroness of the city of Rome.[2] He visited the basilica again forty days after his election, and on that occasion he spoke about the fact that Our Lady is always concerned about the health of her children. "Mary is the mother, and a mother worries above all about the health of her children," Pope Francis said. "Like a buona mamma [good mom]," he added, "she helps us grow, to confront life, to be free." Throughout his life as a priest, bishop, and now pope, the Holy Father has revealed a tender devotion to Mary under numerous titles. Many years ago, before he was made a bishop, Father Bergoglio told the Jesuits in his care, "The magisterium will tell you who Mary is, but it is our believing people who will teach you how to love Mary."[3] There are particular Jesuit devotions to Our Lady of Montserrat and the Madonna della Strada (Our Lady of the Way), which were devotions especially favored by St. Ignatius of Loyola.[4] Alongside these, Pope Francis has indicated his own personal devotion to Mary under three other titles: Our Lady of Luján, patroness of Argentina; Our Lady of Aparecida, patroness of Brazil; and Mary, Undoer of Knots.[5] When the Holy Father was archbishop of Buenos Aires he often used to assist in the spiritual ministry to pilgrims coming to Our Lady of Luján's shrine in Buenos Aires, including celebrating Mass, hearing confessions, and giving spiritual direction. Archbishop Bergoglio, as a member and then-president of the Latin American Bishops' Conference, would often go to meetings at the Marian shrine of Aparecida in Brazil. He returned there for World Youth Day in 2013 and once more reverenced the statue of the Black Virgin. According to legend fishermen were inundated with fish to catch soon after finding an image of a black Virgin Mary. Since then Our Lady of Aparecida has become one of Brazil's most popular and important saints. His other favorite title for Mary, Our Lady, Undoer of Knots, is a devotion that came from Germany, where he was sent for studies after his ordination. He discovered in Augsburg a painting of the Blessed Virgin titled *Undoer of Knots* and took a postcard copy back to Argentina.

Many years later, when he became bishop, Jorge Bergoglio asked that copies of the painting be displayed in churches and chapels throughout the Archdiocese of Buenos Aires. So great was his devotion that as a cardinal he had a chalice made with this image of Mary, Undoer of Knots, and he presented this chalice to Pope Benedict following the latter's election as pope. Perhaps we may glimpse why this devotion so appeals to him through a remark he made on St. Valentine's Day, 2015, when he spoke to 25,000 engaged couples in St. Peter's Square and said: "We all know the perfect family does not exist. The perfect husband does not exist, and the perfect wife does not exist. Let's not even talk about perfect mother-in-laws!"[6] The crowd clearly appreciated the Holy Father's sense of humor.

It is apparent that Pope Francis is in touch with ordinary people and knows much of the everyday problems they face. It is these problems and difficulties—these knots—that he suggests should be taken to Our Lady.[7] Addressing a crowd in St. Peter's Square in October 2013 he said: "We know one thing: nothing is impossible for God's mercy! Even the most tangled knots are loosened by his grace. And Mary, whose 'yes' opened the door for God to undo the knot of the ancient disobedience, is the Mother who patiently and lovingly brings us to God, so that he can untangle the knots of our soul by his fatherly mercy."[8]

In 2018 the Holy Father instituted a new feast for the universal church, Mary, Mother of the Church.[9] This feast was first celebrated on the day following Pentecost Sunday.[10] Before every international journey, and after returning, it has been the custom of Pope Francis to visit the Basilica of St. Mary Major to pray, asking for the intercession of Our Lady for the safety and success of his journey before he leaves, and to offer prayers of gratitude after he returns. If Jesus is mercy, as we have seen that Pope Francis asserts, then Mary is clearly the Mother of Mercy. As he has stated, "No one has penetrated the profound mystery of the incarnation like Mary. Her entire life was patterned after the presence of mercy made flesh.[11]

Reflecting particularly on Mary's title as "Mother of Mercy," Pope Francis opened the Holy Door at the Basilica of St. Mary Major on January 1, 2016, beginning the Extraordinary Jubilee of Mercy. He said: "It is most fitting that on this day we invoke the Blessed Virgin Mary above all as 'mother of mercy.'"[12] Later he said: "The door we have opened is, in fact, a Door of Mercy. . . . Those who cross its threshold are called to enter into the merciful love of the Father with complete trust and freedom from fear; they can leave this Basilica knowing that Mary is ever at their side."[13]

It is clear that for Pope Francis Mary shares to an eminent degree in the divine mercy. She constantly procures for us the compassion of her Son, and here the words of Pope St. John Paul II resonate with those of Pope Francis: "Mary is the one who has the deepest knowledge of the mystery of God's mercy. She knows its price, she knows how great it is. In this sense we call her 'Mother of mercy,' 'Virgin most merciful' each one of these titles having a profound theological meaning. Each of them expresses the special preparation of her soul, of her whole personality, so that she would be able to perceive through the complexity of events, first of all directed to Israel, then to every individual and ultimately to the whole of humanity, the need for that abounding mercy of hers in which 'from generation to generation' people become sharers according to the eternal design of the Most Holy Trinity."[14]

Cardinal Joseph Ratzinger saw Mary as the reflection of Divine Mercy in the message of mercy that was revealed throughout the life of Pope John Paul II. Of him he said at his funeral Mass: "Divine Mercy: the Holy Father found the purest reflection of God's mercy in the Mother of God. He, who at an early age had lost his own mother, loved his divine mother all the more. He heard the words of the

crucified Lord as addressed personally to him: 'Behold your Mother.'
And so he did as the beloved disciple did: he took her into his own
home [cf. John 19:27]—*Totus tuus*. And from the mother he learned
to conform himself to Christ."[15] The wonder of the mercy of God
was proclaimed by St. Thomas Aquinas when he stated: "It is greater
for God to draw good from evil than to create something new out of
nothing; the justification of a sinner by grace is an act greater than the
creation of the whole of the universe of heaven and earth."[16]

In Mary, mercy is united to the piety of a mother. She always leads
the faithful to the throne of grace. The title "Mother of Mercy," won
by her fiat in Nazareth and at the foot of the cross on Calvary, is one
of the greatest and most beautiful of the names of Mary. As the Marian
prayer insists, she is our comfort and our safeguard. As *Lumen Gentium* asserts: "By her maternal charity, she cares for the brethren of
her Son, who still journey onwards on earth beset by dangers and
difficulties, until they are led to their heavenly home. Therefore the
Blessed Virgin is invoked throughout the Church under the titles of
Advocate, Helper, Benefactress."[17] The merciful Virgin is the Refuge
of Sinners. In her we find a safe harbor from the storm. After her
Son, no one detests sin more than Mary does. But she does not reject
sinners; instead she welcomes them and moves them to repentance.
St. Bernard asked: "Who then, shall be able to comprehend what is
the breadth and length and height and depth (Eph. 3:18) of thy mercy,
O Virgin most blessed? It reaches forward, extending even as far as
the end of time, to succour all that invoke it. Its breadth is as broad as
the vast universe, so that of thee too it can be said, 'the whole earth is
full of thy mercy' (Ps. 32:5)."[18]

Two other relevant titles ascribed to Mary and encompassed
within the title Mother of Mercy are Comfort of the Afflicted and
Help of Christians. In June 2020 Pope Francis also approved three
other titles to be ascribed to Mary and appended to the Litany of
Loreto: Mary, Mother of Mercy, Mother of Hope, and Solace of Migrants.[19] Throughout her life, the Blessed Virgin must have been a
source of consolation and support to anyone afflicted by a weight
too heavy to bear alone. Across generations she has never ceased to
comfort those who are oppressed by sorrow, loneliness, or suffering; overwhelmed by apparently insoluble difficulties; crushed by illness; daunted by seeming failure; threatened by discouragement. Our

Lady is Help of Christians because it is a human reality to favor those we love, and nobody has had a greater love than Mary for those who belong to her Son's family. Thus she is confidently called upon for aid to fight against temptation and for assistance in work.

During the Year of Mercy there was a special weekend, October 7–9, 2016, dedicated to Mary. The Marian Jubilee opened on October 7 with Mass in the Basilica of St. Mary Major. The Mass was followed by the recitation of the Rosary in St. Peter's Square and a Prayer to the Queen of the Holy Rosary of Pompeii. Adoration and confessions were then available until midnight in the parishes of Santa Maria in Valicella, also called "Chiesa Nuova," and San Salvatore in Lauro.

Jubilee activities continued Saturday morning with a pilgrimage to the Holy Doors of the four major basilicas in Rome: St. Mary Major, St. Paul Outside the Walls, St. John Lateran, and St. Peter's. Groups of various Marian delegations from national communities and shrines then participated in a special procession to St. Peter's Square, where Pope Francis led pilgrims in praying the Glorious Mysteries of the Rosary before delivering his address. In his speech the Pope noted how, from the earliest centuries of the Church, Mary has been invoked as the "Mother of Mercy," explaining that the prayer of the Rosary in many ways is a "synthesis of the history of God's mercy, which becomes a history of salvation for all who let themselves be shaped by grace." By reflecting on the important moments in Jesus's life, he said, we see how his mercy is shown to everyone from all walks and stages of life, adding that Mary always accompanies us on this journey, pointing us in the direction of her Son, "who radiates the very mercy of the Father."[20] The celebrations finished with a closing Mass in St. Peter's Square on Sunday morning.

Pope Francis sees Mary as an expert in mercy and believes that her heart is in perfect harmony with her son, Jesus Christ. "Mary's entire life was patterned after the presence of mercy made flesh," he has said. "The Mother of the Crucified and Risen One has entered the sanctuary of divine mercy because she participated intimately in the mystery of his love."[21] Nowhere was this more evident than at the foot of the Cross, where "Mary, together with John, the disciple of love, witnessed the words of forgiveness spoken by Jesus. This supreme expression of mercy towards those who crucified him shows us the point to which the mercy of God can reach. Mary attests that the mercy of the Son of God knows no bounds and extends to everyone, without exception."[22]

In his book *The Church of Mercy* Pope Francis reiterates that nothing is impossible for God's mercy and that even the most entangled matters can be unravelled by his grace. He speaks also of Mary as the one whose fiat opened the way for the incarnation and the salvation promised from of old. He speaks of Mary as "the Mother who patiently and lovingly brings us to God, so that he can untangle the knots of our soul by his fatherly mercy."[23] In the apostolic exhortation *Evangelii Gaudium*, Pope Francis reminds his readers that from the cross Christ led us to Mary: "He brought us to her because he did not want us to journey without a mother, and our people read in this maternal image all the mysteries of the Gospel."[24]

Pope Francis calls Mary the star of the new evangelization and emphasizes the important way in which she let herself be "guided by the Holy Spirit on a journey of faith towards a destiny of service and fruitfulness."[25] A significant part of that fruitfulness is the way in which she lives out her title of Mother of Mercy within the life of the Church. He sees a Marian dimension or "style" to the way in which the Church evangelizes and believes that this involves the strength of gentleness and humility: "Whenever we look to Mary, we come to believe once again in the revolutionary nature of love and tenderness. In her we see that humility and tenderness are not virtues of the weak but of the strong who need not treat others poorly in order to feel important themselves."[26] No wonder the title of Mother of Mercy is particularly one that Pope Francis appreciates. Mary encapsulates all those characteristics of humility, tenderness, and gentle strength that he desires to see in members of the merciful Church.

NOTES

Preface

1. Francis, Homily, Casa Santa Marta, Vatican City, October 22, 2013, www.vatican.va/content/francesco/en/cotidie/2013/documents/papa-francesco -cotidie_20131022_contemplation.html.

2. Francis, Homily, Solemnity of the Most Sacred Heart of Jesus, June 3, 2016, www.vatican.va/content/francesco/en/homilies/2016/documents/papa -francesco_20160603_omelia-giubileo-sacerdoti.html.

3. A term Pope Francis used in his Homily for the Closing of the Jubilee Year of Mercy, November 20, 2016, www.vatican.va/content/francesco /en/homilies/2016/documents/papa-francesco_20161120_omelia-chiusura -giubileo.html.

4. Archbishop Donald Bolen, "Mercy," in *A Pope Francis Lexicon*, edited by Joshua J. McElwee and Cindy Wooden, 126–134 (Collegeville MN: Liturgical Press, 2018).

5. Pope Francis defines the gospel as "the book of God's mercy; to be read and reread, because everything that Jesus said and did is an expression of the Father's mercy." Francis, "Draw From the Well of the Father's Mercy, and Bring It to the World!" Homily on Divine Mercy Sunday, April 3, 2016, www .vatican.va/content/francesco/en/homilies/2016/documents/papa-francesco _20160403_omelia-giubileo-divina-misericordia.html.

6. I write "supposed closure" because Pope Francis was very clear that the substantive imperative of mercy was one that should continue in the Church. Francis, Homily, November 20, 2016. See n. 3 above.

Introduction

1. "The Creation of Adam," to which I refer, is one of the nine ceiling panels in the Sistine Chapel depicting scenes from the book of Genesis. In 1508 Pope Julius (1503–1513) hired Michelangelo to paint the ceiling, and he painted it between 1508 and 1512. The Chapel was built in 1479 by Pope Sixtus IV, who gave it his name ("Sistine" derives from "Sixtus"). Since the sixteenth century

this chapel has been the space where cardinals of the Catholic Church gather to elect a new pope as they did in March 2013, when Pope Francis was elected.

2. The first covenant was established with Abram, who became Abraham, with the new name he was given by God as a sign of the covenant. In Genesis 12, God calls Abram into relationship with himself and promises that he will make of Abraham a great nation. He will be given a land of his own, and through him and his offspring (Isaac and Ishmael) all nations of the world would be blessed. The history of the children of Israel is one of the unbounded love of God in the face of numerous infidelities on the part of his people.

3. The Acts of the Apostles relate the history of the early Church after the resurrection and ascension of Jesus and the Pentecost outpouring of the Holy Spirit on the apostles.

4. The election of Pope Francis took place on March 13, 2013, and his installation Mass was held on the Feast of St. Joseph, March 19.

5. Pope Francis's first words after his election were these: "Brothers and sisters, good evening. You all know that the duty of the Conclave was to give a bishop to Rome. It seems that my brother Cardinals have come almost to the ends of the Earth to get him . . . but here we are. I thank you for the welcome that has come from the diocesan community of Rome." He continued by asking the crowd to pray with him for Pope Benedict XVI and concluded by asking the crowd to pray for him before he gave his blessing to them: "And now I would like to give you my blessing, he said. "But before I do, I would like to ask you a favour: before the bishop blesses the people, I ask you to pray to the Lord that He bless me . . . the prayer of the people for a blessing upon their bishop. Let us take a moment of silence for you to offer your prayer for me." Francis, first greeting of the Holy Father Pope Francis, March 13, 2013, www.vatican .va/content/francesco/en/speeches/2013/march/documents/papa-francesco _20130313_benedizione-urbi-et-orbi.html.

6. This was an almost unheard-of phenomenon in the hectic pace of contemporary journalism.

7. For example, his care for the poorest and most vulnerable was clearly seen in the early days of the papal general audiences when, at the general audience of November 6, 2013, he spotted a disfigured man in the crowd and, descending from his Popemobile, embraced the man, who was afflicted with neurofibromatosis, and kissed his disfigured head.

8. An example of Pope Francis's belief in the fruitfulness of tension and disagreement is the injunction that he gave to the bishops at the beginning of the first Extraordinary Synod on the Family: "Do not say: I cannot say this, if I do they will think badly of me. Speak freely of everything you believe." He continued: "It is necessary to say everything that in the Lord we feel must be said," without any concern that it might contradict the pope, he said. Holding back discussion "is not good," Francis added, even as he exhorted the participants to "listen with humility and accept with an open heart all that our brothers say." Pope Francis, Address to the Synod of Bishops, October 6, 2014, www .vatican.va/content/francesco/en/speeches/2014/october/documents/papa -francesco_20141006_padri-sinodali.html.

9. This statement was verified by a senior official from the Secretariat of State at the Vatican.

10. Francis, *Misericordia et Misera*, apostolic letter written at the conclusion of the Extraordinary Jubilee of Mercy, November 20, 2016, www.vatican.va/content/francesco/en/apost_letters/documents/papa-francesco-lettera-ap_20161120_misericordia-et-misera.html.

11. Hans Urs von Balthasar (1905–1988) was a Swiss theologian, Romano Guardini (1885–1968) an Italian-born German Catholic priest, theologian, and philosopher.

12. According to Massimo Faggioli, "There is no question that there is truth to this newly fractured Catholicism, at least in the EuroWestern hemisphere. If there is one thing on which Catholics of different sensibilities easily agree, it is the polarization within the Catholic Church. In the Western world, and especially in the English-speaking world, this phenomenon takes different shapes and has different histories. The intra-Catholic polarization in the United States, Australia, and the United Kingdom, as well as in continental Europe, is not exactly the same in every place. But there is a consensus that it started as political polarization among Catholics, especially around the hot-button 'life issues' such as contraception and, most of all, abortion. It gradually spread to other levels and dimensions of Catholic life and is progressively deepening the rift. There is theological polarization over different interpretations of Vatican II. We also have liturgical polarization over different tastes for liturgy, spanning from support for an enculturated liturgy to the pre-Vatican II Mass. . . . Polarization in the Church has caused a crisis of membership, in the sense that some faithful are so disgusted by this verbally violent atmosphere that they leave. And it is also a crisis of ecclesial citizenship, whereby many Catholics have forgotten how to live their lives of faith in a Church that is not polarized. In addition to this, it is also a crisis of scholarship, in the sense that it has become difficult to think about religion, theology and the Church in non-polarized terms. This polarization has, in fact, become the default disposition towards all sensitive issues." Massimo Faggioli, "Polarization in the Church and the Crisis of the Catholic Mind," *La Croix*, November 27, 2017.

13. Francis, tweet, October 29, 2016, @Pontifextwitter.com/pontifex/status/792327628409573380.

14. Gill Goulding, *A Church of Passion and Hope: The Formation of an Ecclesial Disposition* (London: Bloomsbury, 2016).

15. That was Regis College, the Jesuit Graduate School of Theology, at the University of Toronto.

16. Nicholas of Cusa (1401–1464). Simply put, God as *non aliud* highlights the limitations of finite comprehension. Human understanding of the infinite transcendent God always eludes all our attempts to comprehend God.

17. Hans Urs von Balthasar, *Theo-Drama*, vol. 3: *Theological Dramatic Theory III: The Dramatis Personnae, Persons in Christ*, edited by Graham Harrison (San Francisco: Ignatius Press, 1993), 518.

18. It is true that certain publications of papers by Pope Emeritus Benedict appeared to indicate a difference of understanding between the two popes,

or at least they were claimed by certain factions and media outlets to indicate such. An example would be the publication of a three-part reflection on clerical sexual abuse by Pope Benedict that he had asked Pope Francis if he could publish, which appeared first in a periodical for Bavarian clergy.

19. Francis, *Lumen Fidei*, encyclical, June 29, 2013, www.vatican.va /content/francesco/en/encyclicals/documents/papa-francesco_20130629 _enciclica-lumen-fidei.html. Cardinal Walter Kasper, *Pope Francis' Revolution of Tenderness and Love* (New York: Paulist Press, 2015), 10.

20. In reply to a question, "In regard to your relations with your predecessor, Benedict XVI, have you ever asked him for advice?," Pope Francis replied: "Yes, the Pope Emeritus isn't a museum statue. It's an institution we're not used to. Sixty or seventy years ago, the figure of the Bishop Emeritus didn't exist. That came after Vatican Council II and now it's an institution. The same has to happen with the Pope Emeritus. Benedict is the first and perhaps there will be others. We don't know that. He is discrete, humble, he doesn't want any bother. We spoke about it and together we came to the conclusion that it would be better if he saw people, that he come out and participate in the life of the Church. Once he came here on the occasion of the blessing of the statue of St. Michael the Archangel, then for a lunch in Santa Marta and, after Christmas, I returned the invitation to participate in the Consistory and he accepted. His wisdom is a gift from God. Some would have liked him to retire to a Benedictine Abbey far from the Vatican. And then I thought of grandparents, who with their wisdom and advice give strength to the family and do not deserve to end in a retirement home." Francis, interview with the author, Corriere Della Sera, March 5, 2014.

21. John Paul II, *Dives in Misericordia*, encyclical, November 30, 1980, www.vatican.va/content/john-paul-ii/en/encyclicals/documents/hf_jp-ii_enc _30111980_dives-in-misericordia.html. I am stressing here that a certain continuity of concern for papal teaching on mercy can be detected across these three popes, though expressed in diverse ways and reaching an abundant emphasis of centrality in the papacy of Pope Francis. I am not intending to give the impression that such continuity embraces other areas. I am also aware that in some practical decision-making there has been clear discontinuity between Pope Francis and his two immediate predecessors.

22. Ignatius of Loyola, *The Spiritual Exercises of St. Ignatius of Loyola* (New York: Catholic Book Publishing, 1948).

Chapter 1

1. Francis, *Misericordia et Misera*, apostolic letter issued at the conclusion of the Extraordinary Jubilee of Mercy, November 20, 2016, www.vatican .va/content/francesco/en/apost_letters/documents/papa-francesco-lettera-ap _20161120_misericordia-et-misera.html.

2. Francis, Address at a Meeting with the Bishops of Mexico, February 13, 2016, www.vatican.va/content/francesco/en/speeches/2016/february /documents/papa-francesco_20160213_messico-vescovi.html. In the same

address he also stated: "Do not be led by empty efforts to change people as if the love of God is not powerful enough to bring about change. Rediscover the wise and humble constancy that the fathers of faith of this country passed onto successive generations with the language of divine mystery. They did this by first learning and then teaching the grammar needed to dialogue with God; a God concealed within centuries of searching and then brought close in the person of his Son Jesus Christ."

3. Francis, *Evangelii Gaudium: The Joy of the Gospel*, apostolic exhortation, November 24, 2013, 88, www.vatican.va/content/francesco/en/apost_exhortations/documents/papa-francesco_esortazione-ap_20131124_evangelii-gaudium.html. In this same paragraph Pope Francis also states: "The Christian ideal will always be a summons to overcome suspicion, habitual mistrust, fear of losing our privacy, all the defensive attitudes which today's world imposes on us. . . . True faith in the incarnate Son of God is inseparable from self-giving, from membership in the community, from service, from reconciliation with others." Here we have elaborated the characteristics of that tenderness that Pope Francis so passionately advocates.

4. Ibid., 3.

5. Francis, *Misericordia et Misera*, 1. These sentiments echo the dynamic thrust of the document that inaugurated the year of mercy, namely *Misericordiae Vultus: The Face of Mercy*, in which Pope Francis states: "We need constantly to contemplate the mystery of mercy. It is a wellspring of joy, serenity and peace. . . . Mercy: the ultimate and supreme act by which God comes to meet us. Mercy: the fundamental law that dwells in the heart of every person who looks sincerely into the eyes of his brothers and sisters on the path of life. Mercy: the bridge that connects God and man, opening our hearts to a hope of being loved forever despite our sinfulness. At times we are called to gaze even more attentively on mercy so that we may become a more effective sign of the Father's action in our lives" (2–3). Francis, *Misericordiae Vultus*, apostolic letter, April 11, 2015, www.vatican.va/content/francesco/en/apost_letters/documents/papa-francesco_bolla_20150411_misericordiae-vultus.html.

6. "Pope in Santa Marta: Hope Is the Strongest Virtue but the Least Understood," *Rome Reports*, January 17, 2017, www.romereports.com/en/2017/01/17/pope-in-santa-marta-hope-is-the-strongest-virtue-but-the-least-understood/.

7. Pope Francis developed this theme in later homilies when he said: "Living in hope is journeying towards a reward, yes, toward a happiness that we do not have but we will have there. It is a difficult virtue to understand. It is a humble virtue, very humble. It is a virtue that never disappoints: if you hope, you will never be disappointed. Never, never. It is also a concrete virtue. . . . It is an encounter. Jesus always emphasizes this part of hope, this living in expectation, encountering." Francis, Homily, daily Mass, Casa Santa Marta, Vatican, Rome, October 23, 2018. www.vaticannews.va/en/pope-francis/mass-casa-santa-marta/2018-10/pope-francis-homily-daily-mass-hope-encounter-jesus.html. And in a strong injunction at the Easter Vigil in 2019 Pope Francis exhorted the congregation: "Do not bury hope!" Instead he urged them "to

rediscover in the Risen Christ the one who rolls back from our heart the heaviest of stones." Francis, Homily, Easter Vigil Mass, April 20, 2019, www.vatican.va/content/francesco/en/homilies/2019/documents/papa-francesco_20190420_omelia-vegliapasquale.html.

8. Pope Francis went on to say: "Brothers and sisters, you represent the large and varied world of voluntary workers. You are among the most precious things the Church has, you who every day, often silently and unassumingly, give shape and visibility to mercy. You express one of the most noble desires of the human heart, making a suffering person feel loved. Francis, Homily, Holy Mass and Canonization of Blessed Mother Teresa of Calcutta, Jubilee for Workers of Mercy and Volunteers, September 3, 2016, www.vatican.va/content/francesco/en/homilies/2016/documents/papa-francesco_20160904_omelia-canonizzazione-madre-teresa.html.

9. Ibid. he concluded: "Indeed wherever there is a cry for help, there your active and selfless witness is found. . . . Let your work of mercy be a humble and eloquent continuation of Jesus' presence who continues to bend down to our level to take care of the little ones who suffer."

10. The papacy of Pope Benedict XVI lasted from 2005 to 2013, when he resigned as pope and became pope emeritus. Pope John Paul II's pontificate lasted from 1978 to 2005.

11. As I wrote earlier: "Ignatius came to interpret and to symbolize the profound contradiction that lies central to all human history, not as a struggle between social or even religious forces, but between impersonal forces as our society might interpret this contradiction today. He saw it primarily as a battle between persons and even communities. This enormous and continual struggle in history is not between human beings but about human beings and the very destiny of human life. Fundamentally it is a struggle of the human versus the anti-human and the battle field is the human heart." Gill Goulding, CJ, *A Church of Passion and Hope: The Formation of An Ecclesial Disposition from Ignatius Loyola to Pope Francis* (London: Bloomsbury, 2016), 63–64.

12. Francis, "Forgiveness on the Cross," general audience, September 28, 2016, www.vatican.va/content/francesco/en/audiences/2016/documents/papa-francesco_20160928_udienza-generale.html. In that same address he also stated: "God's salvation is for everyone, without exception. It is offered to everyone. . . . The Church is not only for those who are good or those who seem good or believe they are good; the Church is for everyone, and even preferably for those who are bad, because the Church is mercy. To the one who is nailed to a hospital bed, to one who lives locked in a prison, to those who are trapped by war, I say: look at the Crucifix; God is with you all, he remains with you on the cross and offers himself as Savior to all of us. . . . On the cross, his last act confirms the fulfillment of this plan of salvation. From beginning to end, He revealed Himself as Mercy, He revealed Himself as the definitive and unrepeatable Incarnation of the Father's love. Jesus is truly the face of the Father's mercy."

13. Since 1300, when Pope Boniface VIII declared the first Holy Year, the Roman Catholic Church has regularly celebrated "Holy Years," usually every

twenty-five years. A major aspect of the Holy Year is a pilgrimage to Rome. An important symbolic action for the pilgrim is to pass through the Holy Door at St. Peter's Basilica. The Holy Door is opened every twenty-five years. The Holy Door of St. Peter's Basilica was last opened by Pope Francis for the Jubilee Year of Mercy on December 8, 2015. Prior to this, Pope John Paul II opened the door on December 24, 1999, when he simplified the ceremony for the Jubilee Year of 2000.

14. Francis, Address to the Newly Appointed Bishops, September 16, 2016, www.vatican.va/content/francesco/en/speeches/2016/september/documents /papa-francesco_20160916_corso-formazione-nuovi-vescovi.html. He also stated in this same address: "It is good to let oneself be pierced by the loving knowledge of God. It is consoling to know that He truly knows who we are and is not alarmed by our smallness. It is reassuring to keep in our heart the memory of His voice that in fact called us, despite our shortcomings. It gives peace to abandon oneself to the certainty that it will be Him, and not us, who will bring to fulfillment what He Himself has initiated. . . . In crossing the Holy Door, do so carrying on your shoulders your flock: not by yourselves!—with the flock on your shoulders. . . . Do not be afraid to propose Mercy as the summary of all that God offers to the world, because man's heart cannot aspire to anything greater."

15. Ibid. He continued: "All that is great needs a way to get in—all the more so divine Mercy, which is inexhaustible! Once gripped by Mercy, it exacts an introductive way, a path, a road, an initiation. . . . God's Mercy is the only reality that enables man not to be definitively lost, even when unfortunately, he seeks to flee from its fascination."

16. Ibid. Pope Francis continued: "Men are in need of Mercy; although unaware of it, they are in search of it. They know well they are wounded, they feel it, they know well that they are 'half dead' (cf. Luke 10:30), although being afraid to admit it. When they see Mercy approaching unexpectedly, then exposing themselves they stretch out their hand to beg for it. They are fascinated by its capacity to stop, when so many pass by, of bending down, when a certain rheumatism of soul impedes bending; of touching the wounded flesh, when the preference prevails for all that is aseptic."

17. Ibid.

18. Regarding clergy, he said: "First of all accompany your clergy with solicitous patience; be close to your clergy. I beg you to take to your priests the pope's embrace and appreciation of their active generosity. Try to revive in them the awareness that Christ is their 'destiny,' their 'share and source of inheritance,' their part is to drink from the 'cup' (cf. Ps. 16[15]:5). Who can fill the heart of a servant of God and of His Church other than Christ? I also beg you to act with great prudence and responsibility in receiving candidates or incardinating priests into your local Churches." Ibid.

Regarding families, he said: "Take special care of all families, rejoicing with their generous love and encouraging the immense good that they lavish on this world. Above all, follow the most wounded. Do not 'pass by' in face of their frailties. Stop to let your heart of Pastors be pierced by the vision of their wound; approach them with delicacy and without fear. Put before their eyes the *joy of* genuine *love* and the grace with which God raises it to participation in His own Love. So many are in need of rediscovering it, others have never known it, some expect to recover it, not a few will have to bear the weight of having lost it irremediably. I beg you to accompany them in discernment and with empathy."

19. Francis, Address at a Meeting with the Bishops of Brazil, July 28, 2013, www.vatican.va/content/francesco/en/speeches/2013/july/documents/papa -francesco_20130727_gmg-episcopato-brasile.html.

20. Francis, *Evangelii Gaudium*, 169.

21. Cf. Ibid., 170.

22. Ibid. Pope Francis continued: "Listening helps us to find the right gesture and word which shows that we are more than simply bystanders. Only through such respectful and compassionate listening can we enter on the paths of true growth and awaken a yearning for the Christian ideal: the desire to respond fully to God's love and to bring to fruition what he has sown in our lives. Reaching a level of maturity where individuals can make truly free and responsible decisions calls for much time and patience. . . . Today more than ever we need men and women who, on the basis of their experience of accompanying others, are familiar with processes which call for prudence, understanding, patience and docility to the Spirit. . . . We need to practice the art of listening" (171).

23. The pope makes clear that "someone good at such accompaniment does not give in to frustrations or fears." Indeed, it is our own personal experience of being accompanied that enables us to be good accompaniers, since "our personal experience of being assisted, and of openness to those who accompany us, will teach us to be patient and compassionate with others, and to find the right way to gain their trust, their openness and their readiness to grow." Ibid., 172.

24. Ibid., 173. In this paragraph Pope Francis also cites the example of Paul's relationships with both Timothy and Titus, which "provide an example of this accompaniment and formation which takes place in the midst of apostolic activity. . . . Missionary disciples accompany missionary disciples." Cf. an earlier section in which Pope Francis stated: "Spiritual accompaniment must lead others closer to God. . . . To accompany them would be counterproductive, if it became a sort of therapy supporting their self-absorption and ceased to be a pilgrimage with Christ to the Father." Ibid., 170.

25. E.g., in Kathryn Spink, *Mother Teresa: An Authorized Biography*, revised edition (New York: HarperCollins, 2011); *Mother Teresa: Come Be My Light: The Private Writings of the Saint of Calcutta*, edited and with commentary by Brian Kolodiejchuk, MC (New York: Image, Doubleday, 2007); Kerry Walters, *St. Teresa of Calcutta: Missionary, Mother, Mystic* (Cincinnati: Franciscan Media, 2016).

26. Pope Francis acknowledged the many volunteers during his homily when he said: "We heard in the Gospel, 'Large crowds were travelling with Jesus' (Luke 14:25). Today, this 'large crowd' is seen in the great number of volunteers who have come together for the Jubilee of Mercy. You are that crowd who follows the Master and who makes visible his concrete love for each person. I

repeat to you the words of the Apostle Paul: 'I have indeed received much joy and comfort from your love, because the hearts of the saints have been refreshed through you' (Philem. 1:7). How many hearts have been comforted by volunteers! How many hands they have held; how many tears they have wiped away; how much love has been poured out in hidden, humble and selfless service! This praiseworthy service gives voice to the faith—it gives voice to the faith!—and expresses the mercy of the Father, who draws near to those in need." Francis, Homily, Holy Mass and Canonization of Blessed Mother Teresa of Calcutta.

27. Ibid.

28. Ibid. Recalling the words of the new saint, Pope Francis said: "Mother Teresa loved to say, 'Perhaps I don't speak their language, but I can smile.' Let us carry her smile in our hearts and give it to those whom we meet along our journey, especially those who suffer. In this way, we will open up opportunities of joy and hope for our many brothers and sisters who are discouraged and who stand in need of understanding and tenderness." He also made the point that he thought we would continue to call the new saint Mother Teresa, as "her holiness is so near to us, so tender and so fruitful." Ibid.

29. Cf. Francis, Homily, Jubilee for Socially Excluded People, November 13, 2016, www.vatican.va/content/francesco/en/homilies/2016/documents/papa-francesco_20161113_giubileo-omelia-senza-fissa-dimora.html. Pope Francis also indicated in this homily that we are called to a significant discernment: "Amid the din of so many voices, the Lord asks us to distinguish between what is from him and what is from the false spirit. This is important: to distinguish the word of wisdom that God speaks to us each day from the shouting of those who seek in God's name to frighten, to nourish division and fear."

30. "These two riches do not disappear!" he said. "These are the greatest goods; these are to be loved. Everything else—the heavens, the earth, all that is most beautiful, even this Basilica—will pass away; but we must never exclude God or others from our lives." Ibid.

31. "We should be worried when our consciences are anaesthetized and we no longer see the brother or sister suffering at our side, or notice the grave problems in our world, which become a mere refrain familiar from the headlines on the evening news." Ibid.

32. Francis, Homily, Mass for the Closing of the Jubilee Year of Mercy, November 20, 2016, www.vatican.va/content/francesco/en/homilies/2016/documents/papa-francesco_20161120_omelia-chiusura-giubileo.html. Cf. The questions posed toward the end of the first week of the Spiritual Exercises: What have I done for Christ? What am I doing for Christ? What shall I do for Christ?

33. Pope Francis continued: "This Year of Mercy invites us to rediscover the core, to return to what is essential. This time of mercy calls us to look to the true face of our King, the one that shines out at Easter, and to rediscover the youthful, beautiful face of the Church, the face that is radiant when it is welcoming, free, faithful, poor in means but rich in love, on mission." Ibid.

34. Pope Francis, Homily, Mass for the Closing of the Jubilee Year of Mercy November 20, 2016.

35. Ibid.

36. Francis, First Meditation, Spiritual Retreat Given by His Holiness Pope Francis on the Occasion of the Jubilee for Priests, June 2, 2016, www.vatican.va/content/francesco/en/speeches/2016/june/documents/papa-francesco_20160602_giubileo-sacerdoti-prima-meditazione.html. The pope continued: "This all-embracing character means that everyone can appreciate what it means to be merciful, to feel compassion for those who suffer, sympathy for those in need, visceral indignation in the face of patent injustice and a desire to respond with loving respect by attempting to set things right. If we reflect on this natural feeling of mercy, we begin to see how God himself can be understood in terms of this defining attribute by which Jesus wished to reveal him to us. God's name is mercy."

37. Ibid. Pope Francis continued: "We can concentrate on mercy because it is what is most essential and definitive. By the stairway of mercy (cf. *Laudato Si'*, 77), we can descend to the depths of our human condition—including our frailty and sin—and ascend to the heights of divine perfection: 'Be merciful (perfect) as your Father is merciful.' But always for the sake of 'reaping' even greater mercy."

38. Ibid. He continued: "As God believes in us, infinitely beyond any merits we have, so too we are called to instill hope and provide opportunities to others."

39. He said, "I like to use 'mercy' as a verb: We have to 'show mercy' [*misericordiar* in Spanish—to mercify: we have to stretch the language a little] in order to 'receive mercy' [*ser misericordiados*—to be mercified]. 'But Father, this is not a real word!'—'True, but it is the form I have found useful to grasp this reality: to show mercy, *misericordiar* and receive mercy, *ser misericordiados*.'" Ibid.

40. Cf. Francis, First Meditation, Spiritual Retreat Given by His Holiness Pope Francis on the Occasion of the Jubilee for Priests. Basilica of St. John Lateran, June 2, 2016.

41. Ibid.

42. Those he called out were St. Paul, St. Peter, St. John, St. Augustine, and St. Francis, to name only a few. As Pope Francis stated: "Almost all the great saints were great sinners or, like Saint Therese, knew that it was by sheer grace that they were not." . . . "*Paul* received mercy in the harsh and inflexible vessel of his judgement, shaped by the Law. His harsh judgement made him a persecutor. Mercy so changed him that he sought those who were far off, from the pagan world, and, at the same time showed great understanding and mercy to those who were as he had been. Paul's approach can be summed up in this way: he did not judge even himself, but instead let himself be justified by a God who is greater than his conscience, appealing to Jesus as the faithful advocate from whose love nothing and no one could separate him. Paul's understanding of God's unconditional mercy was radical. . . . Peter was healed of the deepest wound of all, that of denying his friend." Francis, Second Meditation, Spiritual Retreat Given by His Holiness Pope Francis on the Occasion of the Jubilee for Priests, June 2, 2016, www.vatican.va/content/francesco/en/speeches/2016/june/documents/papa-francesco_20160602_giubileo-sacerdoti-seconda-meditazione.html.

43. Ibid. Pope Francis also indicated the endless forgiveness of God that underlies this gaze: "God keeps forgiving, even though he sees how hard it is for his grace to take root in the parched and rocky soil of our hearts. He never stops sowing his mercy and his forgiveness." . . . "With the very threads of our poverty and sinfulness, interwoven with the Father's love, [God's mercy] so weaves us that our soul is renewed and recovers its true image, the image of Jesus." Ibid.

44. Francis, Third Meditation, Spiritual Retreat Given by His Holiness Pope Francis on the Occasion of the Jubilee for Priests, June 2, 1996, www.vatican.va/content/francesco/en/speeches/2016/june/documents/papa-francesco_20160602_giubileo-sacerdoti-terza-meditazione.html.

45. Second Meditation Given by His Holiness Pope Francis on the Occasion of the Jubilee for Priests.

46. Third Meditation, Spiritual Retreat Given by His Holiness Pope Francis on the Occasion of the Jubilee for Priests.

47. Francis, Homily, Casa Santa Marta, Vatican, Rome, April 7, 2014.

48. Third Meditation, Spiritual Retreat Given by His Holiness Pope Francis on the Occasion of the Jubilee for Priests. The pope sees such a focus on the comprehensive need to let themselves be shown mercy as of fundamental importance for priests and bishops: "Being merciful is not only 'a way of life,' but '*the* way of life.' There is no other way of being a priest." He continued: "To see needs and to bring immediate relief, and even more, to anticipate those needs: this is the mark of a father's gaze. This priestly gaze—which takes the place of the father in the heart of Mother Church—makes us see people with the eyes of mercy. It has to be learned from seminary on, and it must enrich all our pastoral plans and projects. We desire, and we ask the Lord to give us, a gaze capable of discerning the signs of the times, to know 'what works of mercy our people need today' in order to feel and savor the God of history who walks among them." Ibid.

49. Francis, *Misericordia et Misera*, 2.

50. Ibid.

51. Francis, *Misericordia et Misera*, 3.

52. Francis, *Misericordiae Vultus*, 2.

53. Joseph Ratzinger, Homily, Mass for the Election of the Roman Pontiff, April 18, 2005, www.vatican.va/gpII/documents/homily-pro-eligendo-pontifice_20050418_en.html.

54. Ibid.

55. Synod of Bishops, XIII Ordinary General Assembly on the New Evangelization and the Transmission of the Christian Faith, October 7–28, 2012, www.vatican.va/roman_curia/synod/documents/rc_synod_doc_20110202_lineamenta-xiii-assembly_en.html.

56. Goulding, *A Church of Passion and Hope*, 276. This movement recalls the dynamic of the Ignatian Spiritual Exercises.

57. Benedict, Homily, pastoral visit to the Roman parish of Dio Padre Misericordioso, March 26, 2006, www.vatican.va/content/benedict-xvi/en/homilies/2006/documents/hf_ben-xvi_hom_20060326_parrocchia-roma.html.

58. Ibid.

59. Benedict XVI, Farewell Address to the Eminent Cardinals Present in Rome, February 28, 2013, www.vatican.va/content/benedict-xvi/en/speeches /2013/february/documents/hf_ben-xvi_spe_20130228_congedo-cardinali.html.

60. Pope Benedict XVI, *Deus Caritas Est: God Is Love*, encyclical, December 25, 2005, 1, www.vatican.va/content/benedict-xvi/en/encyclicals/docu ments/hf_ben-xvi_enc_20051225_deus-caritas-est.html.

61. Ibid., 6.

62. Pope Benedict wrote: "Anyone who wishes to give love must also receive love as a gift. Certainly, as the Lord tells us, one can become a source from which rivers of living water flow (cf. John 7:37–38). Yet to become such a source, one must constantly drink anew from the original source, which is Jesus Christ, from whose pierced heart flows the love of God (cf. John 19:34)." Ibid., 7.

63. Ibid., 10. He continued: "It is so great that it turns God against himself, his love against his justice. Here Christians can see a dim pre-figuration of the mystery of the Cross: so great is God's love for man that by becoming man he follows him even into death, and so reconciles justice and love."

64. Ibid.

65. Francis, *Misericordia et Misera*, 2.

66. Ibid., 12.

67. Ibid., 13. Pope Francis continued: "Union with God through sharing in Jesus' self-gift, sharing in his body and blood. The sacramental 'mysticism,' grounded in God's condescension towards us, operates at a radically different level and lifts us to far greater heights than anything that any human mystical elevation could ever accomplish."

68. Ibid. What is more, "This can only take place on the basis of an intimate encounter with God, an encounter which has become a communion of will, even affecting my feelings."

69. Ibid., 18.

70. Benedict XVI, *Deus Caritas Est*, 1, cited in *Evangelii Gaudium*, 7. Focus on the Christology underpinning the theology of mercy as interpreted by Popes Benedict and Francis will be a feature of chapter 4.

71. Benedict XVI, Homily, Mass for the Inauguration of the Fifth General Conference of the Bishops of Latin American and the Caribbean, May 13, 2007, www.vatican.va/content/benedict-xvi/en/homilies/2007/documents/hf_ben -xvi_hom_20070513_conference-brazil.html.

72. Benedict XVI, Address for the Fortieth Anniversary of the Decree *Ad Gentes*, March 11, 2006, www.vatican.va/content/benedict-xvi/en/speeches /2006/march/documents/hf_ben-xvi_spe_20060311_ad-gentes.html.

73. Benedict XVI, Address to the Brazilian Bishops in the Cathedral of São Paulo, Brazil, May 11, 2007, 86, www.vatican.va/content/benedict-xvi /en/speeches/2007/may/documents/hf_ben-xvi_spe_20070511_bishops-brazil .html.

74. Francis, *Evangelii Gaudium*, 86.

75. Joseph Ratzinger, "The Current Situation of Faith and Theology," address given at the Meeting with the Doctrinal Commissions of Latin America,

May 7, 1996, www.vatican.va/roman_curia/congregations/cfaith/incontri/rc
_con_cfaith_19960507_guadalajara-ratzinger_en.html.

76. Benedict XVI, Homily, Mass for the Opening of the Year of Faith,
October 11, 2012, www.vatican.va/content/benedict-xvi/en/homilies/2012
/documents/hf_ben-xvi_hom_20121011_anno-fede.html.

77. Francis *Evangelii Gaudium*, 86.

78. Benedict XVI, Address for the Screening of the Documentary
Film *Art and Faith—Via Pulchritudinis*, October 25, 2012, www.vatican.va
/content/benedict-xvi/en/speeches/2012/october/documents/hf_ben-xvi_spe
_20121025_arte-fede.html. He continued: "This brings to mind what Jesus said
to his disciples: to you the secret of the Kingdom of God has been given, but to
those on the 'outside' everything is said 'in parables' (Mark 4:10–12)."

79. Benedict XVI, *Intima Ecclesiae Natura: On the Service of Charity*,
motu proprio, November 11, 2012, www.vatican.va/content/benedict-xvi/en
/motu_proprio/documents/hf_ben-xvi_motu-proprio_20121111_caritas.html.

80. Benedict XVI, *Caritas in Veritate*, encyclical, June 29, 2009, 2, www
.vatican.va/content/benedict-xvi/en/encyclicals/documents/hf_ben-xvi_enc
_20090629_caritas-in-veritate.html.

81. Benedict XVI, *Deus Caritas Est*, 16.

82. Ibid., 39.

83. John Paul II, *Dives in Misericordia*, encyclical, November 30, 1980,
www.vatican.va/content/john-paul-ii/en/encyclicals/documents/hf_jp-ii_enc
_30111980_dives-in-misericordia.html.

84. Ibid., 11.

85. He went on to write: "Moral uneasiness is destined to become even
more acute. It is obvious that a fundamental defect, or rather a series of defects,
indeed a defective machinery is at the root of contemporary economics and
materialistic civilization, which does not allow the human family to break free
from such radically unjust solutions." Ibid.

86. Ibid., 12.

87. Ibid, 13.

88. This is a theme to which we shall return in later chapters.

89. Cf. Francis, *Amoris Laetitia*, Apostolic Exhortation on Love in the
Family, April 8, 2016, especially chapter IV, www.vatican.va/content/dam
/francesco/pdf/apost_exhortations/documents/papa-francesco_esortazione
-ap_20160319_amoris-laetitia_en.pdf.

90. John Paul II, *Dives in Misericordia*, 14.

91. He wrote: "In reality the one who gives is always also a beneficiary. In
any case, he too can easily find himself in the position of one who receives, who
obtains a benefit, who experiences merciful love; he too can find himself the
object of mercy." Ibid.

92. Ibid. Later Pope John Paul continued: "Human opinions . . . see mercy
as a unilateral act or process, presupposing and maintaining a certain distance
between the one who is practicing mercy and the one benefitting from it, between the one who does good and the one who receives it. Hence the attempt
is made to free interpersonal and social relationships from mercy and to base

them solely on justice. However such opinions about mercy fail to see the fundamental link between mercy and justice spoken of by the whole biblical tradition, and above all by the messianic mission of Jesus Christ. . . . Mercy that is truly Christian is also, in a certain sense, *the most perfect incarnation* of 'equality' between people, and therefore also the most perfect incarnation of *justice* as well, insofar as justice aims at the same result in its own sphere. However, the equality brought by justice is limited to the realm of objective and extrinsic goods, while love and mercy bring it about that people meet one another in that value which is man himself, with the dignity that is proper to him. At the same time, 'equality' of people through 'patient and kind' love (cf. Francis, *Amoris Laetitia*, chapter 4) does not take away differences: the person who gives becomes more generous when he feels at the same time benefitted by the person accepting his gift; and vice versa, the person who accepts the gift with the awareness that, in accepting it, he too is doing good is in his own way serving the great cause of the dignity of the person; and this contributes to uniting people in a more profound manner."

93. Francis, *Amoris Laetitia*.

94. John Paul II, *Dives in Misericordia*, 14. He continued: "Forgiveness is also the fundamental condition for reconciliation, not only in the relationship of God with man, but also in relationships between people."

95. Ibid.

96. Ibid. He continued: "May this cry be full of that truth about mercy which has found such rich expression in Sacred Scripture and in Tradition, as also in the authentic life of faith of countless generations of the People of God. . . . The mystery of Christ obliges me to have recourse to that mercy and to beg for it at this difficult, critical phase of the history of the Church and of the world" (15).

97. Pope John Paul wrote: "Not only for the Church herself as the community of believers but also in a certain sense for all humanity, this mystery is the *source* of a life different from the life which can be built by man, who is exposed to the oppressive forces of the threefold concupiscence active within him. It is precisely in the name of this mystery that Christ teaches us to forgive always. . . . The Church rightly considers it her duty and the purpose of her mission *to guard the authenticity of forgiveness*, both in life and behavior and in educational and pastoral work. She protects it simply by guarding its *source*, which is the mystery of the mercy of God Himself as revealed in Jesus Christ." Ibid.

98. Francis, Apostolic Letter of His Holiness to All Consecrated People on the Occasion of the Year of Consecrated Life, November 21, 2014, www.vatican.va/content/francesco/en/apost_letters/documents/papa-francesco_lettera-ap_20141121_lettera-consacrati.html.

99. Francis, interview with Antonio Spadaro, SJ, editor-in-chief, *La Civiltà Cattolica*, September 21, 2013, www.vatican.va/content/francesco/en/speeches/2013/september/documents/papa-francesco_20130921_intervista-spadaro.html.

100. Francis, "Catholic Schools and Universities in the Service of the Growth of Humanity, Dialogue and Hope," February 9, 2017, press.vatican.va/content/salastampa/en/bollettino/pubblico/2017/02/09/170209b.html.

101. Ibid. He continued: "Unfortunately there are many forms of violence, poverty, exploitation, discrimination, marginalization and restrictions on freedom that create a culture of waste."

102. Ibid.

103. Archbishop Pablo Puente, Homily to the Conference of Religious, Swanwick, UK, January 31, 2001.

104. David L. Schindler, "On the Catholic Common Ground Project: The Christological Foundations of Dialogue," *Communio* 23, no. 4 (1996), 825–851. For a more extensive presentation, see Gill Goulding, IBVM, *Creative Perseverance: Sustaining Life-Giving Ministry in Today's Church* (Ottawa: Novalis, 2003), chap. 4—Dialectical Process: Conversation, 79–102. Chapter 3 of this book outlines the Christological lynchpins of mercy and returns to the consideration of how these, with their ecclesiological ramifications, inform the theological underpinning of mercy.

105. Though a detailed analysis is beyond the scope of this work, it is clear that the importance of hearing the voice of suffering has been a major determinant in the papacy of Pope Francis. Listening to those who are survivors of clergy sexual abuse, refugees who have been abused, and survivors of human trafficking has been a keynote of his engagement with these diverse groups of people who continue to suffer.

106. Scholas Occurrentes is a worldwide network of schools promoted by Pope Francis. The goal is the integration of educational communities around the world, with special emphasis on those with fewer resources. Since its inception, Pope Francis has looked to the possibility of giving a concrete response to the times. He proposed an educational process that would educate students in openness to others. This was part of his desire to create a new culture of encounter. Today Scholas Occurrentes is constituted as an International Organization of Pontifical Rite, with its network in 190 countries, integrating more than 400 thousand educational centers and reaching more than a million children and young people around the world.

107. Francis, "In Dialogue, Everybody Wins," Pope Francis to Scholas Occurrentes, May 30, 2016, press.vatican.va/content/salastampa/en/bollettino /pubblico/2016/05/30/160530b.html. He continued: "In arguments there is someone who wins and someone who loses, or both lose. Dialogue is gentleness, it is the capacity to listen, it is putting yourself in the other person's shoes, and building bridges."

108. Francis, *Amoris Laetitia*, 136.

109. Ibid., 137.

110. Ibid.

111. Ibid., 138. Cf. The presupposition of the Spiritual Exercises, in which attention is given to the good that the other is trying to say. This will be considered in more detail in the next chapter.

112. Ibid., 139.

113. Ignatius of Loyola, *The Spiritual Exercises of Ignatius of Loyola* (New York: Catholic Book Publishing, 1948), 15. See chapter 2 of this book for further elaboration.

114. Francis, "How to Create Dialogue," morning meditation in the chapel of Casa Santa Marta, January 24, 2014, www.vatican.va/content/francesco /en/cotidie/2014/documents/papa-francesco-cotidie_20140124_create-dialogue .html.

115. Ibid.

116. Ibid.

117. Ibid.

118. Francis, interview with Ulf Jonsson, SJ, on the occasion of his apostolic trip to Sweden, September 24, 2016, www.archivioradiovaticana.va /storico/2016/10/28/pope_francis_gives_interview_ahead_of_trip_to_sweden /en-1268511. In the same interview Pope Francis also commented, in response to a question, on the work of the Jesuits in Sweden: "I believe that the first task of the Jesuits in Sweden is that of favoring dialogue in every way with those who live in the secularized society and with believers: talking, sharing, understanding, standing alongside. Then clearly favoring ecumenical dialogue is necessary."

119. Francis, "Sisters and Priests Free from Idolatry."

120. Francis, Discourse at the 36th General Congregation of the Society of Jesus, October 24, 2016, press.vatican.va/content/salastampa/en/bollettino /pubblico/2016/10/24/161024a.html.

121. Francis, "Pope Urges Jesuits to Teach Discernment in Seminaries to Counter Rigidity," Catholic Voices Comment, August 26, 2016, cvcomment .org/2016/08/26/pope-urges-jesuits-to-teach-discernment-in-seminaries-to -counter-rigidity/.

122. Ibid.

123. Ibid.

124. Ibid.

125. As the pope wrote: "We have long thought that simply by stressing doctrinal, bioethical and moral issues, without encouraging openness to grace, we were providing sufficient support to families, strengthening the marriage bond and giving meaning to marital life. We find it difficult to present marriage more as a dynamic path to personal development and fulfilment than as a lifelong burden. We also find it hard to make room for the consciences of the faithful, who very often respond as best they can to the Gospel amid their limitations, and are capable of carrying out their own discernment in complex situations. We have been called to form consciences, not to replace them." Francis, Amoris Laetitia: Apostolic Exhortation on Love in the Family, March 29, 2016, 37, www.vatican.va/content/dam/francesco/pdf/apost_exhortations/documents /papa-francesco_esortazione-ap_20160319_amoris-laetitia_en.pdf.

126. Francis, Evangelii Gaudium, 33. Indeed, the pope stated: "I encourage each particular Church to undertake a resolute process of discernment, purification and renewal." Ibid., 30.

127. Ibid., 33.

128. "You need to say all that you feel with parrhesia," he continued. "And, at the same time, you should listen with humility and accept with an open heart what your brothers say." "PopeFrancis' Remarks at First Session of Synod of

Bishops on the Family," *Salt + Light Media*, October 6, 2015, slmedia.org/blog
/pope-francis-remarks-at-first-session-of-synod-of-bishops-on-the-family.
129. This will be explored in more depth in chapter 5.
130. Francis, Homily, Mass for the Closing of the Jubilee Year of Mercy.

Chapter 2

1. Francis, interview with Antonio Spadaro, SJ, editor-in-chief, *La Civiltà
Cattolica*, September 21, 2013, www.vatican.va/content/francesco/en/speeches
/2013/september/documents/papa-francesco_20130921_intervista-spadaro
.html.
2. See, for example, Joyce Huggett, "Why Ignatian Spirituality Hooks
Protestants," *The Way Supplement* 68 (1990): 22–34, www.theway.org.uk/back
/s068Huggett.pdf. Also, Sarita Tamayo-Moraga, "Buddhist and Ignatian Spiritualities: Reports on a Trial Run of an Interfaith Retreat Based on 'Ignatius and
Buddha in Conversation: A Resource for a Religiously Plural Dialog Juxtaposing the Spiritual Exercises of Ignatius and Buddhist Wisdom,'" *Buddhist-
Christian Studies* 37 (2017): 131–143, www.jstor.org/stable/44632362#metadata
_info_tab_contents.
3. "Holiness is the most attractive face of Church," Pope Francis wrote
in *Gaudete et Exsultate*, an apostolic exhortation on the call to holiness in today's world, March 19, 2018, 9, www.vatican.va/content/francesco/en/apost
_exhortations/documents/papa-francesco_esortazione-ap_20180319_gaudete
-et-exsultate.html.
4. Ibid., 166.
5. Pope Francis saw this gift of discernment as particularly necessary in
our contemporary context, in which technology has enabled multi-tasking and
virtual reality. "Contemporary life offers immense possibilities for action and
distraction," he wrote, "and the world presents all of them as valid and good.
All of us, but especially the young, are immersed in a culture of zapping. We
can navigate simultaneously on two or more screens and interact at the same
time with two or three virtual scenarios. Without the wisdom of discernment,
we can easily become prey to every passing trend." Ibid., 167.
6. It is this freedom of love attuned to the spirit of Christ that the Church
desires in her formation of consciences. As Pope Francis stated: "We have long
thought that simply by stressing doctrinal, bioethical and moral issues, without
encouraging openness to grace, we were providing sufficient support to families, strengthening the marriage bond and giving meaning to marital life. We find
it difficult to present marriage more as a dynamic path to personal development
and fulfilment than as a lifelong burden. We also find it hard to make room
for the consciences of the faithful, who very often respond as best they can to
the Gospel amid their limitations, and are capable of carrying out their own
discernment in complex situations. We have been called to form consciences,
not to replace them." *Amoris Laetitia*, Apostolic Exhortation on Love in the
Family, April 8, 2016, 37, www.vatican.va/content/dam/francesco/pdf/apost

_exhortations/documents/papa-francesco_esortazione-ap_20160319_amoris
-laetitia_en.pdf. This document focuses on the principle of accompaniment in truth toward right relationships, emphasizing small steps with human accompaniment in truth toward the maturity of right relationships.

7. Francis, Address to the General Superiors of Men's Religious Orders, November 25, 2016, www.myspiritfm.com/News?blogid=8267&view=post&articleid=153069&link=1&fldKeywords=&fldAuthor=&fldTopic=0.

8. Cardinal Vincent Nichols, "St. Brigid's Day Annual Lecture," Belfast, February 7, 2017, stbrigidsparishbelfast.org/assets/documents/Cardinal-Vincent-Nichols-2017.pdf.

9. Ibid. He continued: "It takes humility to recognize our limitations, to let go of the last vestiges of seeing myself as a hero and to acknowledge that I stand in need, constantly, of forgiveness, especially from those who love me most. And we also have to embrace our deepest desires: that pervading longing to be better, the lingering hope of holiness; the marvelous moments when we catch a glimpse through the clouds of our everyday lives, of the bright horizon of our hopes and dreams, and everything again seems possible."

10. Pope Francis, Address to the Students, Teachers, and Family Members of the Jesuit Schools in Italy and Albania, June 7, 2013, www.vatican.va/content/francesco/en/speeches/2013/june/documents/papa-francesco_20130607_scuole-gesuiti.html.

11. Ignatius of Loyola, *Spiritual Exercises of St. Ignatius*, translation and and commentary by George E. Ganss, SJ (Chicago: Loyola Press, 1992), 15.

12. Francis, *Laudato Si': On Care for Our Common Home*, encyclical, May 24, 2015, 201, www.vatican.va/content/francesco/en/encyclicals/documents/papa-francesco_20150524_enciclica-laudato-si.html.

13. Pope Francis insists that "we are free, with the freedom of Christ. Still, [Christ] asks us to examine what is within us—our desires, anxieties, fears and questions—and what takes place all around us—'the signs of the times'—and thus to recognize the paths that lead to complete freedom." Francis, *Gaudete et Exsultate*, 168.

14. As Pope Francis writes: "Discernment is necessary not only at extraordinary times, when we need to resolve grave problems and make crucial decisions. It is a means of spiritual combat for helping us to follow the Lord more faithfully. . . . Often discernment is exercised in small and apparently irrelevant things, since greatness of spirit is manifested in simple everyday realities. It involves striving untrammeled for all that is great, better and more beautiful, while at the same time being concerned for the little things, for each day's responsibilities and commitments. . . . Discernment also enables us to recognize the concrete means that the Lord provides in his mysterious and loving plan, to make us move beyond mere good intentions." Ibid., 169.

15. Karl Rahner, SJ, speaks of the imitation of Christ in this sense of reciprocal intimacy: "The imitation of Christ consists in a true entering of *His* life and *in Him*, entering into the inner life of God that has been given to us." Karl Rahner, *The Spiritual Exercises* (London: Sheed and Ward, 1976), 118.

16. Pope Francis states: "We must remember that prayerful discernment must be born of a readiness to listen: to the Lord and to others, and to reality

itself, which always challenges us in new ways. Only if we are prepared to listen, do we have the freedom to set aside our own partial or insufficient ideas, our usual habits and ways of seeing things. In this way, we become truly open to accepting a call that can shatter our security, but lead us to a better life. It is not enough that everything be calm and peaceful. God may be offering us something more, but in our comfortable inadvertence, we do not recognize it." Francis, *Gaudete et Exsultate*, 172.

17. The pope continues: "Even though it includes reason and prudence, it goes beyond them, for it seeks a glimpse of that unique and mysterious plan that God has for each of us which takes shape amid so many varied situations and limitations. . . . It has to do with the meaning of my life before the Father who knows and loves me, with the real purpose of my life, that nobody knows better than he." Ibid., 170.

18. Ibid., 171. Pope Francis continues: "In this way, we allow the birth of a new synthesis that springs from a life inspired by the Spirit."

19. Gill K. Goulding CJ, *A Church of Passion and Hope: The Formation of an Ecclesial Disposition* (London: Bloomsbury, 2016), 59. Cf. Pope Francis, when he emphasizes that an attitude of listening that lies at the heart of discernment always "entails obedience to the Gospel as the ultimate standard, but also to the Magisterium that guards it. . . . It is not a matter of applying rules or repeating what was done in the past, since the same solutions are not valid in all circumstances and what was useful in one context may not prove so in another. The discernment of spirits liberates us from rigidity, which has no place before the perennial 'today' of the risen Lord. The Spirit alone can penetrate what is obscure and hidden in every situation, and grasp its every nuance, so that the newness of the Gospel can emerge in another light." Francis, *Gaudete et Exsultate*, 173.

20. Francis, First Meditation, Spiritual Retreat Given on the Occasion of the Jubilee for Priests, June 2, 2016, www.vatican.va/content/francesco/en/speeches/2016/june/documents/papa-francesco_20160602_giubileo-sacerdoti-prima-meditazione.html.

21. Ibid.

22. Francis, Address to the Students, Teachers, Family Members, June 7, 2013, www.vatican.va/content/francesco/en/speeches/2013/june/documents/papa-francesco_20130607_scuole-gesuiti.html.

23. Francis, interview with Antonio Spadaro, September 30, 2013.

24. Pope Francis, Discourse at the 36th General Congregation of the Society of Jesus, October 24, 2016.

25. Francis, interview with Antonio Spadaro on the Occasion of His Apostolic Trip in Sweden, *Civiltà Cattolica*, October 28, 2016.

26. Ibid.

27. Francis, *Gaudete et Exsultate*, 174.

28. Francis, Catechesis at General Audience, March 11, 2015, www.vatican.va/content/francesco/en/audiences/2015/documents/papa-francesco_20150311_udienza-generale.html.

29. Francis, *Amoris Laetitia*, 193. He continued: "Listening to the elderly tell their stories is good for children and young people; it makes them feel

connected to the living history of their families, their neighbourhoods and their country."

30. Francis, "Christ Is the Door to the Kingdom," Homily, Casa Santa Marta, April 22, 2013, www.vatican.va/content/francesco/en/cotidie/2013 /documents/papa-francesco-cotidie_20130422_christ-door.html.

31. Francis, *Gaudete et Exsultate*, 174.

32. "Jesus Savior of Men." The Christogram IHS is a monogram symbolizing Jesus Christ. It is the first three letters of his name in Greek, ΙΗΣΟΥΣ (Jesus).

33. Francis, Homily, Feast of St. Ignatius, July 31, 2013, www.vatican.va /content/francesco/en/homilies/2013/documents/papa-francesco_20130731 _omelia-sant-ignazio.html.

34. As Pope Francis wrote: "This entails a readiness to make sacrifices, even to sacrificing everything. For happiness is a paradox. We experience it most when we accept the mysterious logic that is not of this world: 'This is our logic,' says Saint Bonaventure [*Collationes in Hexaemeron*, 1, 30], pointing to the cross. Once we enter into this dynamic, we will not let our consciences be numbed and we will open ourselves generously to discernment." Francis, *Gaudete et Exsultate*, 174.

35. Ibid., 20.

36. Ibid.

37. Cf. "I dream of a 'missionary option,' that is, a missionary impulse capable of transforming everything, so that the church's customs, ways of doing things, times and schedules, language and structures can be suitably channeled for the evangelization of today's world rather than for her self-preservation." Ibid., 27.

38. Ibid., 39.

39. Francis, Address to the General Superiors of Men's Religious Orders, November 25, 2016.

40. Francis, *Evangelii Gaudium: The Joy of Gospel*. Apostolic exhortation, November 24, 2013, 49, www.vatican.va/content/francesco/en/apost _exhortations/documents/papa-francesco_esortazione-ap_20131124_evangelii -gaudium.html.

41. Ibid., 273.

42. Goulding, *A Church of Passion and Hope*, 65.

43. Francis, Address to the Young People of Paraguay, July 12, 2015, www.vatican.va/content/francesco/en/speeches/2015/july/documents/papa -francesco_20150712_paraguay-giovani.html.

44. Ibid.

45. As the pope wrote: "In all aspects of life we can continue to grow and offer something greater to God, even in those areas we find most difficult. We need, though, to ask the Holy Spirit to liberate us and to expel the fear that makes us ban him from certain parts of our lives. God asks everything of us, yet he also gives everything to us.... Discernment, then, is not a solipsistic self-analysis or a form of egotistical introspection, but an authentic process of leaving ourselves behind in order to approach the mystery of God, who helps

us to carry out the mission to which he has called us, for the good of our brothers and sisters." Francis, *Gaudete et Exsultate*, 175.

46. Francis, Address to the Young People of Paraguay, July 12, 2015. The pope continued: "Friends, the devil makes promise after promise, but he never delivers. He'll never really do anything he says. He doesn't make good on his promises." The devil, he said a bit later, "makes you want things which he can't give, whether you get them or not. He makes you put your hopes in things which will never make you happy. That's his game, his strategy. He talks a lot, he offers a lot, but he doesn't deliver."

47. Ibid.
48. Ibid.
49. Ibid.
50. Ibid.
51. Ignatius of Loyola, *Spiritual Exercises*, 167.
52. The pope wrote: "A Colloquy should be made with Our Lady. I beg her to obtain for me grace from her Son and Lord that I may be received under his standard; and first, in the most perfect spiritual poverty; and also, if his Divine Majesty should be served and if he should wish to choose me for it, to no less a degree of actual poverty; and second, in bearing reproaches and injuries, that through them I may imitate him more, if only I can do this without sin on anyone's part and without displeasure to the Divine Majesty. Then I will say a Hail Mary. A Second Colloquy will be to ask the same grace from the Son, that he may obtain it for me from the Father. Then I will say the Soul of Christ. A third colloquy will be to ask the same grace from the Father, that he may grant it to me. Then I will say an Our Father." Ignatius of Loyola, *Spiritual Exercises*, 155.
53. Goulding, *A Church of Passion and Hope*, 66.
54. Francis, Homily, Casa Santa Marta, September 12, 2013, www.vatican.va/content/francesco/en/cotidie/2013/documents/papa-francesco-cotidie_20130912_meek-suffering.html.
55. Pope Francis, *Gaudete et Exsultate*, 82. In this same paragraph he states: "Jesus does not say, 'Blessed are those who plot revenge.' He calls blessed those who forgive and do so 'seventy times seven' (Matt. 18:22). We need to think of ourselves as an army of the forgiven. All of us have been looked upon with divine compassion."
56. Francis, Address to the Marian Fathers of the Immaculate Conception, Vatican, Rome, February 18, 2017. press.vatican.va/content/salastampa/en/bollettino/pubblico/2017/02/18/170218a.html.
57. Ibid.
58. Francis, *Laudato Si'*, 224.
59. As he has said: "Father Arrupe used to say that wherever there is pain, the Society [of Jesus] is there." Francis, Address to the Members of the 36th General Congregation of the Society of Jesus, October 24, 2016. Fr. Pedro Arrupe, SJ (1907–1991), was the twenty-eighth superior general of the Society of Jesus from 1965 to1983.
60. Ibid.

61. Cf. "The Lord who looks at us with mercy and chooses us, sends us out to bring with all its effectiveness that same mercy to the poorest, to sinners, to those discarded people, and those crucified in the present world, who suffer injustice and violence." Ibid. Also cf. this description of something that happened to Fr. Bergoglio one day: "Going to confession one day he had a profound experience of conversion and the grace that flowed from this encounter with Christ. This experience of God's merciful compassion for him marked his life both in his relationship to God and in the call he experienced to have compassion for others. . . . So deep was the imprint of this experience that when he came to choose a motto for his episcopal consecration, it was to this experience that he looked for inspiration." Goulding, *A Church of Passion and Hope*, 264.

62. Francis, Address to the Members of the 36th General Congregation of the Society of Jesus, October 24, 2016.

63. Pope Francis, Meeting with the 88th General Assembly of the Union of Superiors General, November 25, 2016. He continued: "There is a kind of small daily asceticism, which is a constant mortification. I am reminded of a phrase of St. Ignatius that helps us to be freer and happier. He said that mortification in all things possible helps us follow the Lord. . . . But only if it helps you to be freer, not if you need it to show yourself that you are strong."

64. The pope wrote: "Whatever weariness and pain we may experience in living the commandment of love and following the way of justice, the cross remains the source of our growth and sanctification. We must never forget that when the New Testament tells us that we will have to endure suffering for the Gospel's sake, it speaks precisely of persecution." Francis, *Gaudete et Exsultate*, 92. Later in the document Pope Francis starkly states: "Given these uncompromising demands of Jesus, it is my duty to ask Christians to acknowledge and accept them in a spirit of genuine openness . . . without any 'ifs or buts' that could lessen their force. Our Lord made it very clear that holiness cannot be understood or lived apart from these demands, for mercy is 'the beating heart of the Gospel' (*Misericordiae Vultus*, April 11, 2015, 12)." Ibid., 97.

65. Francis, *Evangelii Gaudium*, 1.

66. Francis, *Amoris Laetitia*, 1.

67. Francis, *Laudato Si'*, 222. He continued: "Christian spirituality proposes a growth marked by moderation and the capacity to be happy with little. It is a return to that simplicity which allows us to stop and appreciate the small things, to be grateful for the opportunities which life affords us, to be spiritually detached from what we possess, and not to succumb to sadness for what we lack."

68. Francis, Discourse at the 36th General Congregation of the Society of Jesus, October 24, 2016. He continued: "Let the enemy of our human nature not rob us of our joy, neither by despair before the magnitude of the evils of the world, and the misunderstandings between those who want to do good, nor let him replace it with foolish joys that are always at hand in all human enterprises."

69. Ibid.

70. Ibid. The pope continued: "In an age of instant gratification and unabated consumption, the search for joy should not be confused with the search

for 'a spiritual effect.' . . . Ignatius opens the eyes and wakes us up to the discernment of Spirits to discover the difference between long-lasting joys and transient joys."

71. Ibid.

72. This progress is to go from good to better, and it includes "every increase in faith, hope and charity and every interior joy." Ignatius of Loyola, *Spiritual Exercises*, 316.

73. Francis, Discourse at the 36th General Congregation of the Society of Jesus, October 24, 2016.

74. Bishop Jorge Eduardo Lozano of Gualeguaychú, who was Cardinal Bergoglio's auxiliary bishop in Buenos Aries for six years. Cited in Paul Vallely, *Pope Francis: Untying the Knots* (London: Bloomsbury, 2013), 142.

75. This is not to say that Pope Francis cannot act at times decisively and with what may appear to be a certain ruthlessness when he considers that a matter calls for such action. The way in which he handled the crisis in the leadership of the Order of Malta 2016–2017 was exemplary of this approach. It is clear that Pope Francis leads by being very well informed, by not giving early indications of his thinking, and by making decisions that often take the Curia by surprise. He has spoken out very clearly against a form of clericalism that he sees as a sterile reality that can impede the vitality of the Church. At the same time, if the pope has not been well informed, real difficulties can arise, as on his visit to Chile in 2018, when he was not given accurate data concerning an abusive priest and the way this man had been protected by a number of bishops. His response to the victims of the priest's abuse at that time was considered very insensitive. After the visit and in the light of both criticism from the press and obtaining further information concerning the situation in Chile, Pope Francis took decisive action, not least of which included apologizing for "serious errors of judgment and perception of the situation." Jason Horowitz, "Pope Accepts Resignation of Chilean Bishop Tied to Abuse Scandal," *New York Times*, June 11, 2018, www.nytimes.com/2018/06/11/world/europe/pope-francis-chile-abuse.html. He followed this by sending two senior clerics to investigate matters and then called the entire Chilean episcopacy to Rome.

76. Austen Ivereigh, "Pope Francis and the Uses of Disagreement as a Mechanism of Ecclesial Reform," presentation at the Von Hugel Institute, Cambridge, December 2, 2016.

77. The 3rd Extraordinary Synod of Bishops on the Family of October 5–19, 2014, "The Pastoral Challenges of the Family in the Context of Evangelization," was followed the next year by the Ordinary Synod of Bishops of October 4–25, 2015, "The Vocation and Mission of the Family in the Church and in the Contemporary World," on the same theme. The 16th Ordinary General Assembly of the Synod of Bishops continued the work of the 3rd Extraordinary General Assembly by "reflect[ing] further on the points discussed so as to formulate appropriate pastoral guidelines" for the pastoral care of the person and the family. Synod of Bishops, "The Pastoral Challenges of the Family in the Context of Evangelization," *Instrumentum Laboris*, 3rd Extraordinary

General Assembly of the Synod of Bishops, October 5–19, 2014, www.vatican
.va/roman_curia/synod/documents/rc_synod_doc_20140626_instrumentum
-laboris-familia_en.html.

78. Cf. Francis, *Evangelii Gaudium*, 67.

79. Cf. Pope Francis's discourse at the 36th General Congregation of the Society of Jesus on October 24, 2016, noted above.

80. Pope Francis has referenced these on a number of occasions in his written works. I am indebted here, though, to a talk given by Austen Ivereigh at the Von Hugel Institute, St. Edmund's College, on December 2, 2016: "Catholic Dis/Agreement: Pope Francis and the Uses of Disagreement as a Mechanism of Ecclesial Reform, Austen Ivereigh and Eamon Duffey," a part of the 2016–2017 Dynamics of Dis/Agreement lecture series, www.vhi.st-edmunds.cam.ac.uk/resources-folder/audio-visual. As the pope has written: "A constant tension exists between fullness and limitation. Fullness evokes the desire for complete possession, while limitation is a wall set before us. Broadly speaking, 'time' has to do with fullness as an expression of the horizon, which constantly opens before us, while each individual moment has to do with limitation as an expression of enclosure. People lived poised between each individual moment and the greater, brighter horizon of the utopian future as the final cause which draws us to itself. Here we see a first principle for progress in building a people: time is greater than space." Francis, *Evangelii Gaudium*, 222.

81. Ibid., 223.

82. As Pope Francis wrote: "Conflict cannot be ignored or concealed. It has to be faced. But if we remain trapped in conflict, we lose our perspective, our horizons shrink and reality itself begins to fall apart. In the midst of conflict, we lose our sense of the profound unity of reality." Ibid., 226. Also, "There is a third way, and it is the best way to deal with conflict. It is the willingness to face conflict head on, to resolve it and to make it a link in the chain of a new process." Ibid., 227.

83. Ibid., 230.

84. Eamon Duffey, response to Austen Ivereigh, "Pope Francis and the Uses of Disagreement as a Mechanism of Ecclesial Reform," December 2, 2016.

85. Francis, Greeting of Pope Francis to the Synod Fathers during the First General Congregation of the Third Extraordinary General Assembly of the Synod of Bishops, October 6, 2014. www.vatican.va/content/francesco/en/speeches/2014/october/documents/papa-francesco_20141006_padri-sinodali.html. The pope had also expressed his concern following the communication of one of the Cardinals following a consistory in February 2014 in which the family was discussed: "A Cardinal wrote to me, saying: what a shame that several Cardinals did not have the courage to say certain things out of respect for the Pope, perhaps believing that the Pope might think something else. This is not good." Ibid.

86. Francis, *Evangelii Gaudium*, 231. He continued: "Realities simply are, whereas ideas are worked out. There has to be continuous dialogue between the two, lest ideas become detached from realities. It is dangerous to dwell in the realm of words alone, of images and rhetoric. . . . Realities are greater

than ideas. This calls for rejecting the various means of masking reality: angelic forms of purity, dictatorships of relativism, empty rhetoric, objectives more ideal than real, brands of ahistorical fundamentalism, ethical systems bereft of kindness, intellectual discourse bereft of wisdom."

87. Ibid., 232. In the same paragraph he stated: "Ideas—conceptual elaborations—are at the service of communication, understanding, and praxis. Ideas disconnected from realities give rise to ineffectual forms of idealism and nominalism, capable at most of classifying and defining, but certainly not calling to action. . . . Formal nominalism has to give way to harmonious objectivity. Otherwise, the truth is manipulated. . . . We have politicians—and even religious leaders—who wonder why people do not understand and follow them, since their proposals are so clear and logical. Perhaps it is because they are stuck in the realm of pure ideas and end up reducing politics or faith to rhetoric. Others have left simplicity behind and have imported a rationality foreign to most people."

88. Cardinal Vincent Nichols, "St. Brigid's Day Annual Lecture," February 7, 2017, rcdow.org.uk/cardinal/addresses/st-brigids-day-annual-lecture/.

89. Francis, *Evangelii Gaudium*, 233, where Pope Francis also stated: "The principle of reality of a word already made flesh and constantly striving to take flesh anew, is essential to evangelization. It helps us to see that the Church's history is a history of salvation, to be mindful of those saints who inculturated the Gospel in the life of our peoples and to reap the fruits of the Church's rich bi-millennial tradition, without pretending to come up with a system of thought detached from this treasury, as if we wanted to reinvent the Gospel. At the same time, this principle impels us to put the word into practice, to perform works of justice and charity which make that world fruitful. Not to put that word into practice, not to make it reality is . . . to remain in the realm of pure ideas and to end up in a lifeless and unfruitful self-centredness and Gnosticism."

90. As the pope wrote: "The polyhedron . . . reflects the convergence of all its parts, each of which preserves its distinctiveness. Pastoral and political activity alike seek to gather in this polyhedron the best of each. There is a place for the poor and their culture, their aspirations and their potential. Even people who can be considered dubious on account of their errors have something to offer which must not be overlooked. It is the convergence of peoples who, within the universal order, maintain their own individuality; it is the sum total of persons within a society which pursues the common good, which truly has a place for everyone." Ibid., 236.

91. In the political sphere, the pope wrote, "an innate tension also exists between globalization and localization. We need to pay attention to the global so as to avoid narrowness and banality. Yet we also need to look to the local, which keeps our feet on the ground. Together, the two prevent us from falling into one of two extremes. In the first, people get caught up in an abstract, globalized universe, falling into step behind everyone else. . . . At the other extreme they turn into a museum of local folklore, a world apart, doomed to doing the same things over and over, and incapable of being challenged by

novelty or appreciating the beauty which God bestows beyond their borders."
Ibid., 234.

92. Francis *Evangelii Gaudium*, 235. He continued: "But this has to be
done without evasion or uprooting. We need to sink our roots deeper into
the fertile soil and history of our native place, which is a gift of God. We can
work on a small scale, in our own neighbourhood, but with a larger perspective. Nor do people who wholeheartedly enter into the life of a community
need to lose their individualism or hide their identity; instead, they receive
new impulses to personal growth. The global need not stifle, or the particular
prove barren."

93. Francis, Discourse at the 36th General Congregation of the Society of
Jesus, October 24, 2016. He continued: "Journeying and progressing in the
following of the Lord, the Society moves towards harmonizing the tensions
brought about by the diversity of the men whom it brings together and of the
mission it receives."

94. Jesuit Constitutions Formula Instituti, 3. In John W. Padberg, SJ, ed.,
Constitutions of the Society of Jesus and Their Complementary Norms, edited
by (St. Louis: Institute of Jesuit Sources, 1996), 6–7.

95. Francis, Discourse at the 36th General Congregation of the Society of
Jesus, October 24, 2016.

96. Throughout his pontificate Pope Francis has raised the importance of
popular piety as a contribution to the life of the Church.

97. St. Claude de la Colombiere, SJ (1641–1682), was a Jesuit priest and
confessor to St. Margaret Mary Alacoque (1647–1690), a Visitation Sister living
in the French town of Paray-le-Monial to whom the Lord revealed in a vision
his compassionate heart for the world.

98. Pedro Arrupe, "Rooted and Grounded in Love." In 1985 a collection
of Fr. Arrupe's writings on the Sacred Heart, including this address, was published under the title *In Him Alone Is Our Hope: Texts on the Heart of Christ*
(1966–1983) (St. Louis: Institute of Jesuit Sources, 1985).

99. Ibid. He continued: "If you want my advice, I would say to you, after
fifty-three years of living in the Society and almost sixteen of being its General,
that there is a tremendous power latent in this devotion to the heart of Christ.
Each of us should discover it for himself—if he has not already done so—and
then, entering deeply into it, apply to his personal life in whatever way the Lord
may suggest and grant. There is here an extraordinary grace that God offers us."

100. Ibid.

101. Ibid.

102. Francis, Angelus address, June 9, 2013, www.vatican.va/content/fran
cesco/en/angelus/2013/documents/papa-francesco_angelus_20130609.html.

103. Francis, Homily, Mass for the Sacred Heart of Jesus, Jubilee of Priests,
June 3, 2016, popefrancisdaily.com/popes-homily-at-mass-for-sacred-heart-of
-jesus-jubilee-for-priests/.

104. Ibid. He continued: "The Heart of the Good Shepherd tells us that
his love is limitless; it is never exhausted and it never gives up. There we see
his infinite and boundless self-giving; there we find the source of that faithful and meek love which sets free and makes others free; there we constantly

discover anew that Jesus loves us 'even to the end' (John 3:1), without ever being imposing."

105. St. Ignatius's description of "colloquy" in the *Spiritual Exercises* is an exploration of such "heart speaking to heart."

Chapter 3

1. *Cor ad cor loquitor*, "Heart speaks to heart," was a favorite expression of St. Ignatius of Loyola in discussing the colloquy in the Spiritual Exercises; it was also the motto adopted by St. John Henry Newman.

2. Joseph Ratzinger, *Behold the Pierced One* (San Francisco: Ignatius Press, 1986), 69. Cf. "Adoring contemplation of the side pierced by the spear makes us sensitive to God's salvific will. It enables us to entrust ourselves to his saving and merciful love, and at the same time strengthens us in the desire to take part in his work of salvation, becoming his instruments." Benedict XVI, Letter to the Superior General of the Society of Jesus, May 15, 2006, www.vatican.va /content/benedict-xvi/en/letters/2006/documents/hf_ben-xvi_let_20060515_50 -haurietis-aquas.html. Once more we have exemplified the critical continuity and resonance of the spiritual understanding of Pope Benedict and Pope Francis.

3. Indeed, Philip McCosker has spoken of the "significant generative theological heart" of *Evangelii Gaudium*. Philip McCosker, "From the Joy of the Gospel to the Joy of Christ: Situating and Expanding the Christology of *Evangelii Gaudium*," *Ecclesiology* 12 (2016): 34–53.

4. Walter Kasper, *Pope Francis' Revolution of Tenderness and Love*, translated by William Madges (New York: Paulist Press, 2015), 10. He continued: "Pope Francis himself does not skip any opportunity to emphasize this agreement."

5. In the Middle Ages the heart of Jesus became a specific object of adoration as the center and wellspring of Jesus's passionate and infinite love for us. The Sacred Heart also represented Jesus's woundedness, both the physical wound incurred by his physical heart on the cross (by the centurion's spear), and the spiritual wound of a love so great that he gave up his own life, even though this love was scorned by those for whom it was so generously given. Devotion to the Sacred Heart began to flourish in the Middle Ages through a renewed attentiveness to Jesus's humanity and his Passion. It was associated with the figures of St. Bonaventure (1221–1274), St. Gertrude (1232–1292), and St. Catherine of Siena (1347–1380). In the seventeenth century, the French School of St. Francis de Sales (1567–1622), St. John Eudes (1601–1680), St. Jane Frances de Chantal (1572–1641), and St. Margaret Mary Alacoque (1647–1690) offered a tender, compassionate spirituality that helped to renew the Church and counter Jansenism's severity and sectarianism. From 1673 to 1675, at the Visitation convent of Paray-le-Monial, Margaret Mary received a series of four revelations from Christ about his heart. It was from these revelations that devotion to the Sacred Heart reached its enduring form in the following practices: personal consecration to the Sacred Heart, the observance of an hour of prayer on Thursday nights between 11 o'clock and midnight as a way of sharing in

Christ's suffering in Gethsemane, and the reception of communion on the first Friday of the month as reparation for the indignities inflicted upon the blessed sacrament by those indifferent and ungrateful.

6. Romano Guardini (1885–1968) was a Roman Catholic priest, academic, and author. Though born in Verona, Italy, he grew up in Mainz, Germany, where his father was Italian consul. Ordained to the priesthood in 1910, from 1923 to 1939 he was a university professor of the philosophy of religion and Catholic *Weltanschauung* at the University of Berlin. Expelled by the Nazis, after the war he returned to university life in a similar position at the University of Tubingen and finally at the University of Munich from 1948 to 1963. Jorge Bergoglio started a doctorate in 1986 while in Germany focused on the work of Romano Guardini, but he did not complete it.

7. Romano Guardini, *The Lord*, translated by Elinor Castendyk Briefs (Washington, DC: Gateway Editions, 1962), 629. He continued: "This revolution is difficult to accept and still more difficult to realize and the more openly the world contradicts Christ's teaching, the more earnestly it defines those who accept it as fools, the more difficult that acceptance and realization. Nevertheless, to the degree that the intellect honestly attempts this right-about-face, the reality known as Jesus Christ will surrender itself. From this central reality, the doors of all other reality will swing open, and it will be lifted into the hope of the new creation."

8. Ibid.

9. Francis, *Evangelii Gaudium: The Joy of Gospel*, apostolic exhortation, November 24, 2013, 25, www.vatican.va/content/francesco/en/apost _exhortations/documents/papa-francesco_esortazione-ap_20131124_evangelii -gaudium.html.

10. Cf. "The encounter with God means also, at the same time, that I myself become open, torn from my closed solitude and received into the living community of the Church. That living community is also a mediator of my encounter with God, though that encounter touches my heart in an entirely personal way." Benedict XVI, "Interview with Fr. Jacques Servais, SJ," *Osservatore Romano*, March 17, 2016, www.catholicnewsagency.com/news/33591 /full-text-of-benedict-xvis-recent-rare-and-lengthy-interview.

11. Francis, Homily, Casa Santa Marta, September 13, 2016, www.vatican .va/content/francesco/en/cotidie/2016/documents/papa-francesco-cotidie _20160913_for-a-culture-of-encounter.html.

12. Ibid. Cf. "If the Christian faith essentially constitutes obedience to God's word of grace, then the moment of simple faithfulness through personal engagement steps more and more to the fore." Hans Urs von Balthasar, *Romano Guardini: Reform from the Source* (San Francisco: Ignatius Press, 2010), 89.

13. Francis, Homily, Casa Santa Marta, September 13, 2016.

14. Ibid.

15. Francis, Message for the 51st World Communications Day, January 24, 2017, www.vatican.va/content/francesco/en/messages/communications/docu ments/papa-francesco_20170124_messaggio-comunicazioni-sociali.html.

16. Cf. Guardini: Seeing is "the response to the fact that there is something that can be seen; the object and the eye, form and its perception, constitute . . . one of the original reference points within which existence is held in balance." Romano Guardini, *Die Sinne und die religiöse Erkenninis: Zwei Versuche über die christliche Vergewisserung* (Wurzburg, 1950), 17, cited in Balthasar, *Romano Guardini*, 22.

17. Romano Guardini, *Die Situation des Menschen* (Munich: Akademievorträge, 1953).

18. Romano Guardini, "Die Begegnung." In *Begegnung und Bildung*, by Romano Guardini and Otto Friedrich Bollnow, 4th ed., 9–24. Wurzburg, 1965, 99.

19. Balthasar, *Romano Guardini*, 23.

20. St. Bonaventure (1221–1274) was a renowned theologian and minister general of the Franciscan order. It is interesting to note that Joseph Ratzinger focused his doctoral work on Bonaventure. St. Bonaventure and St. Augustine were the two major influences on his theological formation. He said in later life: "I discovered an aspect of Bonaventure's theology not found in the previous literature, namely, his relation with the new idea of history conceived by Joachim of Fiore in the twelfth century. Joachim saw history as progression from the period of the Father (a difficult time for human beings under the law), to a second period of history, that of the Son (with more freedom, more openness, more brotherhood), to a third period of history, the definitive period of history, the time of the Holy Spirit. "According to Joachim," he wrote, "this was to be a time of universal reconciliation, reconciliation between east and west, between Christians and Jews, a time without the law (in the Pauline sense), a time of real brotherhood in the world. The interesting idea which I discovered was that a significant current among the Franciscans was convinced that St. Francis of Assisi and the Franciscan Order marked the beginning of this third period of history, and it was their ambition to actualize it; Bonaventure was in critical dialogue with this current." Joseph Ratzinger, self-presentation of His Eminence Cardinal Joseph Ratzinger as a member of the Pontifical Academy of Sciences, April 19, 2005, www.vatican.va/content/benedict-xvi/en/biography/documents/hf_ben-xvi_bio_20050419_self-presentation.html. Accordingly, It might be argued that Ratzinger drew from Bonaventure a conception of human history as unfolding in a purposeful way, toward a specific goal, a time of deepened spiritual insight, an "age of the Holy Spirit."

21. Romano Guardini, *Die Lehre des heil: Bonaventura von der Erlösung; Ein Beitrag zur Geschichte und zum System der Erlösungslehre* (Dusseldorf: L. Schwann, 1921), 48.

22. Cf. Francis, *Evangelii Gaudium*, 34–39, 264–67, 270.

23. Romano Guardini, *The Lord* (Washington, DC: Regnery/Gateway Editions, 1982), 40.

24. Joseph Ratzinger, *Introduction to Christianity* (San Francisco: Ignatius Press, 2004), 188.

25. Romano Guardini. *Die menschliche Wirklichkeit des Herrn: Beitrage zu einer Psychologie Jesu*, 3rd ed.. (Mainz, 1991). He continued: "The Christ who is of concern as much to theologians as to Christian believers is he who

encounters us in the fullness of the apostolic proclamation, but not because it is a matter here of the 'Christ of Faith' in contrast to the 'historical Jesus.' . . . The apostles never say *more* than what the historical Jesus was, but always say *less*, . . . and what they say always leads us toward him while lagging behind the fullness of his Incarnation. . . . That is also why anyone who reads the New Testament correctly will sense a reality behind each of its sentences that transcends what is being said." *Romano Guardini Werke*, edited by Franz Henrich under the direction of the committee of experts for the literary estate of Romano Guardini with the Catholic Academy in Bayern, published jointly by Matthias Grünewald, Mainz, and Ferdinand Schöningh (Paderborn, 1991), cited in Hans Urs von Balthasar, *Romano Guardini: Reform from the Source* (San Francisco: Ignatius Press, 2010).

26. Pope Francis, *Misericordiae Vultus: The Face of Mercy*, apostolic letter, April 11, 2015, 8.

27. Francis, "Draw From the Well of the Father's Mercy, and Bring It to the World!," homily on Divine Mercy Sunday, April 3, 2016, aleteia.org/2016/04/03/pope-francis-draw-from-the-well-of-the-fathers-mercy-and-bring-it-to-the-world/.

28. Francis, Angelus address, March 5, 2017, www.vatican.va/content/francesco/en/angelus/2017/documents/papa-francesco_angelus_20170305.html.

29. Ibid.

30. For example, he did so after giving the Angelus address on April 13, 2014.

31. Francis, "Preface," *Youcat: Youth Bible of the Catholic Church* (San Francisco: Ignatius Press, 2017).

32. Ibid.

33. Ibid.

34. Robert A, Kreig, CSC, *Romano Guardini: A Precursor of Vatican II* (Notre Dame, IN: University of Notre Dame Press, 2001), 154.

35. Joseph Ratzinger, "Guardini on Christ in Our Century," *Crisis*, June 1996, 14.

36. "His aim" in this work "was not to present a comprehensive theology of the liturgy." Emery de Gaál, *The Theology of Pope Benedict XVI: The Christocentric Shift* (New York: Palgrave Macmillan, 2010), 252. He continued: "Almost overnight, it became the foundational text for the twentieth-century liturgical movement. Guardini argued that the Eucharist is the premier expression of the Church's essence."

37. Ibid., 253.

38. Cf. "As a member of the faithful, one is able to address the transcendent object, God. Thus in the Christian liturgy, the believer and God become subjects of *opus Dei*, of the one work of God. In Ratzinger's estimation, this is precisely what Romano Guardini wished to convey when he stated that, in the Church's liturgy, God in Jesus Christ shares human time. In this sense, the Eucharist is the real presence of God, that is, it is humans' partaking in the eternal, triune communication of Father, Son, and Holy Spirit. Both Guardini and

Ratzinger understand the liturgy as living in three ontological dimensions: cosmic, historic, and mysterious. Every attempt to depart from the Spirit-inspired past deprives the contemporary liturgy of its inherent quality as *opus Dei* and leads it to degenerate into human self-celebration. . . . The Incarnation occurs anew when body and voice praise God in Jesus Christ." De Gaál, *The Theology of Pope Benedict XVI*, 263.

39. Such a witness to the transcendent reality of the Mass and the Trinitarian action could possibly "assist the present culture in gaining an appreciation for interiority and living in the silence of God." Ibid.

40. Francis, "Justice and Mercy," morning meditation in the chapel of Casa Santa Marta, February 24, 2017, www.vatican.va/content/francesco/en/cotidie /2017/documents/papa-francesco-cotidie_20170224_justice-and-mercy.html.

41. Francis, *Amoris Laetitia*, Apostolic Exhortation on Love in the Family, March 29, 2016, 65, www.vatican.va/content/dam/francesco/pdf/apost _exhortations/documents/papa-francesco_esortazione-ap_20160319_amoris -laetitia_en.pdf. In the same paragraph he continues: "We need to enter into the mystery of Jesus' birth, into that 'yes' given by Mary to the message of the angel, when the Word was conceived in her womb, as well as the 'yes' of Joseph, who gave a name to Jesus and watched over Mary. We need to contemplate the joy of the shepherds before the manger, the adoration of the Magi and the flight into Egypt, in which Jesus shares his people's experience of exile, persecution and humiliation."

42. Walter Kasper, *Mercy: The Essence of the Gospel and the Key to Christian Life*, translated by William Madges (New York: Paulist Press, 2013).

43. Ibid. 62.

44. Cf. Pope Francis: "We need to contemplate the religious expectation of Zechariah and his joy at the birth of John the Baptist." Francis, *Amoris Laetitia*, 65.

45. Cf. Balthasar: "To focus the Incarnation on the Passion enables both theories to reach a point where the mind is flooded by the same perfect thought: in serving, in washing the feet of his creatures, God reveals himself even in that which is most intimately divine in him, and manifests his supreme glory." Hans Urs von Balthasar, *Mysterium Paschale: The Mystery of Easter*, translated by Aidan Nichols, OP (Grand Rapids, MI: Eerdmans, 1993), 11.

46. Francis, *Amoris Laetitia*, 64.

47. E.g., with Lazarus and his sisters (Luke 10:38) and with Peter and his family (Mark 8:14).

48. Cf. John Paul II, *Dives in Misericordia*, 4, where he states: "The concept of 'mercy' in the Old Testament has a long and rich history. We have to refer back to it in order that the mercy revealed by Christ may shine forth more clearly. By revealing that mercy both through His actions and through His teaching, Christ addressed Himself to people who not only knew the concept of mercy, but who also, as the People of God of the Old Covenant, had drawn from their age-long history a special experience of the mercy of God. This experience was social and communal, as well as individual and interior." Earlier in this text, Pope John Paul II stated explicitly: "In Christ and through Christ,

God also becomes especially visible in His mercy; that is to say, there is emphasized that attribute of the divinity which the Old Testament, using various concepts and terms, already defined as 'mercy.' Christ confers on the whole of the Old Testament tradition about God's mercy a definitive meaning. Not only does He speak of it and explain it by the use of comparisons and parables, but above all He Himself makes it incarnate and personifies it. He Himself, in a certain sense, is mercy. To the person who sees it in Him—and finds it in Him—God becomes 'visible' in a particular way as the Father who is rich in mercy." Ibid. 2. John Paul II, *Dives in Misercordia*, encyclical, November 30, 1980, www.vatican.va/content/john-paul-ii/en/encyclicals/documents/hf_jp-ii_enc_30111980_dives-in-misericordia.html.

49. Francis, *Amoris Laetitia*, 64.

50. This narrative is profoundly Christological. God's attitude toward suffering humanity is gratuitous loving tenderness, and Jesus is the concretion of God's charity at the heart of the parable.

51. Kasper, *Pope Francis' Revolution of Tenderness and Love*, 33. He continues: "Mercy is God's own justice, which does not condemn the sinner who wants to be converted, but rather makes him or her just. Let it, however, be understood: mercy justifies the sinner not the sin."

52. "Saint Thomas Aquinas pointed out that the precepts which Christ and the apostles gave to the people of God 'are very few' (*Summa Theologiae* I-II, q. 107, a.4). Citing Saint Augustine, he noted that the precepts subsequently enjoined by the Church should be insisted upon with moderation 'so as not to burden the lives of the faithful' and make our religion a form of servitude, whereas God's mercy has willed that we should be free' (ibid.)." Francis, *Evangelii Gaudium*, 43.

53. Cf. John Paul II: "Man cannot be manifested in the full dignity of his nature without reference—not only on the level of concepts but also in an integrally existential way—to God. Man and man's lofty calling are revealed in Christ *through* the revelation of the mystery of the Father and His love." John Paul II, *Dives in Misericordia*, 1.

54. 1 Peter 1:3: "Blessed be the God and Father of our Lord Jesus Christ! By his great mercy we have been borne anew to a living hope through the resurrection of Jesus Christ from the dead."

55. Cf. Antonio Pitta: "The parables of mercy are located at the borders of the Gospel. Without taking anything away from Jesus' preaching about the kingdom of God, the mercy of God moves out through the parables beyond the circle of disciples and dialogues with everyone who hears them. Even if the parables themselves do not bring salvation—which only happens in a personal encounter with Jesus and his death and resurrection—they do explore new pathways, and they travel on inaccessible roads where the Gospel has not yet reached or where it is unheard. Therefore, if it is unthinkable that salvation can come from merely understanding a parable, it is also undeniable that Jesus' parables indicate paths to salvation in remarkable ways." Antonio Pitta, *The Parables of Mercy* (Rome: Pontifical Council for the Promotion of the New Evangelization, 2015), 85.

56. Benedict XVI, *Jesus of Nazareth: From the Baptism in the Jordan to the Transfiguration*, translated by Adrian Walker (New York: Doubleday, 2007), 188.

57. *Romano Guardini Werke*, 24.

58. Cf. Balthasar: "The Incarnation is ordered to the Cross as to its goal. . . . He who says Incarnation also says Cross. And this is so for two reasons, [first:] The son of God took human nature in its fallen condition, and with it, therefore, the worm in its entrails — mortality, fallenness, self-estrangement, death — which sin introduced into the world. . . . The second reason to be mentioned has to do not with the man assumed, but with the Logos assuming: to become man is for him, in a most hidden yet very real sense, already humiliation — yes indeed, as many would say, a deeper humiliation than the going to the Cross itself." Balthasar, *Mysterium Paschale*, 22–23.

59. Emery de Gaál, *The Theology of Pope Benedict XVI*, 120. He continues: "Biblical titles such as Son and *Kyrios* (Lord) connect him with God's divine being. These titles are so closely linked to him that they became part of his name among people. Office, interpretation, and person blend into one reality. In this vein, Peter can state that Jesus is the Messiah, the Son of the living God. It is in light of this biblical background then, so Ratzinger informs us, that men standing in apostolic succession dared to continue to elaborate on the nature of Jesus."

60. Francis, Homily, Jubilee for Priests, June 3, 2016, www.vatican.va/con tent/francesco/en/homilies/2016/documents/papa-francesco_20160603 _omelia-giubileo-sacerdoti.html.

61. John Paul II, *Crossing the Threshold of Hope*, translated by Jenny McPhee and Martha McPhee (New York: Knopf, 1994), 219. Earlier in that paragraph Pope John Paul II stated: "When, on October 22, 1978, I said the words 'Be not afraid!' in St. Peter's Square, I could not fully know how far they would take me and the entire Church. Their meaning came more from the Holy Spirit, the Consoler promised by the Lord Jesus to His disciples, than from the man who spoke them. Nevertheless, with the passing of the years, I have recalled these words on many occasions. The exhortation 'Be not afraid!' should be interpreted as having a very broad meaning. In a certain sense it was an exhortation addressed to all people, an exhortation to conquer fear in the present world situation, as much in the East as in the West, as much in the North as in the South. Have no fear of that which you yourselves have created, have no fear of all that man has produced, and that every day is becoming more dangerous for him! Finally, have no fear of yourselves! Why should we have no fear? Because man has been redeemed by God. When pronouncing these words in St. Peter's Square, I already knew that my first encyclical and my entire papacy would be tied to the truth of the Redemption. In the Redemption we find the most profound basis for the words 'Be not afraid!': 'For God so loved the world that he gave his only Son' (cf. Jn 3:16). This Son is always present in the history of humanity as Redeemer." John Paul II, *Crossing the Threshold of Hope*, translated by Jenny McPhee and Martha McPhee (New York: Alfred A. Knopf, 2005), 11th printing (original 1994), 218–219.

62. Cf. John 14:10–11. This analogous relationship does not negate the importance of the Fourth Lateran Council's assertion in 1215 that the dissimilarity between human persons and God is always greater than any similarity. Thus, any analogy must be seen in this light.

63. Cf. Guardini: "The Father's will is the Father's love. Through his complete acceptance of it, Jesus enters into the intimacy of God, where all things are luminous with his tenderness and power. This will is constantly forming directives for all needs as they present themselves." Guardini, *The Lord*, 41.

64. Francis, *Evangelii Gaudium*, 285. In *Evangelii Gaudium* Pope Francis reiterates the key apostolic *kerygma*, the proclamation that "Jesus Christ, . . . by his death and resurrection, reveals and communicates to us the Father's infinite mercy." Ibid., 164.

65. Francis, Homily, Jubilee for the Sick and Persons with Disabilities, June 12, 2016, www.vatican.va/content/francesco/en/homilies/2016/documents/papa-francesco_20160612_omelia-giubileo-ammalati-disabili.html. During this very poignant homily Pope Francis also stated: "Each of us, sooner or later, is called to face—at times painfully—frailty and illness, both our own and those of others. How many different faces do these common yet dramatically human experiences take! Yet all of them directly raise the pressing question of the meaning of life. Our hearts may quietly yield to cynicism, as if the only solution were simply to put up with these experiences, trusting only in our own strength. Or we may put complete trust in science, thinking that surely somewhere in the world there is a medicine capable of curing the illness. Sadly, however, this is not always the case, and, even if the medicine did exist, it would be accessible to very few people. Human nature, wounded by sin, is marked by *limitations*. . . . In an age when care for one's body has become an obsession and a big business, anything imperfect has to be hidden away, since it threatens the happiness and serenity of the privileged few and endangers the dominant model. Such persons should best be kept apart, in some 'enclosure'—even a gilded one—or in 'islands' of pietism or social welfare, so that they do not hold back the pace of a false well-being. In some cases, we are even told that it is better to eliminate them as soon as possible, because they become an unacceptable economic burden in time of crisis. Yet what an illusion it is when people today shut their eyes in the face of sickness and disability! They fail to understand the real meaning of life, which also has to do with accepting suffering and limitations. The world does not become better because only apparently 'perfect' people live there—I say 'perfect' rather than 'false'—but when human solidarity, mutual acceptance and respect increase. How true are the words of the Apostle: 'God chose what is weak in the world to shame the strong' (1 Cor. 1:27)!"

66. Ibid.

67. Ibid.

68. Thomas Aquinas, *Summa Theologiae*, pt. I, q.21, a.4, cited in Kasper, *Mercy*, 98.

69. In a homily, the pope said: "Someone with a casuistic mentality might ask, 'But what is more important in God? Justice or mercy?' This, too, is a sick thought, that seeks to go out. . . . What is more important? They are not two

things: it is only one, only one thing. In God, justice is mercy and mercy is justice." Francis, "Justice and Mercy," morning meditation in the chapel of Casa Santa Marta, February 24, 2017, www.vatican.va/content/francesco/en/cotidie/2017/documents/papa-francesco-cotidie_20170224_justice-and-mercy.html. Cf. Pope Pius XII: "Since our divine Redeemer as our lawful and perfect Mediator, out of his ardent love for us, restored complete harmony between the duties and obligations of the human race and the rights of God, he is therefore responsible for the existence of that wonderful reconciliation of divine justice and divine mercy which constitutes the sublime mystery of our salvation." Pius XII, *Haurietis Aquas*, encyclical, May 15, 1956, 37.

70. Pope Francis, General Audience, Vatican, February 3, 2016, www.vatican.va/content/francesco/en/audiences/2016/documents/papa-francesco_20160203_udienza-generale.html.

71. Pope Francis, *Misericoridae Vultus: The Face of Mercy*, apostolic letter, April 11, 2015, 20, www.vatican.va/content/francesco/en/apost_letters/documents/papa-francesco_bolla_20150411_misericordiae-vultus.html. He continued: "Justice is a fundamental concept for civil society; which is meant to be governed by the rule of law. Justice is also understood as that which is rightly due to each individual. In the Bible there are many references to divine justice and to God as 'judge.' In these passages justice is understood as the full observance of the Law and the behavior of every good Israelite in conformity with God's commandments. Such a vision, however, has not infrequently led to legalism by distorting the original meaning of justice and obscuring its profound value. To overcome this legalistic perspective, we need to recall that in Sacred Scripture justice is conceived essentially as the faithful abandonment of oneself to God's will."

72. "If God limited himself to only justice, he would cease to be God, and would instead be like human beings who ask merely that the law be respected." Francis, *Misericordiae Vultus*, 21.

73. Ibid.

74. Francis, Homily, Mass for the Closing of the Jubilee Year of Mercy, November 20, 2016, www.vatican.va/content/francesco/en/homilies/2016/documents/papa-francesco_20161120_omelia-chiusura-giubileo.html. He continued: "So too we are called to instill hope and provide opportunities to others. Because even if the Holy Door closes, the true door of mercy which is the heart of Christ always remains open wide for us. From the lacerated side of the Risen One until the very end of time flow mercy, consolation and hope." In this homily Pope Francis also issued this succinct challenge: "This Year of Mercy invites us to rediscover the core, to return to what is essential. This time of mercy calls us to look to the true face of our King, the one that shines out at Easter, and to rediscover the youthful, beautiful face of the Church, the face that is radiant when it is welcoming, free, faithful, poor in means but rich in love, on mission. Mercy, which takes us to the heart of the Gospel, urges us to give up habits and practices which may be obstacles to serving the Kingdom of God."

75. Francis, *Evangelii Gaudium*, 112. He continued: "He sends his Spirit into our hearts to make us his children, transforming us and enabling us to

respond to his love by our lives. The Church is sent by Jesus Christ as the sacrament of the salvation offered by God. Through her evangelizing activity, she cooperates as an instrument of that divine grace which works unceasingly and inscrutably."

76. See Benedict XVI, *Jesus of Nazareth: Holy Week; From the Entrance into Jerusalem to the Resurrection*, translated by Philip J. Whitmore (San Francisco: Ignatius Press, 2011), 132–133.

77. Benedict XVI, interview with Fr. Jacques Servais. He continued: "Pope Francis is totally in agreement with this line. His pastoral practice is expressed in the fact that he continually speaks to us of God's mercy."

78. Ibid.

79. Kasper, *Mercy*, 75. He continues later: "God reconciles us with himself to such an extent that he re-establishes the covenantal relationship. Augustine says very clearly: the one who created us without us does not want to redeem us without us (Augustine, Sermon 169 c11 n13). The act of redemption enables us to say 'yes' anew in faith."

80. Romano Guardini, *Learning the Virtues That Lead You to God* (Manchester, NH: Sophia Institute Press, 1998), 190.

81. As Kasper wrote: "Jesus's substitutionary atonement is exclusive insofar as he is the one and only mediator of salvation; on the other hand, his substitutionary atonement is inclusive insofar as it includes us in his self-sacrifice. Substitutionary atonement is not an action that replaces what we ourselves can do and must do. It does not replace the individual responsibility of each person, but rather sets it really free again." Kasper, *Mercy*, 76.

82. 1 Cor. 2:2.

83. According to Kasper, it is a freedom that "liberates from the anxious and never successful attempts at self-justification by means of success, money, power, prestige, pleasure, or sex appeal. It liberates us from enslavement to these earthly goods that tyrannize us. It liberates us from fear about the meaninglessness of existence and from the fear of death." Kasper, *Mercy*, 80.

84. Francis, *Misericordiae Vultus*, 21. In the following paragraph, Pope Francis re-emphasizes: "God is always ready to forgive, and he never tires of forgiving in ways that are continually new and surprising." Ibid., 22.

85. Benedict XVI, Angelus address, First Sunday of Lent, February 25, 2007, www.vatican.va/content/benedict-xvi/en/angelus/2007/documents/hf_ben-xvi_ang_20070225.html. He continued: "During these days of Lent, let us not distance our hearts from this mystery of profound humanity and lofty spirituality. Looking at Christ, we feel at the same time looked at by him. He whom we have pierced with our faults never tires of pouring out upon the world an inexhaustible torrent of merciful love. May humankind understand that only from this font is it possible to draw the indispensable spiritual energy to build that peace and happiness which every human being continually seeks." Cf. *Deus Caritas Est*, 12, where Pope Benedict indicated that only by looking at the crucified Lord can the fundamental truth that "God is love" be known and contemplated: "In this contemplation, the Christian discovers the path along which his life and love must move." Benedict XVI, *Deus Caritas Est: God Is*

Love, encyclical, December 25, 2005, www.vatican.va/content/benedict-xvi/en
/encyclicals/documents/hf_ben-xvi_enc_20051225_deus-caritas-est.html.

86. Benedict XVI, interview with Fr. Jacques Servais.

87. Ibid.

88. Ibid.

89. Cardinal Walter Kasper wrote: "They say repeatedly: The just one dies for the unjust in order to make the unjust just. He died so that we could live. The church fathers go a step further and say: God became human so that we would be divinized. In the third Christmas preface, we read: 'for through him the holy exchange that restores our life has shone forth today in splendor: when our frailty is assumed by your word, not only does human mortality receive unending honor but by this wondrous union we, too, are made eternal.' The idea of exchange received its most intense emphasis in Martin Luther, who speaks in many places of the happy change and exchange." Kasper, *Mercy*, 80–81.

90. Cf. Romans 6:23: "For the wages of sin is death, but the free gift of God is eternal life in Christ Jesus our Lord." Also 2 Cor. 5:17: "So if anyone is in Christ, there is a new creation; everything old has passed away; see, everything has become new!" And 2 Cor. 5:18: "It is not we who can reconcile God with us. He is the one who has reconciled himself with us."

91. In chapter 4 we shall consider the Trinitarian horizon of mercy.

92. Benedict XVI, interview with Fr. Jacques Servais.

93. Cf. Augustine's *massa damnata*. Augustine taught that Adam's sin is transmitted by concupiscence, which results in humanity's being a *massa damnata*, with much enfeebled though not destroyed free will.

94. Benedict XVI, interview with Fr. Jacques Servais.

95. Ibid.

96. Henri de Lubac, "Homilies on Ezekiel 6:6," cited by Pope Emeritus Benedict in his interview with Fr. Jacques Servais.

97. De Lubac said: "The Father himself, the God of the universe, he who is overflowing with long-suffering, patience, mercy and compassion, does he also not suffer in a certain sense? 'The Lord your God, in fact, has taken upon himself your ways as the one who takes upon himself his son' (Deut. 1:31). God thus takes upon himself our customs as the Son of God took upon himself our sufferings. The Father himself is not without passion! If He is invoked, then He knows mercy and compassion. He perceives a suffering of love." Ibid.

98. Søren Kierkegaard, *Die Tagebücher*, 1834–1855 (Munich: Kösel, 1949), 239f, cited in Kasper, *Mercy*, 119

99. Cf. Hebrews 4:14–16: "Since then we have a great high priest who has passed through the heavens, Jesus the Son of God, let us hold fast our confession. For we do not have a high priest who cannot sympathize with our weaknesses, but One who has been tempted in all things as we are, yet without sin. Let us therefore draw near with confidence to the throne of grace, that we may receive mercy and may find grace to help in time of need." The many depictions of the throne of grace usually underline the nature of the Trinity. The Father and Son are the two images that merge together to make this one statue: the Father on the throne, Christ on the cross. Simply combining those two images

would be enough to make this statue a powerful visual statement. But there is more to be seen here. Father and Son are linked by the Holy Spirit in the form of a dove who descends from the Father and alights on the top of the cross. He spreads out his wings (echoing the crossbeam of the cross and, more movingly, the son's extended arms) and pitches forward, his head bent solicitously over the head of Jesus.

100. Benedict XVI, interview with Fr. Jacques Servais.

101. Ibid.

102. Benedict XVI, *Spe Salvi*, encyclical, November 30, 2007, 39, www .vatican.va/content/benedict-xvi/en/encyclicals/documents/hf_ben-xvi_enc _20071130_spe-salvi.html. He continues in the same paragraph: "Certainly, in our many different sufferings and trials we always need the lesser and greater hopes too—a kind visit, the healing of internal and external wounds, a favourable resolution of a crisis, and so on. In our lesser trials these kinds of hope may even be sufficient. But in truly great trials, where I must make a definitive decision to place the truth before my own welfare, career and possessions, I need the certitude of that true, great hope of which we have spoken here. For this too we need witnesses—martyrs—who have given themselves totally, so as to show us the way—day after day. We need them if we are to prefer goodness to comfort, even in the little choices we face each day—knowing that this is how we live life to the full. Let us say it once again: the capacity to suffer for the sake of the truth is the measure of humanity. Yet this capacity to suffer depends on the type and extent of the hope that we bear within us and build upon. The saints were able to make the great journey of human existence in the way that Christ had done before them, because they were brimming with great hope."

103. We shall consider this further in chapter 4.

104. Benedict XVI, Homily, Mass for the Election of the Roman Pontiff, April 18, 2005, www.vatican.va/gpII/documents/homily-pro-eligendo-pontifice _20050418_en.html. He continued: "Christ carries the full weight of evil and all its destructive force in his body and his soul. He burns and transforms evil in suffering, in the fire of his suffering love. The day of vindication and the year of favor converge in the Paschal Mystery, in the dead and Risen Christ. This is the vengeance of God: he himself suffers for us, in the person of his Son. The more deeply stirred we are by the Lord's mercy, the greater the solidarity we feel with his suffering—and we become willing to complete in our own flesh 'what is lacking in the afflictions of Christ' (Col. 1:24)."

105. Ibid.

106. Ibid.

107. Ibid.

108. Benedict XVI, interview with Fr. Jacques Servais.

109. Laurent Touze, *Mercy in the Teaching of the Popes* (Vatican: Pontifical Council for the Promotion of the New Evangelization, 2015), 10.

110. *Ramansit misera et Misericordia*: What remained (the two of them remained—Jesus and the adulterous woman) [were] misery and mercy.

111. Paul VI, General Audience, March 20, 1974, www.vatican.va/content/ paul-vi/it/audiences/1974/documents/hf_p-vi_aud_19740320.html. He continued:

"Sin . . . the time has come to examine more clearly this concept, which plays an inferior and negative role in the whole Christian concept of human existence; it is all the more appropriate since the theoretical and practical ideologies of today's world are trying to expunge the name and the reality of sin from modern discourse."

112. Ibid. He went on: "And you know how providential it is: 'Where sin increased, grace abounded even more' (Rom. 5:20). And you know how unpredictable this love was: Christ, the Word of God made man, took upon himself the mission of redemption. 'For our sake he made him to be sin who knew no sin, so that in him we might become the righteousness of God' (2 Cor. 5:21). In other words propitiation was offered in our place, earning for us restitution to a state of grace, that is, the supernatural participation in God's life."

113. Paul VI, General Audience, March 29, 1972, www.vatican.va/content /paul-vi/it/audiences/1972/documents/hf_p-vi_aud_19720329.html.

114. It is also reminiscent of the announcement of each new pope: "Annuntio vobis *gaudium magnum*: HABEMUS PAPAM!"

115. Francis, *Misericordiae Vultus*, 1.

116. Francis, *Evangelii Gaudium*, 164.

117. Ibid., 88.

118. Ibid.

119. Francis, *Evangelii Gaudium*, 231. As Pope Francis makes clear in this paragraph, such espousal of this principle also calls for "rejecting the various means of masking reality: angelic forms of purity, dictatorships of relativism, empty rhetoric, objectives more ideal than real, brands of ahistorical fundamentalism, ethical systems bereft of kindness, intellectual discourse bereft of wisdom."

120. Ibid., 222–225, 226–230, and 234–237.

121. McCosker, "From the Joy of the Gospel to the Joy of Christ," 34–53.

122. The pope wrote: "A constant tension exists between fullness and limitation. Fullness evokes the desire for complete possession, while limitation is a wall set before us. Broadly speaking, 'time' has to do with fullness as an expression of the horizon which constantly opens before us, while each individual moment has to do with limitation as an expression of enclosure. People live poised between each individual moment and the greater, brighter horizon of the utopian future as the final cause which draws us to itself" (Francis, *Evangelii Gaudium*, 222).

123. Philip McCosker asserts: "The Christian community must be pneumatologically ec-centric, seeking ever-greater diversity, and avoiding 'monolithic uniformity at all costs.'" McCosker, "From the Joy of the Gospel to the Joy of Christ," 43.

124. "The unity brought by the Spirit can harmonize every diversity. . . . Diversity is a beautiful thing when it can constantly enter into a process of reconciliation and seal a sort of cultural covenant resulting in a 'reconciled diversity'" (Francis, *Evangelii Gaudium*, 230).

125. Ibid., 228. The pope continued: "In this way it becomes possible to build communion amid disagreement, but this can only be achieved by those

great persons who are willing to go beyond the surface of the conflict and to see others in their deepest dignity."

126. Francis, in *Evangelii Gaudium*, page 234, mentions the tension between "globalization and localization" when he states: "An innate tension also exists between globalization and localization. We need to pay attention to the global so as to avoid narrowness and banality. Yet we also need to look to the local, which keeps our feet on the ground. Together, the two prevent us from falling into one of two extremes. In the first, people get caught up in an abstract globalized universe, falling into step behind everyone else, applauding at all the right times. At the other extreme, they turn into a museum of local folklore, a world apart, doomed to doing the same things over and over, and incapable of being challenged by novelty or appreciating the beauty which God bestows beyond their borders."

127. Cf. McCosker: "We can get lost in an abstract globalized universe at the expense of living in the here and now, or contrariwise we can get trapped into the very particulars of our here and now without relation to the rest of the world or any sense of movement or novelty." McCosker, "From the Joy of the Gospel to the Joy of Christ," 41.

128. The pope wrote: "The polyhedron reflects the convergence of all its parts, each of which preserves its distinctiveness. Pastoral and political activity alike seek to gather in this polyhedron the best of each. There is a place for the poor and their culture, their aspirations and their potential. Even people who can be considered dubious on account of their errors have something to offer which must not be overlooked. It is the convergence of peoples who, within the universal order, maintain their own individuality; it is the sum total of persons within a society which pursues the common good, which truly has a place for everyone" Francis, *Evangelii Gaudium*, 236.

129. By contrast, Pope Francis wrote: "The spirit of suspicion and supposition aims basically for a truth that asserts me against my brother.... In the teaching of Dorotheus of Gaza it is the devil himself who sows suspicion in people's hearts in order to divide them from one another. This phenomenon is the inverse of that resulting from the Incarnation of the Word: the devil aims to *divide* (through means of suspicion) in order to *confuse*; our Lord by contrast, is always God and man, *indivise et inconfuse*—without division of person, without confusion of natures. When the devil sows suspicion, he tries to convince us by means of fallacies, or half-truths, to manipulate our hearts into selfish convictions that lead us into a world closed off from all objectivity. Suspicion, sown by the devil, sets up in the heart a crooked measuring rod, which displaces reality.... It is no longer a question of sorting out this or that wrong idea, but a whole hermeneutic—the way he interprets in a twisted way, because the measure he applies to it is itself crooked." Francis, *The Way of Humility*, translated by Helena Scott (San Francisco: Ignatius Press, 2013), 66–67.

130. Francis, Homily, Easter Sunday, April 16, 2017, www.vatican.va/con tent/francesco/en/homilies/2017/documents/papa-francesco_20170416 _omelia-pasqua.html. The pope continued: "This is the first task: to proclaim forgiveness. This visible sign of His mercy brings with it peace of heart and the joy of a renewed encounter with the Lord."

131. Ibid.

132. The foreword of this book makes the same point based on existential experience.

133. Francis, Homily, Easter Sunday, 2017.

134. Ibid.

135. Ibid.

136. Ibid.

137. *Misericordiae Vultus*, 1. Since Jesus is the revelation of the Father's mercy, Pope Francis emphasized that "we need constantly to contemplate the mystery of mercy. It is a wellspring of joy, serenity, and peace. Our salvation depends upon it." Ibid., 2.

138. He wrote: "Mercy: the word reveals the very mystery of the Most Holy Trinity. Mercy: the ultimate and supreme act by which God comes to meet us.... Mercy: the bridge that connects God and man, opening our hearts to a hope of being loved forever despite our sinfulness." Ibid.

139. Ibid., 5. The fervor of Pope Francis was evident, as in this same paragraph he wrote: "How much I desire that the year to come will be steeped in mercy, so that we can go out to every man and woman, bringing the goodness and tenderness of God! May the balm of mercy reach everyone, both believers and those far away, as a sign that the Kingdom of God is already present in our midst!"

140. Ibid., 8. He continued by writing that in the person of Jesus there is "nothing but love, a love given gratuitously.... The signs he works, especially in the face of sinners, the poor the marginalized, the sick, and the suffering, are all meant to teach mercy.... What moved Jesus in all of these situations was nothing other than mercy, with which he read the hearts of those he encountered and responded to their deepest need."

141. Ibid., 9. He continued: "Jesus reveals the nature of God as that of a Father who never gives up until he has forgiven the wrong and overcome rejection with compassion and mercy."

142. Francis, *Evangelii Gaudium*, 24. Here Pope Francis also stresses the vital importance of becoming involved in the everyday lives of others, a goal that lies at the heart of the Church as an evangelizing community. He writes that "it bridges distances, it is willing to abase itself if necessary, and it embraces human life, touching the suffering flesh of Christ in others. Evangelizers thus take on the 'smell of the sheep' and the sheep are willing to hear their voice."

143. John Paul II, *Dives in Misericordia*, 15, encyclical, November 30, 1980, www.vatican.va/content/john-paul-ii/en/encyclicals/documents/hf_jp-ii_enc _30111980_dives-in-misericordia.html. He continued: "It likewise obliges me to have recourse to that mercy and to beg for it at this difficult, critical phase of the history of the Church and of the world." Cf. "The Church lives an authentic life when she professes and proclaims mercy—the most stupendous attribute of the Creator and of the Redeemer—and when she brings people close to the sources of the Savior's mercy, of which she is the trustee and dispenser." Ibid., 13.

144. Ibid., 2. He continues: "The word and the concept of 'mercy' seem to cause uneasiness in man, who, thanks to the enormous development of science

and technology never before known in history, has become the master of the earth and has subdued and dominated it (cf. Gen. 1:28). This dominion over the earth, sometimes understood in a one-sided and superficial way, seems to have no room for mercy. . . . And this is why, in the situation of the Church and the world today, many individuals and groups guided by a lively sense of faith are turning, I would say almost spontaneously, to the mercy of God."

145. Francis, *Misericordia et Misera*, apostolic letter November 20, 2016, 1, www.vatican.va/content/francesco/en/apost_letters/documents/papa-francesco -lettera-ap_20161120_misericordia-et-misera.html.

146. Ibid. The pope continues: "Jesus looked that woman in the eye and read in her heart a desire to be understood, forgiven and set free. . . . Jesus' only judgement is one filled with mercy and compassion for the condition of this sinner. To those who wished to judge and condemn her to death, Jesus replies with a lengthy silence. His purpose was to let God's voice be heard in the consciences not only of the woman, but also in those of her accusers, who drop their stones and one by one leave the scene. Jesus then says: 'Woman, where are they? Has no one condemned you? . . . Neither do I condemn you. Go your way and from now on do not sin again' (John 8:10–11). Jesus helps the woman to look to the future with hope and to make a new start in life. Henceforth, if she so desires, she can 'walk in charity' (Eph. 5:2). Once clothed in mercy, even if the inclination to sin remains, it is overcome by the love that makes it possible for her to look ahead and to live her life differently."

147. Ibid., 2.

148. Luke 23:34: "Father, forgive them; for they know not what they do."

149. Cf. *Misericordia et Misera*, 2, where Pope Francis states: "*Forgiveness* is the most visible sign of the Father's love, which Jesus sought to reveal by his entire life. Every page of the Gospel is marked by this imperative of a love that loves to the point of forgiveness. Even at the last moment of his earthly life, as he was being nailed to the cross, Jesus spoke words of forgiveness: 'Father, forgive them; for they know not what they do' (Luke 23:34). Nothing of what a repentant sinner places before God's mercy can be excluded from the embrace of his forgiveness. For this reason, none of us has the right to make forgiveness conditional. Mercy is always a gratuitous act of our heavenly Father, an unconditional and unmerited act of love. Consequently, we cannot risk opposing the full freedom of the love with which God enters into the life of every person. Mercy is this concrete action of love that, by forgiving, transforms and changes our lives. In this way, the divine mystery of mercy is made manifest. God is merciful (cf. Ex. 34:6); his mercy lasts for ever (cf. Ps. 136). From generation to generation, it embraces all those who trust in him and it changes them, by bestowing a share in his very life."

150. Cf. The conversion of St. Paul on the road to Damascus (Acts 9: 1–19).

151. Francis, *Misericordia et Misera*, 3. He continued: "It radiates all around us whenever we experience forgiveness. Its source is in the love with which God comes to meet us, breaking through walls of selfishness that surround us, in order to make us in turn instruments of mercy."

152. Cf. particularly his interactions with young people, where Pope Francis has emphasized that they must not let themselves be robbed of this joy. He

reiterates this in *Christus Vivit*, where he states: "Young people are not meant to become discouraged; they are meant to dream great things, to seek vast horizons, to aim higher, to take on the world, to accept challenges and to offer the best of themselves to the building of something better. That is why I constantly urge young people not to let themselves be robbed of hope." Francis, *Christus Vivit*, Post-Synodal Apostolic Exhortation, April 2, 2019, 15, www.vatican .va/content/francesco/en/apost_exhortations/documents/papa-francesco _esortazione-ap_20190325_christus-vivit.html.

153. Cf. *Misericordia et Misera*, 3. Also, Pope Francis is exemplary of the serenity of spirit of which he speaks.

154. Ibid. In that same paragraph Pope Francis calls for true witnesses to such joy: "We need witnesses to hope and true joy if we are to dispel the illusions that promise quick and easy happiness through artificial paradises. The profound sense of emptiness felt by so many people can be overcome by the hope we bear in our hearts and by the joy that it gives."

155. The pope writes: "Our communities can remain alive and active in the work of the new evangelization in the measure that the 'pastoral conversion' to which we are called will be shaped daily by the renewing force of mercy." Ibid., 5.

156. Preface for Sundays in Ordinary Time VII, *Roman Missal*. In *Misericordia et Misera* the Pope continues: "The Fourth Eucharistic Prayer is a hymn to God's mercy: 'For you came in mercy to the aid of all, so that those who seek might find you.' 'Have mercy on us all' [Eucharistic Prayer II] is the insistent plea made by the priest in the Eucharistic Prayer to implore a share in eternal life. After the *Our Father*, the priest continues the prayer by invoking peace and liberation from sin by the 'help of your mercy.' And before the sign of peace, exchanged as an expression of fraternity and mutual love in the light of forgiveness received, the priest prays: 'Look not on our sins but on the faith of your Church' [Communion Rite]," 5.

157. Cf. this from Pope Francis: "In the Church's prayer, then, references to mercy, far from being merely exhortative, are highly *performative*, which is to say that as we invoke mercy with faith, it is granted to us, and as we confess it to be vital and real, it transforms us. This is a fundamental element of our faith, and we must keep it constantly in mind." Francis, *Misericordia et Misera*, 6.

158. Ibid., 11. Earlier in the text he states: "The celebration of mercy takes place in a very particular way in the *Sacrament of Penance and Reconciliation*. Here we feel the embrace of the Father, who comes forth to meet us and grant us the grace of being once more his sons and daughters. We are sinners and we bear the burden of contradiction between what we wish to do and what we do in fact (cf. Rom. 7:14–21). Yet grace always precedes us and takes on the face of the mercy that effects our reconciliation and pardon. God makes us understand his great love for us precisely when we recognize that we are sinners. Grace is stronger than sin: it overcomes resistance, because love conquers all (cf. 1 Cor. 13:7). In the sacrament of Forgiveness God shows us the way to turn back to him and invites us to experience his closeness anew. This pardon can be obtained by beginning, first of all, to live in charity."

159. Pope Francis stated: "I invite priests once more to prepare carefully for the ministry of confession, which is a true priestly mission. I thank all of you from the heart for your ministry, and I ask you to be *welcoming* to all, *witnesses* of fatherly love whatever the gravity of the sin involved, *attentive* in helping penitents to reflect on the evil they have done, *clear* in presenting moral principles, *willing* to walk patiently beside the faithful on their penitential journey, *far-sighted* in discerning individual cases and *generous* in dispensing God's forgiveness." Ibid., 10. Later he states: "The Sacrament of Reconciliation must regain its central place in the Christian life. This requires priests capable of putting their lives at the service of the 'ministry of reconciliation' (2 Cor. 5:18), in such a way that, while no sincerely repentant sinner is prevented from drawing near to the love of the Father who awaits his return, everyone is afforded the opportunity of experiencing the liberating power of forgiveness." Ibid., 11.

160. Cf. Gill Goulding, CJ, *A Church of Passion and Hope: The Formation of an Ecclesial Disposition from Ignatius Loyola to Pope Francis* (London: Bloomsbury, 2016), 285–287.

161. Hans Urs von Balthasar, develops this theme in the five volumes of his *Theo-Drama*.

162. Goulding, *A Church of Passion and Hope*, 285.

163. Francis, *Misericordia et Misera*, 20. He continues in the same paragraph: "The works of mercy affect a person's entire life. For this reason, we can set in motion a real cultural revolution, beginning with simple gestures capable of reaching body and spirit, people's very lives. This is a commitment that the Christian community should take up, in the knowledge that God's word constantly calls us to leave behind the temptation to hide behind indifference and individualism in order to lead a comfortable life free of problems. Jesus tells his disciples: 'The poor will always be with you' (John 12:8). There is no alibi to justify not engaging with the poor when Jesus has identified himself with each of them. The culture of mercy is shaped in assiduous prayer, in docility to the working of the Holy Spirit, in knowledge of the lives of the saints and in being close to the poor."

164. Cf. Dietrich Bonhoeffer: "Suffering has to be endured in order that it may pass away. Either the world must bear the whole burden and collapse beneath it, or it must fall on Christ to be overcome in him. He therefore suffers vicariously for the world. His is the only suffering which has redemptive efficacy. But the Church knows that the world is still seeking for someone to bear its sufferings, and so, as it follows Christ, suffering becomes the Church's lot too and bearing it, it is borne up by Christ. As it follows him beneath the cross, the Church stands before God as the representative of the world." Dietrich Bonhoeffer, *The Cost of Discipleship*, edited by R. H. Fuller (New York: Touchstone, 1959), 81–82.

Chapter 4

1. Pope Francis, *Misericordiae Vultus: The Face of Mercy*, apostolic letter, April 11, 2015, 8, www.vatican.va/content/onotheis/en/apost_letters /documents/papa-francesco_bolla_20150411_misericordiae-vultus.html. Pope

Francis continues: "The mission Jesus received from the Father was that of revealing the mystery of divine love in its fullness. 'God is love' (1 John 4:8, 16) John affirms for the first and only time in all of Holy Scripture. This love has now been made visible and tangible in Jesus' entire life. His person is nothing but love, a love given gratuitously. The relationships he forms with the people who approach him manifest something entirely unique and unrepeatable. The signs he works, especially in the face of sinners, the poor, the marginalized, the sick, and the suffering, are all meant to teach mercy. Everything in him speaks of mercy. Nothing in him is devoid of compassion."

2. Reference is made to the kenosis of Christ, his self-emptying made known in Philippians 2:4–11.

3. Hans Urs von Balthasar, *Theo-Drama*, vol. 3: *Theological Dramatic Theory III: Dramatis Personae; Persons in Christ*, translated by Graham Harrison (San Francisco: Ignatius Press, 1992), 518. Prior to this, Balthasar has asserted: "We must retrace our steps from the God who creates (with the agreement of his Logos to the Father who generates eternally). For, if he-who-is-sent has essentially to reveal the love of him-who-sends, and if he is identical with his divine mission, he must (as the personal bearer of this mission of love) be the divine, that is, eternal Offspring of him-who-sends, whom he himself calls 'Father' in a sense that bursts all analogies. We begin to discern the meaning of 'fatherhood' in the eternal realm when we consider the Son's task, which is to reveal this Father's love (a love that goes to ultimate lengths): such 'fatherhood' can only mean the giving away of everything the Father is, including his entire Godhead (for God, as God, 'has' nothing apart from what he 'is'): it is a giving-away that, in the Father's act of generation—which lasts for all eternity—leaves the latter's womb 'empty.'" Ibid. Later he continues: "As God, however, the Son must be equal to the Father, even though he has come forth from the Father. And since the Father has expressed his whole love—which nothing can hold back—in the Son, the Son is the perfect image of the Father, apt to represent the Father's self-giving in his creation and in every respect. The Father cannot do this himself because he has given everything in and to the Son; he cannot do more than 'pitilessly' hand over this All to the world." Ibid., 518–519.

4. As Balthasar writes: "For the redeeming act consists in a wholly unique bearing of the total sin of the world by the Father's wholly unique Son whose God-manhood (which is more than the 'highest case' of a transcendental anthropology) is alone capable of such an office." Hans Urs von Balthasar, *Mysterium Paschale: The Mystery of Easter*, translated by Aidan Nichols, OP (Grand Rapids, MI: William B. Eerdmans, 1993), 137–138.

5. Clearly the focus here is on the Western Trinitarian tradition based on the understanding of the "filioque," whereby the Spirit proceeds from the Father and the Son.

6. Hans Urs von Balthasar's three volumes of the *Theo-Logic* form the last three volumes of his Trilogy and focus on Truth. There is also a final slim volume, an epilogue.

7. Juan Sara, "*Descensus ad inferos*, Dawn of Hope: Aspects of the Theology of Holy Saturday in the Trilogy of Hans Urs von Balthasar," in *Love*

Alone is Credible: Hans Urs von Balthasar as Interpreter of the Catholic Tradition, edited by David L. Schindler (Grand Rapids, MI: Wm. B. Eerdmans, 2008), 209–240 (225).

8. Ibid.

9. Ibid. Sara continues: "Christ never speaks in the first instance of himself, but of the Father. And in speaking of the Father, he does not emphasize his own authority as the Father's exegete, but leaves his exegesis in being and act in the hands of the Holy Spirit so that the Spirit may do with it as he wills (and the Spirit wishes only to act in perfect creative fidelity; he wishes to 'blow' only in and towards the love of the Father and the Son)."

10. Ibid.

11. Balthasar writes: "The Trinitarian analogy enables the Son, without abolishing the *analogia entis*, simultaneously to do two things: he represents God to the world—but in the mode of the Son who regards the Father as 'greater' and to whom he eternally owes all that he is—and he represents the world to God, by being, as man (or rather as the God-man), 'humble, lowly, modest, docile of heart' (Matt. 11:29). It is on the basis of these two aspects, united in an abiding analogy, that the Son can take up his one, unitary mission." Balthasar, *Theo-Drama*, vol. 3, 68.

12. As the Bible says: "Make your own mind of Jesus: who, being in the form of God, did not count equality with God something to be grasped. But he emptied himself, taking the form of a slave, becoming as human beings are; and being in every way like a human being, he was humbler yet, even to accepting death, death on a cross. And for this God raised him high, and gave him the name which is above all other names; so that all beings in the heavens, on earth and in the underworld, should bend the knee at the name of Jesus and that every tongue should acknowledge Jesus Christ as Lord, to the glory of God the Father." Phil. 2:5–11, New Jerusalem Bible.

13. Karl Barth, *Kirchliche Dogmatik*, IV/I (Zollikon, 1953), cited in Balthasar, *Mysterium Paschale*, 80.

14. Balthasar, *Mysterium Paschale*, 80. Such an emphasis brings into stark relief the Christology of Chalcedon. Balthasar continues in this section: "In his self-emptying, God does not divest himself of his Godhead, but rather does he give it precise confirmation in that he: submits himself to the chains and wretchedness of the human creature; that he, the Lord, becomes a servant, and to that measure, and in exactly this, distinguished thereby from the false gods, *lowers* himself; and that man in Jesus Christ, man without, similarly, loss or mutilation of his humanity, is, in the power of divinity, and so in the power of, and thanks to, the humiliation of God . . . man . . . not divinised but rather . . . divinely exalted. Thus we get: the abasement of *God* and the exaltation of *man*, and indeed the abasement of God is his supreme honour, since it confirms and demonstrates nothing other than his divine being—and the exaltation of man, as a work of God's grace, consists in nothing other than the restoration of his true humanity." Ibid., 80–81.

15. Hans Urs von Balthasar, *Theo-Drama*, vol. 4: *Theological Dramatic Theory IV: The Action*, translated by Graham Harrison (San Francisco: Ignatius

Press), 331. He continues: "The first 'self-limitation' of the same triune God arises through endowing his creatures with freedom. The second, deeper 'limitation' occurs as a result of the covenant, which on God's side is indissoluble, whatever may become of Israel. The third *kenosis*, which is not only Christological but involves the whole Trinity, arises through the Incarnation of the Son alone; henceforth he manifests his Eucharistic attitude [which was always his] in the *pro nobis* of the Cross and Resurrection for the sake of the world."

16. The dramatic nature of this truth is explored in the five volumes of the *Theo-Drama: Theological Dramatic Theory*: vol. 1: *Theological Dramatic Theory I: Prologomena*; vol. 2, *Theological Dramatic Theory II: Dramatis Personae: Man in God*; vol. 3: *Theological Dramatic Theory III: Dramatis Personae; Persons in Christ*; vol. 4: *Theological Dramatic Theory IV*: The Action; and vol. 5: *The Last Act*, all translated by Graham Harrison (San Francisco: Ignatius Press) and the three volumes of the *Theo-Logic*: vol. 1: *Truth of the World*; vol. 2: *Truth of God*; and vol. 3: *The Spirit of Truth*, by Hans Urs von Balthasar, all translated by Adrian J. Walker (San Francisco: Ignatius Press).

17. Hans Urs von Balthasar, *Theo-Drama*, vol. 4, 319.

18. He continues: "It is the drama of the 'emptying' of the Father's heart, in the generation of the Son that contains and surpasses all possible drama between God and the world. The drama of the Trinity lasts forever: the Father was never without the Son, nor were Father and Son ever without the Spirit. Everything temporal takes place within the embrace of the eternal action and as is consequences." Ibid., 327.

19. Balthasar goes on: "The Father strips himself, without remainder, of his Godhead and hands it over to the Son; he 'imparts' to the Son all that is his 'All that is thine is mine' [John 17:10]. . . . Inherent in the Father's love is an absolute renunciation: he will not be God for himself alone. . . . The Son's answer to the gift of Godhead can only be eternal thanksgiving to the Father, the Source—a thanksgiving as selfless and unreserved as the Father's original self-surrender. Proceeding from both, as their subsistent 'We' there breathes the 'Spirit' who is common to both: as the essence of love, he maintains the infinite difference between them, seals it and since he is the one Spirit of them both, bridges it." Ibid., 323–324. Again we return to the activity of divine mercy *ad intra*.

20. Ibid., 326–327. Cf. "God is supremely what he is in giving everything away." Hans Urs von Balthasar, *Theo-Drama*, vol. 2: *Theological Dramatic Theory II: Dramatis Personae; Man in God* (San Francisco: Ignatius Press, 1990), 256. Fundamental to divine mercy is what we may term, analogously, "self-surrender," as is explored later in this chapter.

21. Ben Quash, "The Theo-Drama," in *The Cambridge Companion to Hans Urs von Balthasar*, edited by Edward T. Oakes, SJ, and David Moss (Cambridge, UK: Cambridge University Press, 2004), 143–157.

22. According to Adrienne von Speyr, "Both renounce being a mere 'I' without a 'thou'; this allows us to glimpse the identity of poverty and wealth in the divine love, . . . [and this also applies to the Father, since without the Son he could not be Father]." Adrienne von Speyr, *The World of Prayer* (San Francisco: Ignatius Press, 1985), 64.

23. In *Theo-Logic* vol. 3: *The Spirit of Truth*, Balthasar continues: "This gift, however, is not the calculable total of their love, nor is it the resultant identity of their love: it is an unfathomable *more*, a fruit [as the child is the fruit of the 'one-flesh' relationship of man wife]; for even divine love, and every love that reflects it, is an 'overflowing,' because, in it the pure unmotivated nature of goodness comes to light, as the ultimate face of the Divinity. It is something that overtakes that surprises us [and, since we are in the timelessness of eternity, it does so in ways that are ever new], because we can never plumb the fathomless love of Father and Son. Thus the resultant unit and fruit is the unfathomable Spirit who, as such, brings to light and searches the ever-deeper abysses of the renunciatory love of Father and Son."

24. Again, this is clearly coming from the Western tradition; the Eastern tradition does not acknowledge the *filioque* of the being of the Holy Spirit.

25. Hans Urs von Balthasar, *Theo-Drama*, vol. 5: *Theological Dramatic Theory V: The Last Act*, translated by Graham Harrison (San Francisco: Ignatius Press, 1998), 255.

26. Ibid., 256. Balthasar continues: "So it is a life, a life that rediscovers itself in the Resurrection to eternal life. . . . Thus night ultimately is a transition. Through suffering we are continually being brought back to [merciful] love; suffering keeps us receptive to love. Those who love bear suffering joyfully although the feeling of joy remains hidden. Looking at the Lord, we see that suffering lies at a deep level in love."

27. Ibid. Here there is no attempt to glorify suffering, but to give an indication of the close link between suffering, mercy, and love at the heart of God. "Looking at the Lord," Balthasar writes, "we see that suffering lies at a deep level of love. The love that God shows us in his Son is so great that it embraces not only the joys of love but also its sufferings. Sufferings, understood and accepted as an expression of [merciful] love, lead back to God and increase joy; they bring us close to the suffering Son; the seriousness of suffering teaches us to know the Son at a new and much deeper level. God himself has fashioned these unfathomable depths." Ibid.

28. Bernard Lonergan, SJ, "Theology and Man's Future," in *A Second Collection* (London: Darton, Longman and Todd, 1974), 135–147 (145).

29. Balthasar, *Theo-Drama*, vol. 3, 509. He continues: "Only in this way, in complete freedom, can he reveal himself and give himself to be loved. This is the only way, therefore, in which theo-drama can be ultimately a personal, not a natural event, something that does not undermine dramatic encounters between human beings but undergirds them and makes them—for the first time—truly and authentically personal and significant."

30. Cf. Balthasar, *Theo-Drama*, vol. 3, 141.

31. As Balthasar wrote: "It is not simply knowledge alone that gives joy to God and glorifies him, but the creature's free self-surrender, its bringing him, together with its being and its unconcealment, its love. In this way, the mercy and love that God has lavished on the world in freely turning to the creature is returned to him in the form of a reciprocated love. God shares his truth with creatures inasmuch as he makes his ever deeper mystery visible *as mystery*; and

the creature shares its truth with God insofar as it acknowledges this mystery and gives it back to God." Hans Urs von Balthasar, *Theo-Logic*, vol. 1: *Truth of the World*, translated by Adrian J. Walker (San Francisco: Ignatius Press, 2000), 270.

32. He writes: "Love can never be content with an act of love performed for the present moment only. It wants to abandon itself, to surrender itself, to entrust itself, to commit itself to love. As a pledge of love, it wants to lay its freedom once and for all at the feet of love. As soon as love is truly awakened, the *moment of time is transformed for it into a form of eternity*." Hans Urs von Balthasar, *The Christian State of Life*, translated by Sr. Mary Frances McCarthy (San Francisco: Ignatius Press, 1983), 38–39.

33. Hans Urs von Balthasar, *Prayer* (London: SPCK, 1975), 21.

34. Bernard Lonergan, *Method in Theology* (London: Darton, Longman and Todd, 1975), 171.

35. "In applying it," writes Matthias Scheeben, "everything is to be excluded from the concept of obedience that derives from the relationship between God and the creature insofar as the creature is regarded *qua* creature, that is, as having its origin in nothingness. Everything is to be retained, on the other hand, and translated into the infinite [in the sense of the *via eminentiae*] that pertains to the analogy between God and the creature as the positive image of God, or more properly, of the Trinity. The obedience of which the Son of God gave us an example in his human nature is by no means merely something that is grounded in his human nature and intended as an example for us insofar as we are creatures. Like all his utterances, it is not only borne by his divine person; it is also a positive revelation of his divine person—and hence of his divine nature—translated into human terms. Precisely this filial attitude which looks to the Father in everything and wills to be in everything only the representation and brightness [Heb. 1:3] of the paternal nature, is the manner in which the Son makes love that is, in the Son, a mission received 'by way of generation' the expression of a love that is, in the Father, a mission to generate. In the Third Person of God, the Holy Spirit, this reciprocity of mission becomes the final and fulfilling unity of merciful love whereby the Spirit, in his unique personhood, combines in himself the features of both Father and Son, from whom he proceeds. He is the personification of self-giving, selflessness and mission; of pure and dynamic transparency; of love as service to the love of the Father and Son. When, therefore, the Son reveals to us his love for the Father in the transferred mode of obedience, this revelation is, at the same time, a revelation of the love of the whole Trinity." Matthias Joseph Scheeben, *The Mysteries of Christianity*, translated by Cyril Vollert, SJ (St. Louis: Herder, 1946), 358–359, cited in Hans Urs von Balthasar, *The Christian State of Life*, translated by Sr. Mary Frances McCarthy (San Francisco, Ignatius Press), 1983, 78–79.

36. Balthasar, *Theo-Drama*, vol. 3, 186. He continues: "In thus surrendering himself, the Son, the incarnate One, becomes in one respect a product of the Spirit who brings him forth *ex Maria Virgine*, although within the Trinity itself the Spirit is the product of the united spiration of Father and Son."

37. Hans Urs von Balthasar, *Explorations in Theology III: Creator Spirit*, translated by Brian McNeil, CRV (San Francisco: Ignatius Press, 1993), 122. He

goes on: "But where the Son is nothing more than a human being who sinks down into the darkness of death, he has become the most perfect transparency and instrumentality for God: the ultimate will of the Father coincides with the ultimate obedience of the Son, and the breathing back of the Holy Spirit together with his own expiring spirit allows the humanity of the Son to be taken up definitively into the one principle of the active spiration of the Spirit by Father and the Son."

38. According to Balthasar, this is so "although [the individual] could never find the archetype and ideal of himself by penetrating to the deepest centre of his nature, his superego or his subconscious, or by scrutinizing his own dispositions, aspirations, talents and potentialities." Ibid. Cf. "There are cases where a man's natural endowment is known and presupposed, but the mission that comes to him from God is not added *per accidens* to this original identity; rather, it is given a pre-eminence over it so that his life and being heretofore seem to be instrumental, leading up to what he is to be [and, in the mind of God, has always been]." Balthasar, *Theo-Drama*, vol. 3, 154.

39. John proclaimed a baptism of repentance for the forgiveness of sins (Luke 3:3). As Balthasar writes: "In accordance with this, 'the whole of Judaea and Jerusalem' confess their sins on the occasion of this baptism. Both the penitent confession in conversion and the baptism of the forgiveness of sins, are two sides of one coin: the 'path of righteousness' [Matt. 21:32] on which one may be set through the Baptist in order to go to meet 'the coming one' who is 'greater' and 'to see God's salvation' [Luke 3:6]." Hans Urs von Balthasar, *The Glory of the Lord VII: Theology; The New Covenant*, translated by Brian McNeil, CRV (San Francisco: Ignatius Press, 1989), 55.

40. As Balthasar explains: "When the Baptist responds by 'letting it happen,' the obedience is converted and becomes directly 'Marian' [Luke 1:38], and the new obedience expresses its form in the old: the 'increasing' of the redeemer to the point of his becoming one with all who confess their sins forces the one who declares the promise to 'decrease' [John 3:30] into this inimitable vanishing." Ibid., 56.

41. He continued: "Jesus' initiative attains immediately to its fulfillment, for he 'rises up' out of the waters, and his act of 'coming up from beneath' is answered by the 'coming down from above' of the 'Spirit [of God]': here we see that incarnation is the encounter, to the point of identification, of the Israel who has been made ready and the God of the covenant who descends to Israel." Ibid.

42. "Now it is not possible," Balthasar writes, "for this abolition of the boundary to be an extension of the unfinished work of Christ, as if the *Pneuma* had to round the work off by starting at the point where the *Logos* had had to give up; rather, this perfect accomplishment of work undertaken by the Father must at the same time display the accomplishment of the Son's work: in perfect 'relinquishing' [a condition beyond "authority" and "poverty"], the Son breathes out his Spirit, the Spirit of the love that has gone 'to the end,' and simultaneously the Father ordains something new and different for the *Pneuma*: now that the Son has breathed forth the Spirit of love in absolute

weakness, the Father can demonstrate the absolute power and glory of his Spirit of love, by raising the Son through the *Pneuma* [1 Peter 3:18; cf. Romans 8:11; 1 Tim. 3:16] to be a 'spiritual body' [1 Cor. 15:43f.] i.e. a body that is no longer bound to the earthly demarcations between body and body, between 'I' and 'you,' and can therefore, thanks to the *Pneuma* whose Lord he is [and has become] and in whose boundless sphere he rules, draw in our spirits and bodies too." Ibid., 403.

43. Balthasar maintains that this truth has "in principle" dealt with human refusal from the very beginning. Cf. *Glory of the Lord VII*, 404.

44. Balthasar, *Prayer*, 51.

45. *Theo-Drama*, vol. 3, 159.

46. Ibid., 162.

47. "In the Passion," Balthasar states, "the Father's loving countenance can disappear behind the hard facts of what must be: now, more than ever, this is very much a part of the Trinity's eternal, salvific plan laid before him by the Spirit, the witness of the mutual will of Father and Son. It is as if the Spirit now embodied in the form of a rule, says to them both: this is what you have wanted from all eternity; this is what, from all eternity, we have determined." Ibid., 188. This is the expression of the eternal grace of mercy.

48. Ibid., 162. Balthasar continues: "On the other hand, he makes room within himself, that is, an acting area for dramas of theological moment, involving other, created persons. In this way we begin to see that, while the personal mission of Jesus is unique, it is also capable of 'imitation' by those who are called in him, to participate in his drama."

49. Balthasar writes: "All the acts of self-disclosure in word and deed receive their validity through a Passion that explains everything and makes it all possible. If one sought to understand this Passion as an accident that happened to occur at a certain point through an incidental cause, then every single word, even those of the Sermon on the Mount, would lose its meaning. We cannot take seriously any attempt to separate Jesus' teaching before the Passion, which thus has no relationship to it, from the teaching that is supposedly placed into his mouth after the Passion. The Logos of both his teaching and his action as a whole has to be interpreted in its relationship to 'the hour' that he awaits, to the 'baptism' he desires, to the event that opens up his prophetic mission, which is to bring the old Jewish Covenant to completion in the new sacrificial Covenant, the new blood of the Covenant, the new Covenantal meal." Hans Urs von Balthasar, *Love Alone Is Credible*, translated by D. C. Schindler (San Francisco: Ignatius Press, 2004), 84.

50. As Balthasar writes: "Jesus proclaims himself with his teaching, he is essentially 'handed over' [*traditus*] in it; without conditions and without reservations, he aims at a point beyond all ethics and sociology, a point that lies 'nowhere' [*u-topos*] in the world, into which he casts the whole of his existence, body and soul. And by casting himself, in gratuitous freedom [John 10:18], into this unimaginable abyss [death as abandonment by God (Matt. 27:46) or as followed by the underworld (Rev. 6:8; 1:18) bereft of all hope], he makes himself into an indispensable sacrificial food for all [John 6:51: "My flesh for the life

of the world"; Heb. 13:10–12], not in the freedom of creative genius but in straightforward obedience [John 10:18]." Ibid., 85–86.

51. Balthasar writes, "But for the same reason, he becomes the manifestation of his eternal majesty and kingship which reveals itself most definitively in the servant's ultimate humiliation ["Yes I am a king," John 18:37] but if the kingship of the God who reveals himself as love comes to light precisely in the Son's humble obedience to the Father, then it is clear that this obedience is essentially love." Ibid., 86–87.

52. Balthasar continues: "Precisely in—and *only* in—the kenosis of Christ, the *inner* mystery of God's love comes to light, the mystery of the God who 'is love' [1 John 4:8] in himself and therefore is 'triune.' Though it remains a light inaccessible to the understanding, God's triunity is the sole hypothesis capable of clarifying the phenomenon of Christ [as he is continuously present in the Bible, in the Church, and in history] in a phenomenologically adequate manner without doing violence to the facts." Ibid., 87.

53. Ibid., 88–89. He goes on: "Only non-faith and non-love can imprison Christians in their past; the Spirit has set them free to enter into every age and every future; indeed they move forward fashioning and transforming the world in everything they do in the light of the abundant 'image' that rises before them, not subjectively but objectively, at every moment. The Church and the world live historically in relation to this 'image,' which is an image of the 'Christ who comes again,' while God's Spirit seeks a comprehensive answer from the whole of creation to God's loving Word in Christ and helps to give birth to this answer through the most intense labor pains."

54. As Balthasar writes: "The imitator of the Lord places himself in total 'indifference.' . . . For himself and for others he is still only the agent, the representative of his Lord, like a viceroy, who more perfectly represents the king the more absolutely he places his personal, intellectual and creative powers at the service of the thought and will of his monarch. . . . The idea of representation brings about a new awareness of the manifestation of divine glory in the world." Hans Urs von Balthasar, *Glory of the Lord V: The Realm of Metaphysics in the Modern Age*, translated by Oliver Davies (Edinburgh: T&T Clark, 1992), 106, 107.

55. I am indebted to Christopher Hadley, SJ, for conversations we shared about the Trinitarian understanding of Balthasar and Kasper. He is working on a book—which is a revision of his thesis—on Balthasar's work on the Trinity, in particular the concept of "distance" (*absend*) or space, which maintains both the unity and the distinction of the persons within the Trinity. In addition, at the 2016 CTSA annual convention in Puerto Rico Hadley presented a brief unpublished paper comparing Balthasar and Kasper.

56. Cf. the Fourth Lateran Council.

57. As Kasper writes: "The inner reality of God as self-emptying and self-communicating love, which has become decisively and unsurpassably revealed on the cross, does not remain in itself, but is bestowed on us concretely in the Holy Spirit. In his mercy, God lets us not only see his heart; he creates space for us beside his heart and in his heart through the Holy Spirit. . . . By revealing the Wholly Otherness of his godhead through his love, which empties itself and

gives itself away as gift, God at the very same time bestows the greatest possible closeness to himself." Walter Kasper, *Mercy: The Essence of the Gospel and the Key to a Christian Life*, translated by William Mages (New York: Paulist Press, 2013), 94.

58. Ibid., 93. He continues: "Because everything that concerns God is simply infinite, the Father can communicate his godhead to the Son and to the Spirit through the Son only by retreating in his own infinity and giving space to the other in himself. The *kenosis* (self-emptying) of God is the presupposition for the fact that God, who is infinite, can make room for creation. The incarnation of God in Jesus Christ and, in a more complete way, in Jesus' cross is the unsurpassable apex of God's self-revelation in his trinitarian self-withdrawal."

59. Kasper, *Mercy*, 92. He continues: "In the doctrine of the Trinity, the abstract philosophical definition of God, according to which God is Being Itself, is concretized and qualified. It says: as Being Itself God is love, which communicates and bestows itself as gift to others. . . . As self-radiating love, the one God is at the same time triune. From eternity he has a beloved and a co-beloved; he is thus God as Father, Son and Holy Spirit. . . . Only if God in himself is self-communicating love can he communicate himself externally as the one who he already is." Ibid., 92–93.

60. This form of Theo-drama would be fundamentally biblical in its narrative and intelligibility and deeply focused on *kenosis* as a fundamentally generous act of God's existence in its metaphysical terms. Kasper's biblical theology of mercy encompasses God's compassion for the suffering together with God's passion for justice, as exemplified in the revelation to Moses and the voices of the prophets.

61. Kasper, *Mercy*, 75.

62. Ibid., 76.

63. Ibid., 93–94.

64. Cf. John 14:26: "The advocate, the Holy Spirit whom the Father will send in my name, will teach you everything and remind you of all I have said to you."

65. Benedict XVI, Vigil with Young People, 23rd World Youth Day, July 19, 2008, www.vatican.va/content/benedict-xvi/en/speeches/2008/july/documents/hf_ben-xvi_spe_20080719_vigil.html.

66. Augustine, *De Trinitate* 15.17.31. As Kasper writes: "Augustine could never detach his understanding of God from his Trinitarian conception of God, that is, from his understanding of God as love. He speaks movingly about this in the concluding, fifteenth book of his tractate *On The Trinity*, where he again summarizes, as it were, his understanding of God. He says that the Father's love is nothing other than his nature and his constitutive essence, and he adds: 'As we have often said already and will not tire of repeating it often.' (15.19.37). For Augustine, therefore, God is the God of Christian revelation." Kasper, *Mercy*, 87.

67. He writes: "The inner reality of God as self-emptying and self-communicating love, which has become decisively and unsurpassably revealed on the cross, does not remain in itself, but is bestowed on us concretely in the

Holy Spirit. In his mercy, God lets us not only see into his heart; he creates space for us beside his heart and in his heart through the Holy Spirit." Kasper, *Mercy*, 94.

68. Cf. John 3:1–21, where Jesus teaches Nicodemus.

69. As Balthasar writes: "Thus the Word that the Father utters in the world and which is his Son is fulfilled in such a way that, in giving his life, he gives us his flesh and his Spirit, incorporates us in him, and draws us into the divine love of the Trinity through the two forms of his being as Word. When the risen Christ repeats the action of the Creator, and 'breathes' on those who believe, this communication of his human and divine *pneuma* completes in sensible form, his revelation as Word. It is the 'sacramental' sign of what was, in principle, accomplished at Easter and was to become ecclesiological reality at Pentecost." Balthasar, *Prayer*, 56.

70. Balthasar writes: "[The Spirit] alone can bring about the entry of God's Word into mankind, into history and nature; and so only in the Spirit can man receive, contemplate and understand the Word." Ibid., 58.

71. "The Spirit alone knows 'the inner things of God,' and 'searches all, even the deep things of God,' but in principle, he has revealed these depths to 'those who are spiritual,' the 'spiritual men' who 'possess the Spirit of Christ.' They have access to these things and, with them, to all the mysteries which 'eye has not seen nor ear heard'; and, for that reason, no one who has not received the Spirit 'can understand because it is spiritually examined' [1 Cor. 2:10–16]." Ibid.

72. Balthasar writes: "Through the gift of faith we are taught the truth concerning the Son by the Holy Spirit. . . . The Spirit leads us by degrees into the depths, already opened up, of the truth of God present within us, and this by explaining, interpreting, incorporating Christ's revealed words in the heart of the believer. . . . The depths of the Godhead are opened to those endowed with grace, and they are also made capable of scrutinizing them in the Spirit. Balthasar, *Prayer*, 58–59.

73. Speyr, *The World of Prayer*, 28ff.

74. Ibid., 28. Later she writes: "The eternal dialogue is prayer first and foremost because it is divine vision: vision as the core of contemplation, as a silent listening, a reciprocal beholding, being led, adjusting to the other and getting to know him more, a reciprocal expectation and response. This abundant life streams from one Person to another, since each one always stands in view of the others. There is no self-concealment or reserve between them, only a constant acceptance and surrender, self-opening and self-disclosure, showing and loving. As soon as Father and Son are together, they cause the Spirit to proceed as the witness to their living bond, to the life which consists of their being in unity. And at once, at the very origin of his procession, the Spirit takes on this role of witness to their life. From the very beginning the dialogue between Father and Son sees the signs of fruitfulness in the Spirit, and from the beginning the Spirit, bearing witness, receives a share in their fruitfulness. To the Father he bears witness to the Son's equality of nature; to the Son he testifies to the Father's equality. And the Spirit so fulfills and overfills the expectations of Father and Son that they see more in him than they looked for: In him they experience

a totally unsuspected proof of their love. So they are bound to him in gratitude, just as he to them. Immediately and without any rehearsal he is in the midst of their prayer and dialogue, sharing in their knowledge, discernment, speech, obedience and silence, ensuring that this prayer is a constant adoration and fulfilment. It is adoration because God is in the presence of God; it is fulfilment because God may expect everything from God." Ibid., 32.

75. Balthasar writes: "It is the Spirit who dominates the Mass between the consecration and the communion. He makes the Word newly present, spiritually as well as sacramentally; he is the Pax which the community, on becoming a communion, receives and interchanges amongst its members; indeed, he is that communion which is the essence of the Church. Finally, it is he who empowers the Church to offer herself in her Eucharistic commemoration, while offering the Son to the Father, in a single offering, whose indivisibility derives solely from the unity of feeling wrought by the Spirit, unity of 'spirit' with Christ. Only then can we understand that the Mass is, in the inmost heart of the Church, a free spiritual act supported by grace, an act of reason remembering, that is of contemplation. Then we shall realize, that, by the very nature of the Church, contemplation and the sacrament form an indissoluble unity." Balthasar, *Prayer*, 92.

76. As Balthasar writes: "[The Spirit] is in God, the expression of the unity and the uniting of Father and Son, whose 'spirit' is shown forth in their common and single spiration as itself one, equal, divine and personal. The mysteries of the Spirit are, to the human mind, absolute paradoxes of a unity which does not abolish differences—neither between the divine Persons nor between God and creatures—but utilizes them to create forms of unity that are far more subtle than any conceived by monotheists, pantheists or idealists." Ibid., 61.

77. Ibid., 63. He continues: "Man in prayer does not merely come into the presence of the truth and contemplate it as an object; he lives, as St. John loves to repeat 'in the truth' itself. . . . It is to live in the knowledge that the truth, which is the Spirit dwelling in us, is more interior to us than we are to ourselves, since, in God and in his truth, we were predestined and chosen, before the foundation of the world, before our own creation, to be his children, pure and unstained. Consequently, whatever in us disaccords with this is but a later encroachment in opposition to our real truth, and so an internal contradiction which cancels itself."

78. Aquinas, *Summa Theologiae* II-II, q.30, a.4, cited in Francis, *Evangelii Gaudium: The Joy of the Gospel*, apostolic exhortation, November 24, 2013, 37, www.vatican.va/content/francesco/en/apost_exhortations/documents/papa-francesco_esortazione-ap_20131124_evangelii-gaudium.html.

79. Walter Kasper, *Pope Francis' Revolution of Tenderness and Love: Theological and Pastoral Perspectives*, translated by William Madges (New York: Paulist Press, 2015), 35. Kasper continues that if this is the case, then "through it the most fundamental of all theological questions—the question of God—is posed anew."

80. Aquinas, *Summa Theologiae* I, q.21 a.3, quoted in Kasper, *Mercy*, 89.

81. Kasper, *Pope Francis' Revolution of Tenderness and Love*, 35.

82. Ibid., 89. He continues: "That was the pivotal insight that lay at the basis of the agreement between the Catholic Church and the Lutherans concerning the doctrine of justification. . . . The implication of the central location of mercy for the relation of divine mercy and omnipotence is also important. . . . God is precisely sovereign and omnipotent by being the God who mercifully is for and with the poor and oppressed, he demonstrates his divinity and his omnipotence. . . . It is the omnipotence of his love and his mercy."

83. Ibid., 93. Kasper also asserts that "if mercy is the most fundamental of all divine attributes, then through it the most fundamental of all theological questions—the question of God—is posed anew." Kasper, *Pope Francis' Revolution of Tenderness and Love*, 35.

84. Cf. Lonergan: "It is not propaganda and it is not argument but religious faith that will liberate human reasonableness from its ideological prisons. It is not the promises of men but religious hope that can enable men to resist the vast pressures of social decay. If passions are to quiet down, if wrongs are to be not exacerbated, not ignored, not merely palliated, but acknowledged and removed, then human possessiveness and human pride have to be replaced by religious charity, by the charity of the suffering servant, by self-sacrificing love." Lonergan, *Method in Theology*, 117.

85. Cf. the Chalcedonian reality that in Christ "ultimate immediacy takes place precisely through the Christological paradox, according to which, without confusing the freedom, infinite freedom indwells finite freedom, and so the finite is perfected in the infinite without the infinite losing itself in the finite or the finite in the infinite." Balthasar, *Theo-Drama*, vol. 2, 200.

86. Ibid., 178. Balthasar engages in an interesting way with the work of Cardinal John Henry Newman in the area of freedom. "Newman suggests," he says, "that it may be a law of Providence that God speaks more softly, the more he promises . . . so that our faith is lifted high above reason by its Object, just as in the obscurity of its origins, it sinks below the same reason." Ibid., 130–136 (discussion). He continues, saying that Newman states: "Divine truth is grasped by a subtle and indirect method, which is less tangible than other methods, and this exposes it to contradiction and contempt" (135).

87. Balthasar writes: "This is the paradox of a being which knows that it can only fulfill itself through grateful dependence on a grace on which it has no claim." Balthasar, *Theo-Drama*, vol. 2, 178.

88. Ibid., 217. He continues: "This basic outline, that is, autonomous finite freedom operating within an encompassing Providence, which restrains the former at its limits, is followed through and varied in different ways in the two sketches by Origen and Gregory of Nyssa. . . . As we can see from Clement of Alexandria, who while he is most clearly aware that man only attains his own fulfilment with God's help, yet insists that 'God does not compel us' but rather 'wishes us to be saved on the basis of our own decision.' This then is the essence of the soul: it moves by its own power. This, and the resultant concept of 'synergism,' has nothing to do with Pelagianism. . . . To deny that man has autonomous motion is to deny him rationality. Here we have a clear statement of the inseparability of reason and freedom, on which Thomas [Aquinas] will place such weight." Ibid., 217–218.

89. Within Balthasar's work there is a development that might assist our understanding at this point. There is a movement from the analogy of being into an analogy of freedom or inter-personal love. As John O'Donnell indicates, this raises an interesting philosophical query: "The great philosophical question: why is there being and not nothing, requires the light of revelation for its answer. The great ontological difference between Being and beings finds its ultimate illumination through the biblical revelation of the fact of creation. God is self-subsistent freedom, but God chooses to share his freedom with that which is not God. Thus finite freedom turns out to be a primordial giftedness. Paradoxically, my autonomy is bestowed autonomy. Accordingly, the fundamental attitude of the free creature before God can only be that of thanksgiving." John O'Donnell, *Hans Urs von Balthasar* (London: Geoffrey Chapman, 1992), 69. The analogy of being focuses our attention on the fact that God is true Being, and by our creation in the image of God we are given our being, but it is a being dependent on the goodness of God. Within the analogy of freedom we come to understand that human freedom is a divine gift given by God and guaranteed by divine freedom. Indeed, the dependent graced freedom of each human being must be real and authentic freedom if it is to be a true expression of divine freedom. It is only from this authentic freedom that we can make a truly loving response to God.

90. John Zizioulas's work is particularly significant here. See John D. Zizioulas, *Communion and Otherness*, edited by Paul McPartlan (London: T&T Clark, 2006).

91. O'Donnell, *Hans Urs von Balthasar*, 65–77. I am particularly indebted to the work of the late John O'Donnell, SJ—not least because I was one of his graduate students.

92. Balthasar, *Theo-Logic*, vol. 3, 24.

93. "Outside of this event," Balthasar writes, "there is no truth. The truth of the object exists only as long as infinite or finite spirit turns to it in an act of knowing: the truth of the subject exists only as long as it abides in this act. Outside of this encounter itself, there are natural preconditions of truth, potencies and dispositions, in subject and object alike, that prepare, enable and substantially shape the act of truth. Even in God, the freedom of truth is not caprice but is ordered in conformity with the divine nature. In man, however, there is the additional fact that his spirit emerges out of sub-spiritual nature, so that his spiritual acts have to move in the tracks laid down in advance by his nature." Balthasar, *Theo-Logic*, vol. 1, 79.

94. Thomas Dalzell states: "If God's love, the Holy Spirit, which passes from the Father to the Son in the eternal Trinity can 'blow' from God to the world [Balthasar] believes that when human freedom is exercised as a response of love, the person born of God can 'blow' the Holy Spirit back to God, but he maintains of course that this is only a possibility for created freedom if it acts with and in the incarnate Son." Thomas G. Dalzell, *The Dramatic Encounter of Divine and Human Freedom in the Theology of Hans Urs von Balthasar* (Bern: Peter Lang, 1997), 57.

95. St. Bernard, in a homily titled "In Praise of the Virgin Mother," depicts the scene of the annunciation in a dramatic manner, addressing the Virgin as

follows: "You have heard that you shall conceive and bear a Son, you have heard that you shall conceive not of man, but of the Holy Spirit. The angel is waiting for your answer: it is time for him to return to God who sent him. We too are waiting, O lady, for the word of pity, even we who are overwhelmed in wretchedness by the sentence of damnation. And behold, to you the price of our salvation is offered. If you consent, straightway shall we be freed. In the eternal Word of God were we all made, and lo! We die; by one little word of yours in answer shall we all be made alive. Adam asks this of you, O loving Virgin, poor Adam exiled as he is from paradise with all his poor wretched children; Abraham begs this of you, and David. . . . Believe, speak, receive! Let your humility put on boldness, and your modesty be clothed with trust. Not now should your virginal simplicity forget prudence! In this one thing alone, O prudent Virgin, fear not presumption; for although modesty that is silent is pleasing, more needful now is the loving kindness of your word. Open, O Blessed Virgin, your heart to faith; open your lips to speak; open your bosom to your Maker. Behold! The Desired of all nations is outside, knocking at your door. Oh! If by delay he should pass by, and again in sorrow you should have to begin to seek for him whom your soul loves! Arise, then run and open. Arise by faith, run by the devotion of your heart, open by your word. And Mary said: Behold the handmaid of the Lord: be it done to me according to your word." From the *Office of Readings*, December 20.

96. "My soul proclaims the greatness of the Lord and my spirit exults in God my saviour, because he has looked upon his lowly handmaid. . . . the Almighty has done great things for me. Holy is his name, and his mercy reaches from age to age for those who fear him. . . . He has come to the help of Israel his servant, mindful of his mercy—according to the promise he made to our ancestors—of his mercy to Abraham and his descendants for ever." Luke 1:46–56.

97. Balthasar, *Theo-Drama*, vol. 2, 228. He continues: "The crucial question will be whether and how—if such self-disclosure takes place—finite freedom can fulfill itself in infinite freedom without casting doubt upon the initial datum, but also without making infinite freedom somehow finite, without relegating it to one existent entity among others."

98. Ibid., 229. He continues: "In principle we have access to this condition here and now, although we await its ultimate fulfilment; it is also that state in which 'God will be all in all' (1 Cor. 15:28). But since, on the basis of our presuppositions, this will not abolish finite freedom's self-determination, we must formally assume that this ultimate state is normative for the reciprocal relationship. . . . Only in the preaching of Jesus and the post-Easter meditation upon it in the light of the Holy Spirit does the womb of the Father's divine freedom open so wide and so deep that we begin to suspect what 'the fulfilment of finite freedom in infinite freedom' might mean."

99. Ibid., 257. Balthasar continues: "While the Father from all eternity utters his eternal Word, the latter does not, as it were, keep interrupting him; similarly, the Spirit allows himself to proceed from Father and Son in order to show himself to be the Spirit common to both. True, all temporal notions of 'before' and 'after' must be kept at a distance, but absolute freedom must provide the

acting area in which it is to develop—and develop in terms of love and blessedness. Above all we must fend off that 'all knowing' attitude that is fatal to man, that complacent notion of 'being in the picture'; this eviscerates the joys of expectation, of hope and fulfilment, the joys of giving and receiving and the even deeper joys of finding oneself in the other and of being constantly over-fulfilled by him; and finally—since we are speaking of God—it destroys the possibility of mutual acknowledgement and adoration in the Godhead. 'It is adoration because God may expect everything from God' [Speyr, *The World of Prayer*, 32]."

100. Balthasar asserts: "None is overwhelmed by being known by the others, since each subsists by being *let* be. Thus, finally it becomes clear why finite freedom can really fulfill itself in infinite freedom—the Father *lets* the Son be consubstantial God, and so forth—there is no danger of finite freedom which cannot fulfil itself on its own account [because it can neither go back and take possession of its origins nor can it attain its absolute goal by its own power], becoming alienated from itself in the realm of the infinite. It can only be what it is, that is, an image of infinite freedom, imbued with a freedom of its own, by getting in tune with the [Trinitarian] 'law' of absolute freedom [of self-surrender], and this law is not foreign to it—for after all it is the 'law' of absolute Being—but most authentically its own." Balthasar, *Theo-Drama*, vol. 2, 259.

Chapter 5

1. I met with individuals from the following: the Secretariat of State, Congregation for the Doctrine of the Faith, Congregation for Oriental Churches, Congregation for Divine Worship and the Discipline of the Sacraments, Congregation for the Clergy, Congregation for Institutes of Consecrated Life and Societies of Apostolic Life, Congregation for Catholic Education, Dicastery for Promoting Integral Human Development, Pontifical Council for Promoting Christian Unity, Pontifical Council for Inter-Religious Dialogue, Pontifical Council for Culture, Pontifical Council for Promoting the New Evangelization, Pontifical Academy for Life, Pontifical Theological Academy, Pontifical Commission for the Protection of Minors, and Order of the Holy Sepulcher of Jerusalem. I also met with representatives from the British Embassy to the Holy See, Australian Embassy to the Holy See, and Canadian Embassy to the Holy See.

2. Francis, *Misericordia et Misera*, apostolic letter, November 20, 2016, www.vatican.va/content/francesco/en/apost_letters/documents/papa-francesco-lettera-ap_20161120_misericordia-et-misera.html. This statement was cited at the very beginning of this book and is worth returning to as we approach the end since it indicates the all-encompassing nature of the pope's understanding of mercy.

3. Pope Francis, *Predicate Evangelium*, Apostolic Constitution on the Roman Curia and Its Service to the Church in the World, March 19, 2022, www.vatican.va/content/francesco/en/apost_constitutions/documents/20220319-costituzione-ap-praedicate-evangelium.html.

4. Massimo Borghesi, *The Mind of Pope Francis: Jorge Mario Bergoglio's Intellectual Journey*, translated by Barry Hudock (Collegeville, MN: Liturgical Press, 2018), 258. He continues: "In the contemporary world which no longer knows the gratuitousness of true love, divided as it is between an affectivity and eros, mercy unites beauty and goodness in the communication of truth. *It is this gratuitous love that can respond to the need for beauty, which has been coveted and violated by libertine atheism.*" Ibid., 258–259.

5. Francis, Homily, Holy Mass on the Solemnity of Mary, Mother of God, January 1, 2017, www.vatican.va/content/francesco/en/homilies/2017 /documents/papa-francesco_20170101_omelia-giornata-mondiale-pace.html. He continued: "In this 'monadic' world there is no longer any father or mother, husband or wife, children or siblings. . . . The loss of the ties that bind us, so typical of our fragmented and divided culture, increases this sense of orphanhood and, as a result, of great emptiness and loneliness. The lack of physical (and not virtual) contact is cauterizing our hearts and making us lose the capacity for tenderness and wonder, for pity and compassion. Spiritual orphan-hood makes us forget what it means to be children, grandchildren, parents, grand-parents, friends and believers. It makes us forget the importance of singing, of a smile, of rest, of gratitude."

6. Romano Guardini, *The End of the Modern World: A Search for Orientation* (Wilmington, DE: ISI Books, 1998), 108–109. He continues: "Perhaps it will gain what lies hidden in the key words of the providential message of Jesus: that things are transformed for the man who makes God's will for His Kingdom his first concern (Matt. 6:33). These eschatological conditions will show themselves it seems to me, in the religious temper of the future. With these words I proclaim no facile apocalyptic. . . . If we speak here of the nearness of the End, we do not mean nearness in the sense of time, but nearness as it pertains to the essence of the End, for in essence man's existence is now nearing an absolute decision. Each and every consequence of that decision bears within it the greatest potentiality and the most extreme danger."

7. Hans Urs von Balthasar, *The Church and the World*, translated by A. V. Littledale and N. Dru (Freiburg im Breisgau, Germany: Herder and Herder, 1967), 43.

8. Austen Ivereigh, *Wounded Shepherd: Pope Francis and His Struggle to Convert the Catholic Church* (New York: Henry Holt, 2019) 314. He continues: "Holiness demanded discernment, a constant seeking of God's will in the real, in the flesh, in the now. To discern was not to settle for a religiosity of rules or take refuge in concepts, but courageously to follow Christ, to be a channel of His mercy in a bruised and bruising world. Only the following of Christ in freedom was capable of changing horizons. Discernment, the pope wrote, had to do with 'the meaning of my life before the Father who knows and loves me, with the real purpose of my life, that nobody knows better than he.' It required no special abilities or knowledge or virtue, but a willingness to grow in trust and be aware of the promptings of the Spirit and an ability to spot the bad spirit behind its angel wings."

9. Francis, Message for the Opening of the 37th International Meeting of Friendship among Peoples, August 19, 2016, www.vatican.va/content

/francesco/it/messages/pont-messages/2016/documents/papa-francesco _20160819_messaggio-meeting-amicizia-popoli.html (in Italian). He also indicated: A "true meeting" always requires a "willingness to put yourself in the other person's shoes in order to understand, beneath the surface, what stirs his heart, what he is truly looking for." The pope continued: "We will discover that opening ourselves to others does not impair our gaze, but makes us richer because it enables us to recognize the other person's truth, the importance of his experience and the background of what he says, even when it is hidden behind attitudes and choices that we do not share." The message was signed by Secretary of State Cardinal Pietro Parolin on behalf of the Holy Father.

10. Message to Professor Klaus Schwab, Executive Chairman of the World Economic Forum, January 21, 2020, www.vatican.va/content/francesco /en/messages/pont-messages/2020/documents/papa-francesco_20200115 _messaggio-worldeconomicforum.html. The message continued: "All too often materialistic or utilitarian visions, sometimes hidden, sometimes celebrated, lead to practices and structures motivated largely, or even solely, by self-interest. This typically views others as a means to an end and entails a lack of solidarity and charity, which in turn gives rise to real injustice, whereas a truly integral human development can only flourish when all members of the human family are included in, and contribute to, pursuing the common good. In seeking genuine progress, let us not forget that to trample upon the dignity of another person is in fact to weaken one's own worth. In my Encyclical Letter *Laudato Si'*, I drew attention to the importance of an "integral ecology" that takes into account the full implications of the complexity and interconnectedness of our common home.

11. Francis, *Laudato Si': On Care for Our Common Home*, encyclical, May 24, 2015, 141, www.vatican.va/content/francesco/en/encyclicals/documents /papa-francesco_20150524_enciclica-laudato-si.html. He continues: "Today, the analysis of environmental problems cannot be separated from the analysis of human, family, work-related and urban contexts, nor from how individuals relate to themselves, which leads in turn to how they relate to others and to the environment. There is an interrelation between ecosystems and between the various spheres of social interaction, demonstrating yet again that 'the whole is greater than the part' (*Evangelii Gaudium*, 237)."

12. Francis, Address to the Diplomatic Corps, January 9, 2020, www .vatican.va/content/francesco/en/speeches/2020/january/documents/papa -francesco_20200109_corpo-diplomatico.html. Earlier he had written: "Young people are telling us that this cannot be the case, for at every level we are being urgently challenged to protect our common home and to 'bring the whole human family together to seek a sustainable and integral development' (*Laudato Si'*, 13). They remind us of the urgent need for an *ecological conversion* which "must be understood in an integral way, as a transformation of how we relate to our sisters and brothers, to other living beings, to creation in all its rich variety and to the Creator who is the origin and source of all life." Francis, Message for the Celebration of the 53rd World Day of Peace, December 8, 2019, 4, www .vatican.va/content/francesco/en/messages/peace/documents/papa-francesco _20191208_messaggio-53giornatamondiale-pace2020.html.

13. Francis, Address to the Members of the Diplomatic Corps Accredited to the Holy See, January 11, 2016, www.vatican.va/content/francesco/en/speeches /2016/january/documents/papa-francesco_20160111_corpo-diplomatico .html. In a similar manner, Pope Francis began his address on January 9, 2020, by stating the importance of hope and joy: "A new year is opening before us; like the cry of a newborn baby, it fills us with joy and hope. I would like that word 'hope' which is an essential virtue for Christians, to inspire our way of approaching the times that lie ahead." The pope noted again in 2020 the problems of violence: "Another cause for concern is the proliferation of political crises in a growing number of countries of the American continent, accompanied by tensions and unaccustomed forms of violence that sharpen social conflicts and have grave socioeconomic and humanitarian consequences. Greater polarization does not help to resolve the real and pressing problems of citizens, especially those who are poorest and most vulnerable, nor can violence, which for no reason can be employed as a means of dealing with political and social issues." Francis, Address to the Members of the Diplomatic Corps Accredited to the Holy See, January 9, 2020, www.vatican.va/content/francesco/en/speeches /2020/january/documents/papa-francesco_20200109_corpo-diplomatico.html.

14. Francis, Meeting with the Muslim Community of Bangui, CAR, November 30, 2015, www.vatican.va/content/francesco/en/speeches/2015/november /documents/papa-francesco_20151130_repubblica-centrafricana-musulmani .html.

15. Francis, Address to the Members of the Diplomatic Corps, January 11, 2016. He continued: "Only a distorted ideological form of religion can think that justice is done in the name of the Almighty by deliberately slaughtering defenceless persons, as in the brutal terrorist attacks which occurred in recent months in Africa, Europe and the Middle East."

16. Francis, Address to the Members of the Diplomatic Corps, January 9, 2020. He continued: "In Madagascar, I saw how it is possible to create security where many proclaimed death and destruction." (Cf. Francis, Greeting to the Akamasoa City of Friendship, September 8, 2019, www.vatican.va/content /francesco/en/speeches/2019/september/documents/papa-francesco_20190908 _cittaamicizia-madagascar.html).

17. Ibid. Pope Francis also urged the international community to do more to "support the efforts made by these countries to eliminate the scourge of terrorism that is causing more and more bloodshed in whole parts of Africa, as in other parts of the world. . . . Likewise there is a need to encourage initiatives to foster fraternity among all local cultural, ethnic and religious groups, particularly in the Horn of Africa, in Cameroon and in the Democratic Republic of the Congo, where violence continues, especially in the eastern part of that country. . . . I think also of Sudan, with the fervent hope that its citizens will be able to live in peace and prosperity, and cooperate in the democratic and economic growth of the country. I think also of the Central African Republic, where a global agreement was signed last February to put an end to over five years of civil war. My thoughts turn also to South Sudan, which I hope to be able to visit in the course of this year."

18. This occurred on February 4, 2019, in Abu Dhabi, United Arab Emirates. The document is available at www.vatican.va/content/francesco/en/travels /2019/outside/documents/papa-francesco_20190204_documento-fratellanza -umana.html.

19. Pope Francis, Address to the Members of the Diplomatic Corps, January 9, 2020. Referencing the Document on Human Fraternity for World Peace and Living Together, he stated: "The Document recalls the importance of the *concept of citizenship*, 'based on the equality of rights and duties, under which all enjoy justice.' This requires respect for religious freedom and the resolve to reject the discriminatory use of the term 'minorities,' which engenders feelings of isolation and inferiority, and paves the way for hostility and discord, discriminating between citizens on the basis of their religious affiliation."

20. Francis, Address to the Members of the Diplomatic Corps," January 12, 2015, www.vatican.va/content/francesco/en/speeches/2015/january/docu ments/papa-francesco_20150112_corpo-diplomatico.html. By contrast, in this same address Pope Francis spoke of his time in Albania, which he visited in September 2014, where "despite the painful events of its recent history, the country is marked by the 'peaceful coexistence and collaboration that exists among followers of different religions' (Address to Authorities, Tirana, September 21, 2014) in an atmosphere of respect and mutual trust between Catholics, Orthodox and Muslims. This is an important sign that sincere faith in God makes one open to others, generates dialogue and works for the good, whereas violence is always the product of a falsification of religion, its use as a pretext for ideological schemes whose only goal is power over others."

21. Francis, Address to the Members of the Diplomatic Corps, January 11, 2016, www.vatican.va/content/francesco/en/speeches/2016/january/docu ments/papa-francesco_20160111_corpo-diplomatico.html.

22. Francis, Address to Participants in the International Conference on Violence Committed in the Name of Religion, February 2, 2018, www.vatican .va/content/francesco/en/speeches/2018/february/documents/papa-francesco _20180202_conferenza-tacklingviolence.html.

23. Apostolic Journey to Egypt, April 28–29, 2017, www.vatican.va/con tent/francesco/en/travels/2017/outside/documents/papa-francesco-egitto _2017.html.

24. Francis, Address to Participants in the International Peace Conference, April 28, 2017, www.vatican.va/content/francesco/en/speeches/2017/april /documents/papa-francesco_20170428_egitto-conferenza-pace.html.

25. Francis, Address to Participants in the International Conference on Violence Committed in the Name of Religion, February 2, 2018.

26. Ibid. The Holy Father continued: "The religious person knows that God is the Holy One, and that no one can claim to use his name in order to perpetrate evil. Every religious leader is called to unmask any attempt to manipulate God for ends that have nothing to do with him or his glory. We need to show, with unremitting effort, that every human life is sacred, that it deserves respect, esteem, compassion and solidarity, without regard for ethnicity, religion, culture, or ideological and political convictions. Adherence to a particular

religion does not confer additional dignity and rights upon individuals, nor does non-adherence deny or diminish them. There is a need, then, for a common commitment on the part of political authorities, religious leaders, teachers and those engaged in the fields of education, training and communications, to warn all those tempted by perverse forms of misguided religiosity that these have nothing to do with the profession of a religion worthy of this name. This will help all those people of good will who seek God to encounter him in truth, to encounter the One who sets us free from fear, hatred and violence, and who desires to use the creativity and energy of each person to spread his plan of love and peace, which is offered to all."

27. Francis, Address to the Members of the Diplomatic Corps," January 11, 2016.

28. Ibid.

29. Francis, Address to the Parliament of Europe, November 25, 2014, www.vatican.va/content/francesco/en/speeches/2014/november/documents/papa-francesco_20141125_strasburgo-parlamento-europeo.html.

30. Cf. letter of Mathetes to Diogenetes, 6. subelmonte.weebly.com/letter-to-diognetus.html.

31. Francis, Address to the European Parliament, November 25, 2014. He continued: "We see this in the beauty of our cities, and even more in the beauty of the many works of charity and constructive human cooperation throughout this continent. This history, in large part, must still be written. It is our present and our future. It is our identity. Europe urgently needs to recover its true features in order to grow, as its founders intended, in peace and harmony, since it is not yet free of conflicts."

32. In an address he gave to families gathered in St. Peter's Square in 2013, he stated: "In order to have a healthy family, three words need to be used. And I want to repeat these three words: please, thank you, sorry. Three essential words! We say please so as not to be forceful in family life: "May I please do this? Would you be happy if I did this?" We do this with a language that seeks agreement. We say thank you, thank you for love! Be honest with me, how many times do you say thank you to your wife, and you to your husband? How many days go by without uttering this word? And the last word: sorry. We all make mistakes, and on occasion someone gets offended in the marriage, in the family and harsh words are spoken. But please listen to my advice: don't ever let the sun set without reconciling. Peace is made each day in the family." Francis, Address to the Participants in the Pilgrimage of Families during the Year of Faith, October 26, 2013, www.vatican.va/content/francesco/en/speeches/2013/october/documents/papa-francesco_20131026_pellegrinaggio-famiglie.html.

33. Francis, Address to the Members of the Diplomatic Corps, January 11, 2016. He also notes: "Today there is a widespread fear of the definitive commitment demanded by the family; those who pay the price are the young, who are often vulnerable and uncertain, and the elderly, who end up being neglected and abandoned."

34. Francis, interview with Antonio Spadaro, SJ, August 19, 2013, www.vatican.va/content/francesco/en/speeches/2013/september/documents/papa-francesco_20130921_intervista-spadaro.html.

35. The General Superior of the Society of Jesus, Fr. Arturo Sosa, stated: "Discernment can make a huge difference when people live it as individuals. We have seen that in the last 30–40 years. But it can also make a difference at group level. This has not been so obvious in the last decades and this is where our real growth point can be. This is where the Spirit is calling us. We have a big opportunity. If we learn to discern together it can give us a new way of being. Pope Francis is showing us the way when in each synod he insists on stopping after every four interventions and leaving a time of silence. It is a way of saying: this whole project of Church is not about us and our opinions; it is the Spirit of God who is the real mover. Personally I think this is why Pope Francis can be unperturbed by the politics and the arguments. He knows that we have to go below those levels, those categories of right and left, conservative and liberal. We have to go deeper, below ideologies, to where the Spirit is at work. And we have to let that Spirit do the work." Arturo Sosa, address given in the Discerning Leadership Program, Jesuit Curia, Rome, October 28, 2019, discerningleadership.org/releases/father-general-arturo-sosa-s-j-taking-the-risk-making-discernment-central/. Cf. chapter 1. Pope Francis also asserted in his interview with Antonio Spadaro on August 19, 2013: "The risk in seeking and finding God in all things, then, is the willingness to explain too much, to say with human certainty and arrogance: 'God is here.' We will find only a god that fits our measure. The correct attitude is that of St. Augustine: seek God to find him, and find God to keep searching for God forever. Often we seek as if we were blind, as one often reads in the Bible. And this is the experience of the great fathers of the faith, who are our models. We have to re-read the Letter to the Hebrews, Chapter 11. Abraham leaves his home without knowing where he was going, by faith. All of our ancestors in the faith died seeing the good that was promised, but from a distance. . . . Our life is not given to us like an opera libretto, in which all is written down; but it means going, walking, doing, searching, seeing. . . . We must enter into the adventure of the quest for meeting God; we must let God search and encounter us."

36. Francis, interview with Antonio Spadaro, August 19, 2013.

37. Antonio Spadaro and Marcelo Figueroa, "Evangelical Fundamentalism and Catholic Integralism: A Surprising Encounter," *La Civiltà Cattolica*, January 12, 2018.

38. Francis, Angelus address, January 28, 2018, www.vatican.va/content/francesco/en/angelus/2020/documents/papa-francesco_angelus_20200209.html.

39. Andrea Tornielli, "Card. Parolin: 'Pope Asking Assad for Concrete Initiatives on Behalf of Syrian Population,'" *Vatican News*, July 22, 2019, www.vaticannews.va/en/pope/news/2019-07/card-parolin-pope-asking-assad-to-help-syrian-population.html.

40. On February 9, 2020, Pope Francis expressed his concern for Syrians in Idlib Province in his Angelus address. He stated: "Painful reports are still emerging from Northwestern Syria, particularly regarding the plight of so many women and children, as well as of people forced to flee because of a military escalation." He also appealed to the international community once more and to all parties involved to "make use of diplomatic channels, dialogue and negotiation" to end the conflict and "to safeguard the lives and welfare of civilians."

The Holy Father also invited everyone in St. Peter's Square and those watching the broadcast around the world to pray for "beloved and martyred Syria." Francis, Angelus address, February 9, 2020, www.vatican.va/content/francesco /en/angelus/2020/documents/papa-francesco_angelus_20200209.html.

41. Michael L. Fitzgerald, interview with Gerry O'Connell, *America*, February 3, 2019.

42. Pope Francis, prayer intention for November 2019. The full text reads: "In the Middle East, concord and dialogue among the three monotheistic religions is based on spiritual and historic bonds. The Good News of Jesus, risen out of love, came to us from these lands. Today, many Christian communities, together with Jewish and Muslim communities, work here for peace, reconciliation, and forgiveness. Let us pray that a spirit of dialogue, encounter, and reconciliation emerge in the Middle East."

43. The quotation is from Benedict XVI, *Spe Salvi*, encyclical, November 30, 2007, 1, www.vatican.va/content/benedict-xvi/en/encyclicals/documents/hf _ben-xvi_enc_20071130_spe-salvi.html.

44. Francis, Message for the Celebration of the 53rd World Day of Peace, January 1, 2020, 1, www.vatican.va/content/francesco/en/messages /peace/documents/papa-francesco_20191208_messaggio-53giornatamondiale -pace2020.html. He continued: "The world does not need empty words but convinced witnesses, peacemakers who are open to a dialogue that rejects exclusion or manipulation. In fact, we cannot truly achieve peace without a convinced dialogue between men and women who seek the truth beyond ideologies and differing opinions. Peace 'must be built up continually.'" And once more drawing from the work of his predecessor he stated: "What is true of peace in a social context is also true in the areas of politics and the economy, since peace permeates every dimension of life in common. There can be no true peace unless we show ourselves capable of developing a more just economic system." As Pope Benedict XVI said thirteen years ago in his encyclical *Caritas in Veritate*, "In order to defeat underdevelopment, action is required not only on improving exchange-based transactions and implanting public welfare structures, but above all on gradually increasing openness, in a world context, to forms of economic activity marked by quotas of gratuitousness and communion." Benedict XVI, *Caritas in Veritate*, encyclical, June 29, 2009, 39, www .vatican.va/content/benedict-xvi/en/encyclicals/documents/hf_ben-xvi_enc _20090629_caritas-in-veritate.html.

45. In this regard, Pope Francis particularly emphasizes the importance of reconciliation and forgiveness: "This path of reconciliation is a summons to discover in the depths of our heart the power of forgiveness and the capacity to acknowledge one another as brothers and sisters. When we learn to live in forgiveness, we grow in our capacity to become men and women of peace." Francis, message for the Celebration of the 53rd World Day of Peace, January 1, 2020, 3.

46. Our Lady Queen of Peace is a title of the Blessed Virgin Mary. She is often represented in art as holding a dove and an olive branch—symbols of peace. She is also named mother of the Prince of Peace.

47. This occurred on May 25. Pope Francis's pilgrimage to the Holy Land took place from May 24 to 26, 2014.

48. Address at a meeting with Palestinian Authorities, May 25, 2014, www.vatican.va/content/francesco/en/speeches/2014/may/documents/papa -francesco_20140525_terra-santa-autorita-palestinesi.html. The Holy Father continued: "In expressing my closeness to those who suffer most from this conflict, I wish to state my heartfelt conviction that the time has come to put an end to this situation which has become increasingly unacceptable. For the good of all, there is a need to intensify efforts and initiatives aimed at creating the conditions for a stable peace based on justice, on the recognition of the rights of every individual, and on mutual security. The time has come for everyone to find the courage to be generous and creative in the service of the common good, the courage to forge a peace which rests on the acknowledgment by all of the right of two States to exist and to live in peace and security within internationally recognized borders."

49. Francis, Homily, Mass at Ciudad Juárez, February 17, 2016, www .vatican.va/content/francesco/en/homilies/2016/documents/papa-francesco _20160217_omelia-messico-ciudad-juarez.html. The Holy Father continued: "We cannot deny the humanitarian crisis which in recent years has meant migration for thousands of people, whether by train or highway or on foot, crossing hundreds of kilometers through mountains, deserts and inhospitable zones. The human tragedy that is forced migration is a global phenomenon today. This crisis, which can be measured in numbers and statistics, we want instead to measure with names, stories, families. They are the brothers and sisters of those expelled by poverty and violence, by drug trafficking and criminal organizations. Being faced with so many legal vacuums, they get caught up in a web that ensnares and always destroys the poorest. Not only do they suffer poverty but they must also endure all these forms of violence. Injustice is radicalized in the young; they are "cannon fodder", persecuted and threatened when they try to flee the spiral of violence and the hell of drugs. And what can we say about the many women whose lives have been unjustly robbed?" In April 2019 Pope Francis donated US $500,000 to Mexico-based projects to help migrant communities at the US–Mexico border.

50. Lampedusa is the southernmost island of Italy, south of Sicily and the closest to the African coast. It receives the majority of the migrants and refugees crossing the Mediterranean Sea by boat from Libya to Italy.

51. Pope Francis visited Cuba on September 19 to 22, 2015. While there, he received the crucifix. Measuring over three meters high, the crucifix is crafted from wooden oars tied with ropes to symbolize the reality of migrants who have crossed the Mediterranean by boat.

52. Pope Francis, as Bishop of Rome, is the head of the Roman Catholic Church, and Patriarch Kirill is patriarch of Moscow and all Russia and the primate of the Russian Orthodox Church. Holding the meeting in Cuba brought together the North and the South.

53. Pope Francis visited Bangui to open the Year of Mercy on November 29, 2015.

54. Pope Francis referred to this as "a door of mercy through which anyone who enters will experience the love of God who consoles, pardons and instills hope." Francis, *Misericordiae Vultus: The Face of Mercy*, apostolic letter, April 11, 2015, www.vatican.va/content/francesco/en/apost_letters/documents /papa-francesco_bolla_20150411_misericordiae-vultus.html. Pope Francis designated certain Church doors in Rome as Holy Doors of mercy, and so in dioceses around the world certain churches were designated as having doors of mercy.

55. As an example, when Pope Francis flew to Panama in January 2019 on the way to World Youth Day he sent the following telegram to King Felipe of Spain: "HIS MAJESTY FELIPE VI KING OF SPAIN MADRID I EXTEND CORDIAL GREETINGS TO YOUR MAJESTY, THE MEMBERS OF THE ROYAL FAMILY, AND THE PEOPLE OF SPAIN AS I FLY OVER YOUR COUNTRY ON MY WAY TO PANAMA FOR MY APOSTOLIC VISIT. INVOKING THE BLESSING OF ALMIGHTY GOD UPON THE NATION I PRAY THAT HE MAY GRANT ALL OF YOU PEACE AND WELL-BEING." "Pope Sends Telegrams to Heads of State on Flight to Panama," *Vatican News*, January 23, 2019, www.vaticannews.va/en/pope/news /2019-01/pope-francis-panama-wyd-2019-telegrams-flyover.html.

56. On his way to Japan in November 2019, Pope Francis sent the following telegram to China: "HIS EXCELLENCY XI JINPING PRESIDENT OF THE PEOPLE'S REPUBLIC OF CHINA BEIJING, I SEND CORDIAL GREETINGS TO YOUR EXCELLENCY AS I FLY OVER CHINA ON MY WAY TO JAPAN. I ASSURE YOU OF MY PRAYERS FOR THE NATION AND ITS PEOPLE, INVOKING UPON ALL OF YOU ABUNDANT BLESSINGS OF PEACE AND JOY." "Pope Francis Sends Telegrams In-Flight to Japan," *Vatican News*, November 23, 2019, www.vaticannews.va /en/pope/news/2019-11/pope-francis-telegrams-flight-thailand-japan.html.

57. Pierre Favre's reaction to the political events of his day was typical: he had recourse to prayer. He received an indication of the importance of praying for key figures in the religious conflicts of his times. He saw these men as having grave responsibilities, and his compassion for them was stirred: "I felt great fervor as eight persons became present to me along with the desire to remember them vividly in order to pray for them without taking notice of their faults. They were the sovereign pontiff, the emperor, the king of France, the king of England, Luther, the Grand Turk, Bucer and Philip Melanchthon. That came about through experiencing in my soul how severely these men were judged by many; as a result I felt for them a certain kind of holy compassion accompanied by a good spirit." Pierre Favre, *Memoriale* 25, in *The Spiritual Writings of Pierre Favre*, edited by Edmond C. Murphy, SJ, and John W. Padberg, SJ (St. Louis: Institute of Jesuit Sources, 1996), 79. As I previously wrote: "Here we see an extraordinary ecumenical spirit operative in Favre. He was praying for Pope Paul III; Charles V, the Holy Roman Emperor; Francis I, King of France; Henry VIII, King of England; Martin Luther; Suleiman I, the Grand Turk; Martin Bucer; and Philip Melanchthon, leading lights amongst the reformers. It is important to note here that he prays for them and their good, not against them

and for their downfall. He brings them before the love of God which embraces all human beings. We can see how this focus on the love of God extended to all human persons. In moment of great disillusionment, Favre commends the most important figures in the conflicts that he perceived all around him, to the love and mercy of God." Gill Goulding, CJ, *A Church of Passion and Hope: The Formation of an Ecclesial Disposition from Ignatius Loyola to Pope Francis and the New Evangelization* (London: Bloomsbury, 2016), 131–132.

58. Fr. Jacques Hamel was murdered on July 26, 2016, by two extremist Islamic militants while he was celebrating Mass at St. Étienne-du-Rouvray, France. He was 85 years of age.

59. Pope Francis, in Poland, speaking with journalists on July 27, 2016. He was also concerned to emphasize that he did not mean a war of religion, so he added: "Not a war of religion. There is a war of interests. There is a war for money. There is a war for natural resources. There is a war for domination of peoples. This is the war," he said. "All religions want peace. Others want war. Do you understand?" Joshua J. McElwee, "Francis Declares 'The World Is at War' after French Priest's Slaying," *National Catholic Reporter*, July 27, 2016, www.ncronline.org/francis-declares-world-war-after-french-priests-slaying.

60. Cf. *Evangelii Gaudium* 53, where Pope Francis also asks: "How can it be that it is not a news item when an elderly homeless person dies of exposure, but it is news when the stock market loses two points? This is a case of exclusion. . . . Masses of people find themselves excluded and marginalized: without work, without possibilities, without any means of escape. Human beings are themselves considered consumer goods to be used and then discarded. We have created a 'disposable' culture which is now spreading. It is no longer simply about exploitation and oppression, but something new." Francis, *Evangelii Gaudium: The Joy of the Gospel*, apostolic exhortation, November 24, 2013, www.vatican.va/content/francesco/en/apost_exhortations/documents/papa -francesco_esortazione-ap_20131124_evangelii-gaudium.html.

61. Ibid., 54. Pope Francis continues: "Almost without being aware of it, we end up being incapable of . . . weeping for other people's pain, and feeling a need to help them, as though all this were someone else's responsibility and not our own."

62. Ibid. He continues: "The culture of prosperity deadens us; we are thrilled if the market offers us something new to purchase; and in the meantime all those lives stunted for lack of opportunity seem a mere spectacle; they fail to move us."

63. Pope Francis indicates the total disproportion that exists in society: "While the earnings of a minority are growing exponentially, so too is the gap separating the majority from the prosperity enjoyed by those happy few. This imbalance is the result of ideologies, which defend the absolute autonomy of the marketplace and financial speculation. Consequently they reject the right of states, charged with vigilance for the common good, to exercise any form of control. A new tyranny is thus born, invisible and often virtual, which unilaterally and relentlessly imposes its own laws and rules. Debt and the accumulation of interest also makes it difficult for countries to realize the potential of their

own economies and keep citizens from enjoying their real purchasing power."
Ibid., 56.

64. Ibid., 198. Pope Francis goes on: "This divine preference has consequences for the faith life of all Christians . . . [this is] 'a special form of primacy in the exercise of Christian charity, to which the whole tradition of the Church bears witness' (Pope John Paul II, *Sollicitudo Rei Socialis*, 30 Dec. 1987, 42)." He continues: "This option as Benedict XVI has taught—'is implicit in our Christian faith in a God who became poor for us, so as to enrich us with his poverty' (Benedict, Address at the Inaugural Session of the Fifth General Conference of the Latin American and Caribbean Bishops—13 May 2007)." Also, Walter Kasper writes: "The preferential option for the poor did not remain a Latin American anomaly. John Paul II and Pope Benedict XVI adopted it in their own teaching pronouncements. In his opening speech in Aparecida (at the second plenary assembly of the Latin American episcopate in 2007) [Pope Benedict] repeated this option, grounded it Christologically. In his address at the conclusion of his visit to Germany, on September 25th 2011 in Freiburg, under the heading 'Becoming Unworldly,' Benedict basically addressed nothing other than what Francis is saying today. At that time, to a considerable extent people did not understand him or they did not want to understand him. Now Francis shows clearly, in a programmatic way, what the issue is, not only through his words, but also through his own simple and plain lifestyle the way he appears on the public stage, and through his gestures." Walter Kasper, *Pope Francis' Revolution of Tenderness and Love: Theological and Pastoral Perspectives*, translated by William Madges (New York: Paulist Press, 2015), 70–71.

65. Francis, *Evangelii Gaudium*, 198.

66. Ibid., 56. Pope Francis continues: "In this system, which tends to devour everything which stands in the way of increased profits, whatever is fragile, like the environment, is defenceless before the interests of a deified market, which become the only rule."

67. Ibid., 57. He continues: "A financial reform open to such ethical considerations would require a vigorous change of approach on the part of political leaders. I urge them to face this challenge with determination and an eye to the future, while not ignoring, of course, the specifics of each case. Money must serve, not rule! The Pope loves everyone, rich and poor alike, but he is obliged in the name of Christ to remind all that the rich must help, respect and promote the poor. I exhort you to generous solidarity and a return of economics and finance to an ethical approach which favors human beings." Ibid., 58.

68. The visit took place on July 29, 2016, during Pope Francis's apostolic visit to Poland on July 27 to 31, 2016. Auschwitz was the largest of six dedicated extermination camps. The Holocaust Memorial Museum estimates that 1.3 million people were sent to Auschwitz in occupied Poland. Of these, nearly 1.1 million were Jews, 960,000 of whom died in the camp; the other 200,000 were predominantly non-Jewish Poles, the mentally challenged, Roma people, homosexuals, and Soviet prisoners of war. Some 85 percent of the people sent to Auschwitz were killed there. In January 1945, some 7,000 people were liberated from the camp.

69. Pope Francis, Auschwitz guest book, inscribed July 29, 2016.
70. Fr. Luigi Giussani (1922–2005), an Italian priest and founder of Communion and Liberation, defined fundamentalism as a poor and instrumental conception of sentiment and religious experience.
71. The period of the Cold War in Europe was from 1947 to 1991.
72. The Bosnian War lasted from April 1992 to December 1995.
73. The conflict dates from the early centuries of the common era. Shiites believe that the prophet Mohammed should have been succeeded by his son-in-law, Imam Ali, and that leadership of the Muslim world should pass through the prophet's descendants. Sunnis don't believe that the leadership of the Muslim world should necessarily pass through hereditary succession. There are also other significant differences between the groups that have accrued over time.
74. A personal example may be helpful here. I can recall the first time I visited Africa and how living for a month on that continent gave me a very different perspective. For me Europe shrank in proportion, and new insights became apparent. In a video message Pope Francis sent on July 2, 2016, to be part of an event in Monaco, he stated: "Europe is in a highly complex world becoming increasingly globalized and therefore less and less Eurocentric." Francis, "Message from Pope Francis for #together4europe," Facebook, July 2, 2016, www .facebook.com/watch/?v=604954909673556.
75. Francis, Address to the Members of the Diplomatic Corps Accredited to the Holy See, January 9, 2017, www.vatican.va/content/francesco/en/speeches /2017/january/documents/papa-francesco_20170109_corpo-diplomatico.html.
76. Ibid.
77. Ibid.
78. Pope Francis, Address to "Roma Tre" University, February 17, 2017, www.vatican.va/content/francesco/en/speeches/2017/february/documents /papa-francesco_20170217_universita-romatre..
79. Ibid.
80. Ibid.
81. Here Pope Francis is referencing the regular practice of smuggling people and the often-associated practice of human trafficking, particularly of young women.
82. In April of 2016, the worst month for that year, 1,222 deaths of migrants were recorded. In May of 2017, the worst month for that year, 1,178 deaths were recorded. Every month for those two years, deaths were recorded in the Mediterranean, and in 2018, from January 1 to February 5, 343 deaths were recorded. The sea-worthiness of many of the boats that set sail was highly questionable.
83. Francis, Address to "Roma Tre" University, February 17, 2017.
84. Antonio Spadaro, SJ, "The Diplomacy and Geopolitics of Mercy? The World of Pope Francis," presentation at the University of Notre Dame, Indiana, October 2017, nanovic.nd.edu/events/keeley-vatican-lecture/.
85. Ibid.
86. Shortly after his election in 2013, Pope Francis set up a Council of Cardinals to advise him. The Council originally consisted of eight members:

Cardinal Oscar Rodriguez Maradiaga (Honduras), Cardinal Reinhold Marx (Germany), Cardinal Sean O'Malley (USA), Cardinal Oswald Gracias (India), Cardinal Giuseppe Bertello (Italy), Cardinal George Pell (Australia), Cardinal Javier Errazuriz Ossa (Chile), and Cardinal Laurent Monsengwo Pasinya (Congo). In 2018 the latter three cardinals were released on the grounds of age, having served a five-year term. Cardinal Pietro Parolin was not one of the eight but regularly attended meetings and in 2014 was confirmed as the ninth member.

87. Francis, *Predicate Evangelium*. This apostolic constitution, published on March 19, 2022, entered into full effect on June 5, 2022, the Solemnity of Pentecost. This replaced the apostolic constitution *Pastor Bonus* promulgated by Pope John Paul II and later revised by Pope Benedict XVI.

88. In a message issued on the March 7, 2020, by the Vatican Dicastery for the Laity, Family and Life, there was an invitation for all to face the emergency of coronavirus with seriousness, serenity, and courage. "A person's life has great value in the eyes of God. If in certain circumstances, something attacks the health and life itself of many persons, and perhaps even our own, we must not feel alone in the face of this enemy." The message continued: "As the Dicastery entrusted by the Holy Father with the pastoral care of the laity, the family and life, we wish to manifest—at this difficult time—to those who have been affected by coronavirus or feel threatened by this viral infection, our closeness, our affection and our prayer for them." Dicastery for Laity Family Life, "Message to the Laity and Families," March 6, 2020, www.laityfamilylife.va/content/laityfamilylife/en/news/2020/messaggio-ai-laici-e-alle-famiglie.html. Such an embrace of the reality of the situation, the measures taken by the Italian government, and the hope of a vibrant faith brought much consolation to the populations of the Vatican City State, the people of Rome, and the world.

89. It is important to note that various attempts have been made to use Pope Emeritus Benedict's writings or rare interviews to appear to show dissension between the two men. These did not appear to undermine the deep relationship that existed between the two pontiffs.

90. In 2013 the pre-conclave meetings of cardinals were marred by the revelations of scandal surrounding Cardinal Keith Patrick O'Brien from Scotland. He admitted that he had engaged in sexual misconduct not befitting a priest, archbishop, or cardinal. He resigned as Archbishop of St. Andrews and Edinburgh during this period. In addition, there were still repercussions from the scandal of leaked papal documents and the investigation by three cardinals into what lay behind this leak.

91. Vatican diplomats are priests in Rome and different parts of the world whom people seek out. They are points of reference when people are looking for assistance in navigating a whole variety of difficulties. They are people seeking to be helpful and of service to the Church at a number of different levels. They are offering a different service to humanity, one that is rooted in the outreach of the Holy See to individuals and nations worldwide. They endeavor to show how to look at and contextualize issues. They are part of a service that has been available to the Holy See for many generations.

92. Walter Kasper, *Pope Francis' Revolution of Tenderness and Love*, translated by William Madges (New York: Paulist Press, 2015), 71. Pope Francis sees this as one of the worst temptations that can threaten the Church. However, it is noteworthy that he does not limit this form of "spiritual worldliness" to those who hold clerical office. The challenge he issues is to the whole Church. including the laity and religious. Ibid.

93. Hodges, Susy. "Pope at Mass: Be Bishops for Your Flock, Not for Your Career." *Vatican News*, May 15, 2018. www.vaticannews.va/en/pope-francis /mass-casa-santa-marta/2018-05/pope-mass-santa-marta-bishops-flock.html.

94. Kasper, *Pope Francis' Revolution of Tenderness and Love*, 72.

95. Francis, *Predicate Evangelium*, 1.

96. Cf. ibid., 3.

97. Ibid., 4.

98. Ibid., 7.

99. Ibid., 12.

100. Ibid., Art. 59 (2): "In a particular way, the specific activity of the Missionaries of Mercy contributes to this end."

101. Ibid., 10.

102. Pope Paul VI, Homily for the Solemnity of the Immaculate Conception of the Blessed Virgin Mary at the conclusion of the Second Vatican Ecumenical Council, December 8, 1965, cited in ibid., 12.

103. Pope Francis designates this as a form of worldliness that he deprecates: "Those who have fallen into this worldliness look on from above and afar, they reject the prophecy of their brothers and sisters, they discredit those who raise questions, they constantly point out the mistakes of others and they are obsessed by appearances. Their hearts are open only to the limited horizon of their own immanence and interests, and as a consequence they neither learn from their sins nor are they genuinely open to forgiveness. This is a tremendous corruption disguised as a good. . . . God save us from a worldly Church with superficial spiritual and pastoral trappings! This stifling worldliness can only be healed by breathing in the pure air of the Holy Spirit who frees us from self-centeredness cloaked in an outward religiosity bereft of God. Let us not allow ourselves to be robbed of the Gospel." Francis, *Evangelii Gaudium*, 95.

104. Francis, *Evangelii Gaudium*, 95. He continues: "In this way, the life of the Church turns into a museum piece or something which is the property of a select few. In others, this spiritual worldliness lurks behind a fascination with social and political gain, or pride in their ability to manage practical affairs, or an obsession with programs of self-help and self-realization. It can also translate into a concern to be seen, into a social life full of appearances, meetings, dinners and receptions."

105. Ibid.

106. Kasper, *Pope Francis' Revolution of Tenderness and Love*, 72.

107. Kasper writes: "With this program of a poor church for the poor, Pope Francis directs a serious inquiry at the church. . . . The challenge is directed primarily at affluent churches in an affluent society. . . . The church is not supposed to depend on political and social influence and glamour; it is not to rely

only on programs, planning and organizations, but rather to rely on spiritual radiance. Pope Francis is convinced that we can only overcome the *acedia*, the crippling force that pulls us down, and can direct our attention upward and regain our spiritual momentum if we, as a poor church for the poor, reclaim the joy and spark of the gospel and set our hope on God and his providence." Ibid. 72–73.

108. In *Evangelii Gaudium* there is clear evidence of this, for example, in paragraphs 53–60 and 197–291. It is clear that the problem of violence is involved: "The poor and the poorer peoples are accused of violence, yet without equal opportunities the different forms of aggression and conflict will find a fertile terrain for growth and eventually explode [59]. . . . Just as goodness tends to spread, the toleration of evil, which is injustice, tends to expand its baneful influence and quietly to undermine any political and social system, no matter how solid it may appear [59]. . . . Inequality eventually engenders a violence which recourse to arms cannot and never will be able to resolve" [60].

109. In the Ignatian Spiritual Exercises, voluntary poverty has a real value in itself and also is a prophetic sign of the kingdom of God.

110. *Lumen Gentium*, 8:3. Cf. *Gaudium et Spes*, 1, which states that the Church "shares the joys and the hopes, the griefs and the anxieties of the men of this age, especially those who are poor or in any way afflicted." Paul VI, *Lumen Gentium*, Dogmatic Constitution on the Church, November 21, 1964, www .vatican.va/archive/hist_councils/ii_vatican_council/documents/vat-ii_const _19641121_lumen-gentium_en.html; *Gaudium et Spes*, Dogmatic Constitution on the Church in the World, December 7, 1965, www.vatican.va/archive/hist _councils/ii_vatican_council/documents/vat-ii_const_19651207_gaudium-et -spes_en.html. Walter Kasper makes the point that "in this spirit, shortly before the end of the Council, on November 16, 1965 (the feast of St. Margaret of Scotland), in the catacombs of Domitilla in Rome, forty bishops forged the so-called Catacomb Pact 'For a Servant and Poor Church' which five hundred additional bishops subsequently joined. They committed themselves to a series of voluntary obligations concerning lifestyle, vestments, titles, and engagement on behalf of the poor. Among the first to sign were bishops such as Hélder Câmara and Aloísio Lorscheider and Auxiliary Bishop Julius Angerhausen from Essen, Germany." Kasper, *Pope Francis' Revolution of Tenderness and Love*, 69–70.

111. Though the Vatican is the smallest state in the world, it has a global outreach.

112. Sant'Egidio is a Christian community founded in 1968, right after the Second Vatican Council. An initiative of Andrea Riccardi, it was born in a secondary school in the center of Rome. Over the years, it has become a network of communities. The community pays attention to the periphery and peripheral people, gathering men and women of all ages and conditions, united by a fraternal tie through listening to the Gospel and making a voluntary and free commitment to the poor and peace. Prayer, the poor, and peace are its fundamental points of reference. Prayer is based on listening to the Word of God and is the first action of the community: it accompanies and guides life. The poor are brothers and sisters, friends of the community. Friendship with whoever is in

a moment of need—the elderly, homeless, migrants, disabled people, prisoners, street children—is the distinctive focus of the lives of those who are part of Sant'Egidio on the different continents. The awareness and understanding that war is the mother of all poverties has driven the community to work for peace: to protect it wherever it is threatened and to help re-build it wherever needed, aiding dialogue between parties when it has been lost. The work to foster peace is lived as a Christian responsibility, part of a bigger service of reconciliation. It is also part of the fraternity lived through ecumenical commitment and inter-religious dialogue, in the "Spirit of Assisi," the place where Pope John Paul II first called religious leaders together to pray for peace.

113. There is a covenant between the Anglican Diocese of Qu'Appelle and the Archdiocese of Regina in Saskatchewan, Canada. This was built on relationships that had developed since the 1960s and an agreement that was signed in January 2011. Archbishop Don Bolen, the Roman Catholic Archbishop of Regina, had been involved in ecumenical relations at the highest level, serving on the Pontifical Council for Promoting Christian Unity at the Vatican from 2001 to 2008. In a local news interview in November 2017, Bolen said, "We were created for community, with God and with one another." He said the ecumenical work in Saskatchewan is "a good example for the rest of the country, although we still have more to do." Joanne Shurvin-Martin, "Ecumenical Reps Meet for Workshop," November 19, 2017, archregina.sk.ca/newsstory/anglican-roman-catholic-covenant-action/.

114. Receptive Ecumenism was offered as a possible way forward when ecumenical progress at the beginning of the third millennium appeared to have slowed, and indeed to be stagnating. Three conferences were held at the University of Durham, England, in 2006, 2009, and 2014, taking up aspects of this theme. The essential principle behind Receptive Ecumenism is that the primary ecumenical responsibility is to ask not "What do the other traditions first need to learn from us?" but "What do we need to learn from them?" The assumption is that if all were asking this question seriously and acting on it, then all would be moving in ways that would both deepen our authentic respective identities and draw us into more intimate relationship.

115. One of the most important depictions of Allah for Islam is Allah the Most Merciful.

116. Just as a reminder, these are: to feed the hungry, to give drink to the thirsty, to clothe the naked, to give shelter to travelers, to visit the sick, to visit the imprisoned, and to bury the dead.

117. For example, on March 5, 2018, Pope Francis visited women and their children at Casa Leda, a home for women in semi-detention in Rome; on April 12, 2019, he visited patients with Alzheimer's disease at Emanuele Village on the northern outskirts of Rome.

118. Pope Paul VI, *Nostra Aetate*, Declaration on the Relations of the Church to Non-Christian Religions, October 28, 1965, www.vatican.va/archive/hist_councils/ii_vatican_council/documents/vat-ii_decl_19651028_nostra-aetate_en.html. It stated explicitly: "The Church, therefore, exhorts her sons, that through dialogue and collaboration with the followers of other religions,

carried out with prudence and love and in witness to the Christian faith and life, they recognize, preserve and promote the good things, spiritual and moral, as well as the socio-cultural values found among these men." A particular focus of attention was on the Abrahamic faiths. Thus, regarding Islam it stated: "The Church regards with esteem also the Moslems. They adore the one God, living and subsisting in Himself; merciful and all-powerful, the Creator of heaven and earth, who has spoken to men; they take pains to submit wholeheartedly to even His inscrutable decrees, just as Abraham, with whom the faith of Islam takes pleasure in linking itself, submitted to God. Though they do not acknowledge Jesus as God, they revere Him as a prophet. They also honor Mary, His virgin Mother; at times they even call on her with devotion. . . . This sacred synod urges all to work sincerely for mutual understanding and to preserve as well as to promote together for the benefit of all mankind social justice and moral welfare, as well as peace and freedom."

119. Pope Francis has had a long history of engagement with Judaism stretching back to his time in Buenos Aries. He is very cognizant of the sections of *Nostra Aetate* that encourage ongoing dialogue. A key declaration was its description of the Judaeo-Christian heritage: "The Church of Christ acknowledges that, according to God's saving design, the beginnings of her faith and her election are found already among the Patriarchs, Moses and the prophets. She professes that all who believe in Christ—Abraham's sons according to faith (cf. Gal. 3:7)—are included in the same Patriarch's call, and likewise that the salvation of the Church is mysteriously foreshadowed by the chosen people's exodus from the land of bondage. The Church, therefore, cannot forget that she received the revelation of the Old Testament through the people with whom God in His inexpressible mercy concluded the Ancient Covenant. . . . Indeed, the Church believes that by His cross Christ, Our Peace, reconciled Jews and Gentiles. making both one in Himself (cf. Eph. 2:14–16). . . . God holds the Jews most dear for the sake of their Fathers; He does not repent of the gifts He makes or of the calls He issues—such is the witness of the Apostle (cf. Rom. 11:28–29). . . . Since the spiritual patrimony common to Christians and Jews is thus so great, this sacred synod wants to foster and recommend that mutual understanding and respect which is the fruit, above all, of biblical and theological studies as well as of fraternal dialogue." Paul VI, *Nostra Aetate*.

Conclusion

1. The English College is situated at Via di Monserrato 45, 00186 Roma RM, Italy. The Venerable English College, commonly referred to as the English College, is a Catholic seminary in Rome for the training of priests for England and Wales. The seminary was founded in 1579 as a place for preparing priests to serve on the "English Mission," but there has been an English presence on Via di Monserrato since 1362, when the site was acquired by a confraternity of Englishmen living at Rome. The English Hospice, as it came to be known, offered welcome to generations of pilgrims.

2. Upon receiving news of the martyrdom of one of its alumni, the students began the practice of gathering around the picture to sing a *Te Deum*. This practice continued across the centuries, and still today, each year on "Martyrs' Day," which is December 1, the Feast of St. Edmund Campion, SJ, the students gather to sing the *Te Deum* in front of the painting and the relics of the martyrs, which are venerated by the students.

3. Edmund, King of East Anglia, was born around 840 and was from infancy a Christian. He was crowned at the age of 15 and was an exemplary ruler, strong in faith and prayer and determined to treat all justly. In 869 his kingdom was invaded by the Vikings. They were repulsed but returned in greater numbers. Edmund was captured but refused to renounce his faith. He was martyred in 870. St. Edmund, king and martyr, was adopted as patron saint of England before being replaced by St. George. St. Thomas à Becket of Canterbury was born around 1120, the son of a prosperous London merchant. He was well educated and quickly became an agent to Theobald, archbishop of canterbury, who sent him on several missions to Rome. Becket's talents were noticed by Henry II, who made him his chancellor, and the two became close friends. When Theobald died in 1161, Henry made Becket archbishop. Becket transformed himself from a pleasure-loving courtier into a serious, simply-dressed cleric. The king and his archbishop's friendship was put under strain when it became clear that Becket would now stand up for the Church in its disagreements with the king. In 1164, realizing the extent of Henry's displeasure, Becket fled into exile in France and remained in exile for several years. He returned in 1170. On December 29, 1170, four knights, believing the king wanted Becket out of the way, confronted and murdered him in Canterbury Cathedral. Becket was made a saint in 1173, and his shrine in Canterbury Cathedral became an important focus for pilgrimage.

4. Monsignor Dario Viganò (born in 1962), is prefect emeritus of the Secretariat for Communications.

5. Referencing "The Theology of Pope Francis," a series of eleven books written by eleven different authors and published by Libreria Editrice Vaticana, Pope Benedict wrote: "I applaud this initiative, it contradicts the foolish prejudice of those who see Pope Francis as someone who lacks a particular theological and philosophical formation, while I would have been solely a theorist of theology with little understanding of the concrete lives of today's Christian." Benedict, Letter to Msgr. Dario Edoardo Viganò, February 7, 2018, in Pentin, Edward, "Vatican Reveals Full Text of Benedict XVI's Letter to Msgr. Viganò," National Catholic Register, March 17, 2018, www.ncregister.com/blog/vatican -reveals-full-text-of-benedict-xvi-s-letter-to-msgr-vigano.

6. Aquinas, *Summa Theologiae*, I, q.25, a.3, ad.3.

7. Cf. Francis, *Misericordia et Misera*, apostolic letter, November 20, 2016, 12ff, www.vatican.va/content/francesco/en/apost_letters/documents/papa -francesco_bolla_20150411_misericordiae-vultus.html.

8. Francis, Homily, Mass for the Sacred Heart of Jesus, Jubilee of Priests, June 3, 2016, popefrancisdaily.com/popes-homily-at-mass-for-sacred-heart-of -jesus-jubilee-for-priests/.

9. The heart of Christ, the pope said, "is not only the Heart that shows us mercy, but is itself mercy. There the Father's love shines forth, there I know I am welcomed and understood as I am; there, with all my sins and limitations, I know the certainty that I am chosen and loved." Ibid.

10. Francis, Homily, Mass for the Closing of the Jubilee Year of Mercy, November 20, 2016. www.vatican.va/content/francesco/en/homilies/2016 /documents/papa-francesco_20161120_omelia-chiusura-giubileo.html.

11. Cf. John 14:23ff to the end of John 17.

12. Francis, Catechesis at General Audience, June 13, 2018, www.vatican.va /content/francesco/en/audiences/2018/documents/papa-francesco_20180613 _udienza-generale.html.

13. Ibid.

14. Pope Francis was reflecting on the gospel passage where the young man comes to Jesus to ask, "What must I do to inherit eternal life?" (Mark 10:17–22). Pope Francis recalled that Jesus tells the young man to follow the commandments, but then points him to something greater, because it is clear that the young man does not have a full life. He said that the transition from youth to maturity takes place when one begins to "accept one's limits" and "becomes aware of what is lacking." Ibid.

15. "The quality of mercy is not strained, / It droppeth as the gentle rain from heaven / Upon the place beneath. It is twice blessed; / It blesses him that gives and him that takes." Portia's speech in William Shakespeare, *The Merchant of Venice*, act IV, scene 1.

Postscript

1. Francis, Extraordinary Moment of Prayer, Sagrato of St. Peter's Basilica, Friday March 27, 2020, www.vatican.va/content/francesco/en/homilies /2020/documents/papa-francesco_20200327_omelia-epidemia.html. He continued: "It shows us how we have allowed ourselves to become dull and feeble in the very things that nourish, sustain and strengthen our lives and our communities. The tempest lays bare all our prepackaged ideas and forgetfulness of what nourishes our people's souls; all those attempts that anesthetize us with ways of thinking and acting that supposedly 'save' us, but instead prove incapable of putting us in touch with our roots and keeping alive the memory of those who have gone before us. We deprive ourselves of the antibodies we need to confront adversity."

2. Ibid. He continued: "Greedy for profit, we let ourselves get caught up in things, and lured away by haste. We did not stop at your reproach to us, we were not shaken awake by wars or injustice across the world, nor did we listen to the cry of the poor or of our ailing planet. We carried on regardless, thinking we would stay healthy in a world that was sick."

3. Ibid. The pope went on: "The Lord asks us from his cross to rediscover the life that awaits us, to look towards those who look to us, to strengthen, recognize and foster the grace that lives within us. . . . It means finding the courage

to create spaces where everyone can recognize that they are called, and to allow new forms of hospitality, fraternity and solidarity. By his cross we have been saved in order to embrace hope and let it strengthen and sustain all measures and all possible avenues for helping us protect ourselves and others. Embracing the Lord in order to embrace hope: that is the strength of faith, which frees us from fear and gives us hope."

Appendix

1. Santa Maria Maggiore, or St. Mary Major, is one of the four major basilicas in Rome, along with St. John Lateran, St. Paul Outside the Walls, and St. Peter's. It was the first church in the West to be dedicated to the Virgin Mary. The present church was built by Pope Sixtus III in 431 AD to honor Mary after the Council of Ephesus that year had proclaimed her Mother of God. There were various additions to the building over time up to the thirteenth century.

2. The icon is recounted by pious tradition to have been painted by St. Luke the Evangelist and in the fourth century brought by the Roman emperor Constantine's mother, St. Helena, to Rome, where it was credited with the miraculous delivery of the city from the plague in the sixth century.

3. Jorge Mario Bergoglio, *Meditaciones para religiosos* (Mensajero, 2014), 46–47; Michael C. Barber, SJ, "Pope Francis and the Mother of Mercy," *Columbia Online*, May 1, 2014, www.kofc.org/en/columbia/detail/pope-francis -mother-mercy.html.

4. A statue of Our Lady of Montserrat, which is found at the Santa Maria de Montserrat monastery on Montserrat Mountain in Catalonia, Spain. She is the patron saint of Catalonia dates to at least the twelfth century. Over time the features of Mother and Child became blackened by the candles that were burned before the statue day and night. St. Ignatius of Loyola made a pilgrimage there soon after his conversion. The Madonna della Strada, or Santa Maria della Strada, is the name of the image of the Blessed Virgin Mary that is enshrined in the Gesù, the mother church of the Society of Jesus in Rome. This image, now dated to the end of the thirteenth century or the beginning of the fourteenth, has an interesting history. The painting is first documented in the sixteenth century in the small parish church of Santa Maria della Strada, which preceded the Gesù on the same site in the heart of Rome and at a crossroads along the ceremonial route of the popes. A Jesuit in the eighteenth century claimed that Our Lady of the Way owed her title to the image's original position on the exterior wall of the church facing a main street. (There is no evidence to support that theory.) In all likelihood, the little painting decorated a space somewhere inside Santa Maria della Strada. Ignatius probably first encountered it in 1540, when he preached day after day on an adjacent street corner. Within a year the pope had approved his small band of "reformed priests" as a religious order and given them Santa Maria della Strada as their pastoral home base, effectively making Ignatius caretaker of the painting. Ignatius's attachment to the Virgin ran deep. Visions of the Madonna and Child and accounts of all-night vigils

before crowned images of the holy pair punctuate his autobiography. His devotion could even go hand in hand with conservation. After forsaking his old life as a courtier for that of a pilgrim, he donated part of his last wages "for an image of Our Lady, which was in bad condition, so that it could be repaired and very finely adorned." Years later in Rome, Ignatius showed equal solicitude toward the Madonna della Strada. Before his death in 1556, he instructed the Jesuits to preserve the image and eventually to enshrine it in the new, large church he had planned for but never lived to see replace Santa Maria della Strada. "When the still-unfinished Gesù opened for services in 1575, the painting was installed temporarily above a side altar. Seven years later, the Jesuits transferred it permanently to its own lavishly decorated chapel to the left of the high altar. There it remained, a direct link to Ignatius's own devotion but cut off from its pre-Jesuit history." Gregory Waldrop, "The Dramatic Restoration of the 'Madonna della Strada,'" *America*, December 21, 2009, www.americamagazine.org/faith/2009/12/21/dramatic-restoration-madonna-della-strada.

5. Our Lady of Lujan is the name given to a terracotta image of Our Lady of the Immaculate Conception, fourteen inches tall, that has been venerated in Argentina since its arrival in 1630. According to tradition, the image "chose" to stay in Lujan, some forty miles northwest of Buenos Aires. After three days of traveling in a caravan toward the northern region of Argentina, the two oxen pulling the statue's cart stopped moving near the Lujan River. After much coaxing, it became evident that the oxen would move only if the image was left behind, and the Portuguese rancher who was transporting the statue agreed. El Negro Manuel had been "gifted" to a rancher in Lujan, who allowed the slave to dedicate his life to taking care of the image, which he did until he died, in 1686. When those who "inherited" Manuel tried to take him away from his life-long task in 1674, the people of Lujan came together and bought his freedom. During the process, he would simply say, "I belong to Our Lady, and no one else."

The story of Our Lady of Aparecida is told in an article from *Vatican News*: "Early on the morning of October 12, 1717, three Brazilian fishermen set out on the waters of the Paraiba River, which ran through their village. They were charged with providing the fish for the banquet that would be held a few days later in the village of Guarantinguetá. The three fishermen—Domingos Garcia, Filipe Pedroso, and João Alves—had had no luck that morning; they had been fishing for hours without catching anything. They had almost given up, when João Alves decided to give it one more try. He cast his net into the river and slowly began to draw it in. There was something there, but it wasn't a fish . . . it seemed to be a piece of wood. When they pulled it out of the net, they saw that it was a statue of the Blessed Virgin Mary, with the head missing. João cast his net into the waters once more, and pulling it in, he found another piece of wood, which proved to be the statue's head. As if in response to a strange instinct, he cast his net a third time into the river. When he tried to pull it in, he found it was full of fish. Now his companions cast their nets as well, and likewise found themselves overwhelmed with an abundance of fish. Over the course of the next few days, the three fishermen cleaned and re-assembled the statue, and Filipe Pedroso placed it in his humble abode. Soon after, news of the miraculous catch spread to the neighboring villages, and day by day more of their countrymen came to honor the Blessed Virgin and pray the Rosary. They gave the virgin of the statue the name Nossa Senhora da Conceição Aparecida, that is, Our Lady of the Appeared Conception. As time went on, the crowds became so large that there was no longer room in the little hut. A small chapel was built, and later, in 1737, a larger one. Soon witnesses began to tell of many graces that were received from Our Lady and of the many miracles that took place at the sanctuary." In "Our Lady of Aparecida," *Vatican News*, October 12, 2017.

The history of the devotion to Mary, Undoer of Knots, is traced to 1615, when a couple on the verge of divorce went to see a Jesuit priest, known for his Marian devotion, for counseling. The couple took along their white wedding ribbon, which, according to Bavarian custom, had been used to tie their hands together as a sign of unity during their nuptial Mass. Praying fervently that the couple's problems would be resolved, the priest took the ribbon and held it up before an image of Our Lady and proceeded to untie the ribbon's knots. As the last knot came undone, the ribbon miraculously glowed whiter, and the priest took it as a sign of Our Lady's favor. The couple stayed together, and a painting was later commissioned to commemorate the event. Marie-Albert Boursiquot, "Our Lady Undoer of Knots," *Linacre Quarterly* 84 (3): 203–204, www.ncbi.nlm.nih.gov/pmc/articles/PMC5592300/#:~:text=Its%20roots%2C %20however%2C%20go%2.

6. Francis, Homily, Closing Mass of the Eighth World Meeting of Families, Philadelphia, September 27, 2015, www.vatican.va/content/francesco/en /homilies/2015/documents/papa-francesco_20150927_usa-omelia-famiglie .html.

7. Pope Francis waxed eloquent about these knots: "The 'knot' of disobedience, the 'knot' of unbelief. When children disobey their parents, we can say that a little 'knot' is created. This happens if the child acts with an awareness of what he or she is doing, especially if there is a lie involved. At that moment, they break trust with their parents. You know how frequently this happens! Then the relationship with their parents needs to be purified of this fault; the child has to ask forgiveness so that harmony and trust can be restored. Something of the same sort happens in our relationship with God. When we do not listen to him, when we do not follow his will, we do concrete things that demonstrate our lack of trust in him—for that is what sin is—and a kind of knot is created deep within us. These knots take away our peace and serenity. They are dangerous, since many knots can form a tangle which gets more and more painful and difficult to undo." Francis, Address for the "Marian Day" of the Year of Faith, October 12, 2013, www.vatican.va/content/francesco/en/speeches/2013 /october/documents/papa-francesco_20131012_preghiera-mariana.html.

8. Ibid.

9. The decree on the celebration of the Blessed Virgin Mary, Mother of God, was published by the Congregation for Divine Worship and the Discipline of the Sacraments on February 11, 2018. The text stated: "The joyous veneration given to the Mother of God by the contemporary Church, in light

of reflection on the mystery of Christ and on his nature, cannot ignore the figure of a woman (cf. Gal. 4:4), the Virgin Mary, who is both the Mother of Christ and Mother of the Church." It continued: "Indeed, the Mother standing beneath the cross (cf. John 19:25), accepted her Son's testament of love and welcomed all people in the person of the beloved disciple as sons and daughters to be reborn unto life eternal. She thus became the tender Mother of the Church which Christ begot on the cross handing on the Spirit. Christ, in turn, in the beloved disciple, chose all disciples as ministers of his love towards his Mother, entrusting her to them so that they might welcome her with filial affection. As a caring guide to the emerging Church Mary had already begun her mission in the Upper Room, praying with the Apostles while awaiting the coming of the Holy Spirit (cf. Acts 1:14). In this sense, in the course of the centuries, Christian piety has honoured Mary with various titles, in many ways equivalent, such as Mother of Disciples, of the Faithful, of Believers, of all those who are reborn in Christ; and also as 'Mother of the Church' as is used in the texts of spiritual authors as well as in the Magisterium of Popes Benedict XVI and Leo XIII. Thus the foundation is clearly established by which Blessed Paul VI, on 21 November 1964, at the conclusion of the Third Session of the Second Vatican Council, declared the Blessed Virgin Mary as 'Mother of the Church, that is to say of all Christian people, the faithful as well as the pastors, who call her the most loving Mother' and established that 'the Mother of God should be further honoured and invoked by the entire Christian people by this tenderest of titles.'"

10. The feast was inaugurated on May 21, 2018.

11. Francis, *Misericordiae Vultus: The Face of Mercy*, apostolic letter, April 11, 2015, 24, www.vatican.va/content/francesco/en/apost_letters/documents/papa -francesco_bolla_20150411_misericordiae-vultus.html.

12. Francis, Homily, Holy Mass and Opening of the Holy Door, Basilica of St. Mary Major, January 1, 2016, www.vatican.va/content/francesco /en/homilies/2016/documents/papa-francesco_20160101_giubileo-omelia -portasanta-smmaggiore.html. He continued: "*Salve, Mater Misericordiae!* With this invocation we turn to the Blessed Virgin Mary in the Roman Basilica dedicated to her under the title of Mother of God. It is the first line of an ancient hymn, which we will sing at the conclusion of this Holy Eucharist. Composed by an unknown author, it has come down to us as a heartfelt prayer spontaneously rising up from the hearts of the faithful: Hail Mother of mercy, Mother of God, Mother of forgiveness, Mother of hope, Mother of grace and Mother full of holy gladness.' In these few words we find a summary of the faith of generations of men and women who, with their eyes fixed firmly on the icon of the Blessed Virgin, have sought her intercession and consolation."

13. Ibid. The Pope's remarks came on the Solemnity of Mary, Mother of God. As part of his celebration of the day, the pontiff opened the final Holy Door of the four major basilicas in Rome. His text continued: "She is the Mother of mercy, because she bore in her womb the very Face of divine mercy, Jesus, Emmanuel, the Expectation of the nations, the 'Prince of Peace' (Is. 9:5). The Son of God, made incarnate for our salvation, has given us his Mother, who joins us on our pilgrimage through this life, so that we may never

be left alone, especially at times of trouble and uncertainty. Mary is the *Mother of God, she is the Mother of God who forgives,* who bestows forgiveness, and so we can rightly call her *Mother of forgiveness.* This word—'forgiveness'— so misunderstood in today's world, points to the new and original fruit of Christian faith. A person unable to forgive has not yet known the fullness of love. Only one who truly loves is able to forgive and forget. At the foot of the Cross, Mary sees her Son offer himself totally, showing us what it means to love as God loves. At that moment she heard Jesus utter words which probably reflected what he had learned from her as a child: 'Father, forgive them; for they do not know what they are doing' (Luke 23:24). At that moment, Mary became for all of us the Mother of forgiveness. Following Jesus' example and by his grace, she herself could forgive those who killed her innocent Son. For us, Mary is an icon of how the Church must offer forgiveness to those who seek it. The Mother of forgiveness teaches the Church that the forgiveness granted on Golgotha knows no limits. Neither the law with its quibbles, nor the wisdom of this world with its distinctions, can hold it back. The Church's forgiveness must be every bit as broad as that offered by Jesus on the Cross and by Mary at his feet. There is no other way. It is for this purpose that the Holy Spirit made the Apostles the effective ministers of forgiveness, so what was obtained by the death of Jesus may reach all men and women in every age (cf. John 20:19–23)."

14. John Paul II, *Dives in Misericordia,* encyclical, November 30, 1980, 8, www.vatican.va/content/john-paul-ii/en/encyclicals/documents/hf_jp-ii_enc _30111980_dives-in-misericordia.html. In the same paragraph he also states: "Mary is also the one who obtained mercy in a particular and exceptional way, as no other person has. At the same time, still in an exceptional way, she made possible with the sacrifice of her heart her own sharing in revealing God's mercy. This sacrifice is intimately linked with the cross of her Son, at the foot of which she was to stand on Calvary. Her sacrifice is a unique sharing in the revelation of mercy, that is, a sharing in the absolute fidelity of God to his own love, to the covenant that he willed from eternity and that he entered into in time with man, with the people, with humanity; it is a sharing in that revelation that was definitively fulfilled through the cross. No one has experienced, to the same degree as the Mother of the crucified One, the mystery of the cross, the overwhelming encounter of divine transcendent justice with love: that 'kiss' given by mercy to justice. No one has received into his heart, as much as Mary did, that mystery, that truly divine dimension of the redemption effected on Calvary by means of the death of the Son, together with the sacrifice of her maternal heart, together with her definitive 'fiat.'"

15. Joseph Ratzinger, Homily at the Funeral Mass for Pope John Paul II, April 8, 2005, www.vatican.va/gpII/documents/homily-card-ratzinger_20050408 _en.html.

16. Aquinas, *Summa Theologiae,* I-II, 113, 9.

17. Paul VI, *Lumen Gentium,* Dogmatic Constitution on the Church, No- vember 21, 1964, 62, www.vatican.va/archive/hist_councils/ii_vatican_council /documents/vat-ii_const_19641121_lumen-gentium-en.html. It is important

to note that in this paragraph there is a clear nuancing of all Mary's titles in relation to her Son, such that: "This, however, is to be so understood that it neither takes away from, nor adds anything to, the dignity and efficaciousness of Christ the one Mediator." Ibid.

18. St. Bernard, "Homily on the Assumption of the Blessed Virgin Mary," Office of Readings, December 20, in *The Divine Office*, English edition (London: Collins, 1974), 4.

19. This was published by the Congregation for Divine Worship and the Sacraments on June 20, 2020, the Feast of the Immaculate Heart of Mary. "Pope Adds Three New Invocations to the Litany of the Blessed Virgin Mary," *Vatican News*, June 20, 2020, www.vaticannews.va/en/pope/news/2020-06/pope-francis-loreto-litany-new-invocations.html.

20. Francis, Meditation at the Marian Vigil during the Jubilee of Mercy, October 8, 2016, www.vatican.va/content/francesco/en/speeches/2016/october/documents/papa-francesco_20161008_giubileo-veglia-mariana.html. He also stated in this meditation: "Throughout her life, Mary did everything that the Church is asked to do in perennial memory of Christ." With her faith, "we learn to open our hearts to obey God; in her self-denial, we see the importance of tending to the needs of others; in her tears, we find the strength to console those experiencing pain." In each of these moments, Mary "expresses the wealth of divine mercy that reaches out to all in their daily need."

21. Francis, *Misericordiae Vultus*, 24. He continued: "Chosen to be the Mother of the Son of God, Mary, from the outset, was prepared by the love of God to be the Ark of the Covenant between God and man. She treasured divine mercy in her heart in perfect harmony with her Son Jesus."

22. Ibid. He concluded this section of his meditation by stating: "Let us address her in the words of the *Salve Regina*, a prayer ever ancient and ever new, so that she may never tire of turning her merciful eyes upon us, and make us worthy to contemplate the face of mercy, her Son Jesus."

23. Francis, *The Church of Mercy: A Vision for the Church* (Chicago: Loyola Press, 2014), 137. He continued: "We all have some of these knots, and we can ask in our heart of hearts: what are the knots in my life? ... All the knots of our heart, every knot of our conscience can be undone. Do I ask Mary to help me to be open to God's mercy, to undo those knots, to change? ... She leads us by the hand as a mother, our Mother, to the embrace of our Father, the Father of mercies."

24. Pope Francis, *Evangelii Gaudium: The Joy of Gospel*, apostolic exhortation, November 24, 2013, 285. www.vatican.va/content/francesco/en/apost_exhortations/documents/papa-francesco_esortazione-ap_20131124_evangelii-gaudium.html. He continues: "The close connection between Mary, the Church and each member of the faithful is based on the fact that each in his or her own way brings forth Christ." Later he indicates: "As mother of all, she is a sign of hope for peoples suffering the birth pangs of justice. She is the missionary who draws near to us and accompanies us throughout life, opening our hearts to faith by her maternal love. As a true mother, she walks at our side, she shares our struggles and she constantly surrounds us with God's love." Ibid., 286.

25. Ibid., 287.

26. Ibid., 288. He continues: "Mary is able to recognize the traces of God's Spirit in events great and small. She constantly contemplates the mystery of God in our world, in human history and in our daily lives. She is the woman of prayer and work at Nazareth, and she is also Our Lady of Help, who sets out from her town 'with haste' (Luke 1:39) to be of service to others. This interplay of justice and tenderness, of contemplation and concern for others, is what makes the ecclesial community look to Mary as a model of evangelization. We implore her maternal intercession that the church may become a home for many peoples, a mother for all peoples, and that the way may be opened to the birth of a new world."

BIBLIOGRAPHY

Papal and Other Church Sources

Benedict XVI. Address for the Fortieth Anniversary of the Decree *Ad Gentes*, March 11, 2006. www.vatican.va/content/benedict-xvi/en/speeches/2006 /march/documents/hf_ben-xvi_spe_20060311_ad-gentes.html.

———. Address for the Screening of the Documentary Film "Art and Faith— Via Pulchritudinis," October 25, 2012. www.vatican.va/content/benedict -xvi/en/speeches/2012/october/documents/hf_ben-xvi_spe_20121025 _arte-fede.html.

———. Angelus address, first Sunday of Lent, February 25, 2007. www.vatican .va/content/benedict-xvi/en/angelus/2007/documents/hf_ben-xvi_ang _20070225.html.

———. *Caritas in Veritate*. Encyclical, June 29, 2009. www.vatican.va/content /benedict-xvi/en/encyclicals/documents/hf_ben-xvi_enc_20090629 _caritas-in-veritate.html.

———. *The Church of Mercy: A Vision for the Church*. Chicago: Loyola Press, 2014.

———. "The Current Situation of Faith and Theology." Address given at the Meeting with the Doctrinal Commissions of Latin America, May 7, 1996. www.vatican.va/roman_curia/congregations/cfaith/incontri/rc_con _cfaith_19960507_guadalajara-ratzinger_en.html.

———. *Deus Caritas Est: God Is Love*. Encyclical, December 25, 2005. www .vatican.va/content/benedict-xvi/en/encyclicals/documents/hf_ben-xvi _enc_20051225_deus-caritas-est.html.

———. Farewell Address to the Eminent Cardinals Present in Rome, February 28, 2013. www.vatican.va/content/benedict-xvi/en/speeches/2013 /february/documents/hf_ben-xvi_spe_20130228_congedo-cardinali .html.

———. Homily, Mass for the Inauguration of the Fifth General Conference of the Bishops of Latin American and the Caribbean, May 13, 2007. www .vatican.va/content/benedict-xvi/en/homilies/2007/documents/hf_ben -xvi_hom_20070513_conference-brazil.html.

——. Homily, Mass for the Opening of the Year of Faith, October 11, 2012. www.vatican.va/content/benedict-xvi/en/homilies/2012/documents/hf _ben-xvi_hom_20121011_anno-fede.html.

——. Homily, Pastoral Visit to the Roman Parish of Dio Padre Misericordioso, March 26, 2006. www.vatican.va/content/benedict-xvi/en/homilies /2006/documents/hf_ben-xvi_hom_20060326_parrocchia-roma.html.

——. "Interview with Fr. Jacques Servais, SJ." *L'Osservatore Romano*, March 17, 2016. www.catholicnewsagency.com/news/33591/full-text-of-benedict -xvis-recent-rare-and-lengthy-interview.

——. *Intima Ecclesiae Natura: On the Service of Charity.* Motu proprio, November 11, 2012. www.vatican.va/content/benedict-xvi/en/motu_proprio /documents/hf_ben-xvi_motu-proprio_20121111_caritas.html.

——. *Jesus of Nazareth: From the Baptism in the Jordan to the Transfiguration.* Edited by Adrian Walker. New York: Doubleday, 2007.

——. *Jesus of Nazareth: Holy Week: From the Entrance into Jerusalem to the Resurrection.* Translated by Philip J. Whitmore. San Francisco: Ignatius Press, 2011.

——. Letter to Msgr. Dario Edoardo Viganò, February 7, 2018. In Pentin, Edward, "Vatican Reveals Full Text of Benedict XVI's Letter to Msgr. Viganò," *National Catholic Register*, March 17, 2018, www.ncregister.com /blog/vatican-reveals-full-text-of-benedict-xvi-s-letter-to-msgr-vigano.

——. Letter to the Superior General of the Society of Jesus, May 15, 2006. www.vatican.va/content/benedict-xvi/en/letters/2006/documents/hf_ben -xvi_let_20060515_50-haurietis-aquas.html.

——. *Spe Salvi.* Encyclical, November 30, 2007. www.vatican.va/content /benedict-xvi/en/encyclicals/documents/hf_ben-xvi_enc_20071130_spe -salvi.html.

——. Vigil with Young People, 23rd World Youth Day, July 19, 2008. www .vatican.va/content/benedict-xvi/en/speeches/2008/july/documents/hf _ben-xvi_spe_20080719_vigil.html.

Bernard. "Homily on the Assumption of the Blessed Virgin Mary," Office of Readings, December 20, in *The Divine Office*, English edition (London: Collins, 1974), 4.

Dicastery for Laity Family Life. "Message to the Laity and Families," March 6, 2020. www.laityfamilylife.va/content/laityfamilylife/en/news/2020/mes saggio-ai-laici-e-alle-famiglie.html.

Extraordinary Synod of Bishops on the Family. "The Pastoral Challenges of the Family in the Context of Evangelization." Instrumentum Laboris, 3rd Extraordinary General Assembly of the Synod of Bishops, October 5–19, 2014. www.vatican.va/roman_curia/synod/documents/rc_synod_doc _20140626_instrumentum-laboris-familia_en.html.

Francis. Address to the Members of the Diplomatic Corps, January 9, 2020, www.vatican.va/content/francesco/en/speeches/2020/january/documents /papa-francesco_20200109_corpo-diplomatico.html.

——. Address to the Members of the Diplomatic Corps," January 12, 2015, www.vatican.va/content/francesco/en/speeches/2015/january/documents /papa-francesco_20150112_corpo-diplomatico.html.

———. Address to the Members of the Diplomatic Corps, January 11, 2016. www.vatican.va/content/francesco/en/speeches/2016/january/documents /papa-francesco_20160111_corpo-diplomatico.html

———. Address for the "Marian Day" of the Year of Faith, October 12, 2013. www.vatican.va/content/francesco/en/speeches/2013/october/documents /papa-francesco_20131012_preghiera-mariana.html.

———. Address to the Marian Fathers of the Immaculate Conception, Vatican, Rome, February 18, 2017. Press.vatican.va/content/salastampa/en /bollettino/pubblico/2017/02/18/170218a.html.

———. Address at a Meeting with Palestinian Authorities, May 25, 2014. www .vatican.va/content/francesco/en/speeches/2014/may/documents/papa -francesco_20140525_terra-santa-autorita-palestinesi.html.

———. Address at a Meeting with the Bishops of Brazil, July 28, 2013. www .vatican.va/content/francesco/en/speeches/2013/july/documents/papa -francesco_20130727_gmg-episcopato-brasile.html.

———. Address to the Synod of Bishops, October 6, 2014. www.vatican.va /content/francesco/en/speeches/2014/october/documents/papa-francesco _20141006_padri-sinodali.html.

———. Address at a Meeting with the Bishops of Mexico, February 13, 2016. www.vatican.va/content/francesco/en/speeches/2016/february/documents /papa-francesco_20160213_messico-vescovi.html.

———. Address to the Members of the Diplomatic Corps Accredited to the Holy See, January 12, 2015. www.vatican.va/content/francesco/en/speeches /2015/january/documents/papa-francesco_20150112_corpo-diplomatico .html.

———. Address to the Members of the Diplomatic Corps Accredited to the Holy See, January 11, 2016. www.vatican.va/content/francesco/en/speeches /2016/january/documents/papa-francesco_20160111_corpo-diplomatico .html.

———. Address to the Members of the Diplomatic Corps Accredited to the Holy See, January 9, 2017. www.vatican.va/content/francesco/en/speeches/2017 /january/documents/papa-francesco_20170109_corpo-diplomatico.html.

———. Address to the Members of the Diplomatic Corps Accredited to the Holy See, January 9, 2020. www.vatican.va/content/francesco/en/speeches /2020/january/documents/papa-francesco_20200109_corpo-diplomatico .html.

———. Address to the Newly Appointed Bishops, September 16, 2016. www .vatican.va/content/francesco/en/speeches/2016/september/documents /papa-francesco_20160916_corso-formazione-nuovi-vescovi.html.

———. Address to the Parliament of Europe, November 25, 2014. www.vatican .va/content/francesco/en/speeches/2014/november/documents/papa -francesco_20141125_strasburgo-parlamento-europeo.html.

———. Address to Participants in the General Chapter of the Congregations of the Marian Clerics of the Immaculate Conception of the Blessed Virgin Mary, February 18, 2017. www.vatican.va/content/francesco/en/speeches /2017/february/documents/papa-francesco_20170218_chierici-mariani .html.

———. Address to Participants in the International Conference on Violence Committed in the Name of Religion, February 2, 2018. www.vatican.va /content/francesco/en/speeches/2018/february/documents/papa-francesco _20180202_conferenza-tacklingviolence.html.

———. Address to Participants in the International Peace Conference, April 28, 2017. www.vatican.va/content/francesco/en/speeches/2017/april /documents/papa-francesco_20170428_egitto-conferenza-pace.html.

———. Address to Participants in the Pilgrimage of Families during the Year of Faith, October 26, 2013. www.vatican.va/content/francesco/en/speeches /2013/october/documents/papa-francesco_20131026_pellegrinaggio -famiglie.html.

———. Address to the Students, Teachers, and Family Members of the Je-suit Schools of Italy and Albania, June 7, 2013. www.vatican.va/content /francesco/en/speeches/2013/june/documents/papa-francesco_20130607 _scuole-gesuiti.html.

———. Address to the Young People of Paraguay, July 12, 2015. www.vatican .va/content/francesco/en/speeches/2015/july/documents/papa-francesco _20150712_paraguay-giovani.html.

———. Amoris Laetitia: Apostolic Exhortation on Love in the Family, March 29, 2016. www.vatican.va/content/dam/francesco/pdf/apost_exhortations /documents/papa-francesco_esortazione-ap_20160319_amoris-laetitia_en .pdf.

———. Angelus address, June 9, 2013. www.vatican.va/content/francesco/en /angelus/2013/documents/papa-francesco_angelus_20130609.html.

———. Angelus address, April 13, 2014. www.vatican.va/content/francesco/en /angelus/2014/documents/papa-francesco_angelus_20140413.html.

———. Angelus address, March 5, 2017. www.vatican.va/content/francesco/en /angelus/2017/documents/papa-francesco_angelus_20170305.html.

———. Angelus address, January 28, 2018. www.vatican.va0/content/francesco/ en/angelus/2018/documents/papa-francesco_angelus_20180128.html.

———. Angelus address, February 9, 2020. www.vatican.va/content/francesco /en/angelus/2020/documents/papa-francesco_angelus_20200209.html.

———. Apostolic Journey to Egypt, April 28–29, 2017. www.vatican.va/content /francesco/en/travels/2017/outside/documents/papa-francesco-egitto _2017.html.

———. Apostolic Letter of His Holiness to All Consecrated People on the Occa-sion of the Year of Consecrated Life, November 21, 2014. www.vatican.va /content/francesco/en/apost_letters/documents/papa-francesco_lettera -ap_20141121_lettera-consacrati.html.

———. "Beyond Formalities." L'Osservatore Romano, April 1, 2014.

———. Catechesis at General Audience, March 11, 2015. www.vatican.va/content /francesco/en/audiences/2015/documents/papa-francesco_20150311 _udienza-generale.html.

———. Catechesis at General Audience, June 13, 2018. www.vatican.va/content /francesco/en/audiences/2018/documents/papa-francesco_20180613 _udienza-generale.html.

———. "Catholic Schools and Universities in the Service of the Growth of Humanity, Dialogue and Hope," February 9, 2017. press.vatican.va/content /salastampa/en/bollettino/pubblico/2017/02/09/170209b.html.

———. "Christ Is the Door to the Kingdom." Homily, Casa Santa Marta, April 22, 2013. www.vatican.va/content/francesco/en/cotidie/2013/documents/papa -francesco-cotidie_20130422_christ-door.html.

———. *Christus Vivit*, Post-Synodal Apostolic Exhortation, April 2, 2019. www .vatican.va/content/francesco/en/apost_exhortations/documents/papa -francesco_esortazione-ap_20190325_christus-vivit.html.

———. "Contemplating Jesus, Meek and Suffering." *L'Osservatore Romano*, September 12, 2013.

———. "Contemplation, Closeness, Abundance." *L'Osservatore Romano*, November 1, 2013.

———. Discourse at the 36th General Congregation of the Society of Jesus, October 24, 2016. press.vatican.va/content/salastampa/en/bollettino/pubblico /2016/10/24/161024a.html.

———. Document on Human Fraternity for World Peace and Living Together, February 4, 2019. www.vatican.va/content/francesco/en/travels/2019/out side/documents/papa-francesco_20190204_documento-fratellanza-umana .html.

———. "Draw From the Well of the Father's Mercy, and Bring It to the World!" Homily on Divine Mercy Sunday, April 3, 2016. www.vatican.va/content /francesco/en/homilies/2016/documents/papa-francesco_20160403 _omelia-giubileo-divina-misericordia.html..

———. *Evangelii Gaudium: The Joy of the Gospel*. Apostolic exhortation, November 24, 2013. www.vatican.va/content/francesco/en/apost_exhortations /documents/papa-francesco_esortazione-ap_20131124_evangelii-gaudium .html.

———. Extraordinary Moment of Prayer, Sagrato of St. Peter's Basilica, Friday March 27, 2020. www.vatican.va/content/francesco/en/homilies/2020 /documents/papa-francesco_20200327_omelia-epidemia.html.

———. First greeting of the Holy Father Pope Francis, March 13, 2013. www .vatican.va/content/francesco/en/speeches/2013/march/documents/papa-francesco_20130313_benedizione-urbi-et-orbi.html.

———. First Meditation, Spiritual Retreat Given on the Occasion of the Jubilee for Priests, June 2, 2016. www.vatican.va/content/francesco/en/speeches /2016/june/documents/papa-francesco_20160602_giubileo-sacerdoti -prima-meditazione.html.

———. "For a Culture of Encounter." *L'Osservatore Romano*, September 23, 2016.

———. "Forgiveness in a Caress." *L'Osservatore Romano*, April 7, 2014.

———. "Forgiveness on the Cross." General audience, September 28, 2016. www.vatican.va/content/francesco/en/audiences/2016/documents/papa -francesco_20160928_udienza-generale.html.

———. *Gaudete et Exsultate*. Apostolic exhortation, March 19, 2018. www .vatican.va/content/francesco/en/apost_exhortations/documents/papa -francesco_esortazione-ap_20180319_gaudete-et-exsultate.html.

——. General Audience, February 3, 2016. www.vatican.va/content/francesco /en/audiences/2016/documents/papa-francesco_20160203_udienza -generale.html.

——. "General Audience: The Family–7; The Grandparents," March 11, 2015. www.vatican.va/content/francesco/en/audiences/2015/documents/papa -francesco_20150311_udienza-generale.html.

——. Greeting to the Akamasoa City of Friendship, September 8, 2019. www .vatican.va/content/francesco/en/speeches/2019/september/documents /papa-francesco_20190908_cittaamicizia-madagascar.html.

——. Homily, Casa Santa Marta, October 22, 2013. www.vatican.va/content /francesco/en/cotidie/2013/documents/papa-francesco-cotidie_20131022 _contemplation.html.

——. Homily, Closing Mass of the Eighth World Meeting of Families, Philadel- phia, September 27, 2015. www.vatican.va/content/francesco/en/homilies /2015/documents/papa-francesco_20150927_usa-omelia-famiglie.html.

——. Homily, Easter Sunday, April 16, 2017. www.vatican.va/content/francesco /en/homilies/2017/documents/papa-francesco_20170416_omelia-pasqua .html.

——. Homily, Easter Vigil Mass, April 20, 2019. www.vatican.va/content /francesco/en/homilies/2019/documents/papa-francesco_20190420 _omelia-vegliapasquale.html.

——. Homily, Feast of Saint Ignatius, July 31, 2013. www.vatican.va/content /francesco/en/homilies/2013/documents/papa-francesco_20130731 _omelia-sant-ignazio.html.

——. Homily, Holy Mass and Canonization of Blessed Mother Teresa of Cal- cutta, Jubilee for Workers of Mercy and Volunteers, September 3, 2016. www.vatican.va/content/francesco/en/homilies/2016/documents/papa -francesco_20160904_omelia-canonizzazione-madre-teresa.html.

——. Homily, Holy Mass on the Solemnity of Mary, Mother of God, January 1, 2017. www.vatican.va/content/francesco/en/homilies/2017/documents /papa-francesco_20170101_omelia-giornata-mondiale-pace.html.

——. Homily, Jubilee for Priests, June 3, 2016. www.vatican.va/content /francesco/en/homilies/2016/documents/papa-francesco_20160603 _omelia-giubileo-sacerdoti.html.

——. Homily, Jubilee for the Sick and Persons with Disabilities, June 12, 2016. www.vatican.va/content/francesco/en/homilies/2016/documents/papa -francesco_20160612_omelia-giubileo-ammalati-disabili.html.

——. Homily, Jubilee for Socially Excluded People, November 13, 2016. www.vatican.va/content/francesco/en/homilies/2016/documents/papa -francesco_20161113_giubileo-omelia-senza-fissa-dimora.html.

——. Homily, Jubilee for Workers of Mercy and Volunteers, September 3, 2016. www.vatican.va/content/francesco/en/homilies/2016/documents /papa-francesco_20160904_omelia-canonizzazione-madre-teresa.html.

——. Homily, Mass at Ciudad Juárez, February 17, 2016. www.vatican.va /content/francesco/en/homilies/2016/documents/papa-francesco _20160217_omelia-messico-ciudad-juarez.html.

———. Homily, Mass for the Closing of the Jubilee Year of Mercy, November 20, 2016. www.vatican.va/content/francesco/en/homilies/2016/documents/papa-francesco_20161120_omelia-chiusura-giubileo.html.

———. Homily, Mass for the Sacred Heart of Jesus, Jubilee of Priests, June 3, 2016. popefrancisdaily.com/popes-homily-at-mass-for-sacred-heart-of-jesus-jubilee-for-priests/.

———. "How Harmony Is Created." *L'Osservatore Romano*, April 8, 2016.

———. "How to Create Dialogue." Morning meditation in the chapel of Casa Santa Marta, January 24, 2014. www.vatican.va/content/francesco/en/cotidie/2014/documents/papa-francesco-cotidie_20140124_create-dialogue.html.

———. "In Dialogue, Everybody Wins." Pope Francis to Scholas Occurrentes, May 30, 2016. press.vatican.va/content/salastampa/en/bollettino/pubblico/2016/05/30/160530b.html.

———. Interview with Antonio Spadaro, SJ, August 19, 2013. www.vatican.va/content/francesco/en/speeches/2013/september/documents/papa-francesco_20130921_intervista-spadaro.html.

———. Interview with Antonio Spadaro, SJ, editor-in-chief, *La Civiltà Cattolica*, September 21, 2013. www.vatican.va/content/francesco/en/speeches/2013/september/documents/papa-francesco_20130921_intervista-spadaro.html.

———. Interview with Antonio Spadaro on the Occasion of His Apostolic Trip to Sweden. *La Civiltà Cattolica*, October 31, 2016.

———. Interview with Ulf Jonsson, SJ, on the Occasion of His Apostolic Trip to Sweden, September 24, 2016. www.archivioradiovaticana.va/storico/2016/10/28/pope_francis_gives_interview_ahead_of_trip_to_sweden/en-1268511.

———. "Justice and Mercy." Morning Meditation in the Chapel of Casa Santa Marta, February 24, 2017. www.vatican.va/content/francesco/en/cotidie/2017/documents/papa-francesco-cotidie_20170224_justice-and-mercy.html.

———. "Justice and Mercy." *L'Osservatore Romano*, March 10, 2017.

———. *Laudato Si': On Care for Our Common Home.* Encyclical, May 24, 2015. www.vatican.va/content/francesco/en/encyclicals/documents/papa-francesco_20150524_enciclica-laudato-si.html.

———. *Lumen Fidei.* Encyclical, June 29, 2013. www.vatican.va/content/francesco/en/encyclicals/documents/papa-francesco_20130629_enciclica-lumen-fidei.html.

———. Meditation at the Marian Vigil during the Jubilee of Mercy, October 8, 2016. www.vatican.va/content/francesco/en/speeches/2016/october/documents/papa-francesco_20161008_giubileo-veglia-mariana.html.

———. Meeting with the 88th General Assembly of the Union of Superiors General, November 25, 2016. www.lamennais.org/en/pope-pope-francis-met-the-superiors-general-among-whom-was-bro-yannick-houssay/.

———. Meeting with the Muslim Community of Bangui, CAR, November 30, 2015. www.vatican.va/content/francesco/en/speeches/2015/november/documents/papa-francesco_20151130_repubblica-centrafricana-musulmani.html.

———. Message for the 51st World Communications Day, January 24, 2017. www
.vatican.va/content/francesco/en/messages/communications/documents
/papa-francesco_20170124_messaggio-comunicazioni-sociali.html.

———. Message for the Celebration of the 53rd World Day of Peace, December 8, 2019. www.vatican.va/content/francesco/en/messages/peace/docu
ments/papa-francesco_20181208_messaggio-52giornatamondiale-pace
2019.html.

———. Message for the Opening of the 37th International Meeting of Friend-ship among Peoples, August 19, 2016. www.vatican.va/content/francesco
/it/messages/pont-messages/2016/documents/papa-francesco_20160819
_messaggio-meeting-amicizia-popoli.html (in Italian).

———. Message to Professor Klaus Schwab, Executive Chairman of the World Economic Forum, January 15, 2020. www.vatican.va/content/francesco
/en/messages/pont-messages/2020/documents/papa-francesco_20200115
_messaggio-worldeconomicforum.html.

———. *Misericordia et Misera*. Apostolic letter issued at the conclusion of the Extraordinary Jubilee of Mercy, November 20, 2016. www.vatican.va
/content/francesco/en/apost_letters/documents/papa-francesco-lettera
-ap_20161120_misericordia-et-misera.html.

———. *Misericordiae Vultus: The Face of Mercy*. Apostolic letter, April 11, 2015. www.vatican.va/content/francesco/en/apost_letters/documents/papa
-francesco_bolla_20150411_misericordiae-vultus.html.

———. *Predicate Evangelium*. Apostolic Constitution on the Roman Curia and Its Service to the Church in the World, March 19, 2022. www.vatican
.va/content/francesco/en/apost_constitutions/documents/20220319
-costituzione-ap-praedicate-evangelium.html.

———. Preface. *Youcat: Youth Bible of the Catholic Church*. San Francisco: Ignatius Press, 2017.

———. Second Meditation, Spiritual Retreat Given by His Holiness Pope Francis on the Occasion of the Jubilee for Priests, June 2, 2016. www.vatican.va
/content/francesco/en/speeches/2016/june/documents/papa-Francesco
_20160602_giubileo-sacerdoti-seconda-meditazione.html.

———. "Sisters and Priests Free from Idolatry." morning meditation in the chapel of Casa Santa Marta, March 3, 2014, www.vatican.va/content
/francesco/en/cotidie/2014/documents/papa-francesco-cotidie_20140303
_sisters-and-priests.html.

———. Third Meditation, Spiritual Retreat Given by His Holiness Pope Francis on the Occasion of the Jubilee for Priests, June 2, 1996. www.vatican
.va/content/francesco/en/speeches/2016/june/documents/papa-francesco
_20160602_giubileo-sacerdoti-terza-meditazione.html.

———. *The Way of Humility*. Translated by Helena Scott. San Francisco: Ignatius Press, 2013.

John Paul II. *Crossing the Threshold of Hope*. Translated by Jenny McPhee and Martha McPhee. 11th printing (original 1994). New York: Alfred A. Knopf, 2005, 219.

———. *Dives in Misericordia*. Encyclical, November 30, 1980. www.vatican.va /content/john-paul-ii/en/encyclicals/documents/hf_jp-ii_enc_30111980 _dives-in-misericordia.html.

Paul VI. *Gaudium et Spes*. Dogmatic Constitution on the Church in the World, December 7, 1965. www.vatican.va/archive/hist_councils/ii_vatican_coun cil/documents/vat-ii_const_19651207_gaudium-et-spes_en.html.

———. General Audience, March 29, 1972. www.vatican.va/content/paul-vi/it /audiences/1972/documents/hf_p-vi_aud_19720329.html.

———. General Audience, March 20, 1974. www.vatican.va/content/paul-vi/it /audiences/1974/documents/hf_p-vi_aud_19740320.html.

———. *Lumen Gentium*. Dogmatic Constitution on the Church, November 21, 1964. www.vatican.va/archive/hist_councils/ii_vatican_council/documents /vat-ii_const_19641121_lumen-gentium_en.html.

Pius XII. *Haurietis Aquas*. Encyclical, May 15, 1956. www.vatican.va/content /pius-xii/en/encyclicals/documents/hf_p-xii_enc_15051956_haurietis -aquas.html.

Ratzinger, Joseph. "The Current Situation of Faith and Theology." Address given at the Meeting with the Doctrinal Commissions of Latin America, Guadalajara, Mexico, May 7, 1996. www.vatican.va/roman_curia/congrega tions/cfaith/incontri/rc_con_cfaith_19960507_guadalajara–ratzinger_en.html.

———. Homily, Mass for the Election of the Roman Pontiff, April 18, 2005. www.vatican.va/gpII/documents/homily-pro-eligendo-pontifice_20050418 _en.html.

Synod of Bishops. "The New Evangelization for the Transmission of the Christian Faith." 13th Ordinary General Assembly, October 7–28, 2012. www .vatican.va/roman_curia/synod/documents/rc_synod_doc_20110202 _lineamenta-xiii-assembly_en.html.

———. "The Pastoral Challenges of the Family in the Context of Evangelization." *Instrumentum Laboris*, 3rd Extraordinary General Assembly of the Synod of Bishops, October 5–19, 2014, www.vatican.va /roman_curia/synod/documents/rc_synod_doc_20140626_instrumentum -laboris-familia_en.html.

Secondary Sources

Archdiocese of Regina. "Anglican-Roman Catholic Covenant in Action." archregina.sk.ca/newsstory/anglican-roman-catholic-covenant-action/.

Arrupe, Pedro. *In Him Alone Is Our Hope: Texts on the Heart of Christ (1966–1983)*. St. Louis: Institute of Jesuit Sources, 1985.

Balthasar, Hans Urs von. *The Church and the World*. Translated by A. V. Littledale and N. Dru. Freiburg im Breisgau, Germany: Herder and Herder, 1967.

———. *The Christian State of Life*. Translated by Sr. Mary Frances McCarthy. San Francisco: Ignatius Press, 1983.

——. *Explorations in Theology III: Creator Spirit*. Translated by Brian Mc-Neil, CRV. San Francisco: Ignatius Press, 1993.

——. *Glory of the Lord V: The Realm of Metaphysics in the Modern Age*. Translated by Oliver Davies. Edinburgh: T&T Clark, 1992.

——. *The Glory of the Lord VII: Theology; The New Covenant*. Translated by Brian McNeil, CRV. San Francisco: Ignatius Press, 1989.

——. *Love Alone Is Credible*. Edited by D. C. Schindler. San Francisco: Ignatius Press, 2004.

——. *Mysterium Paschale: The Mystery of Easter*. Translated by Aidan Nichols, OP. Grand Rapids, MI: Eerdmans, 1993.

——. *Prayer*. London: SPCK, 1975.

——. *Romano Guardini: Reform from the Source*. San Francisco: Ignatius Press, 2010. .

——. *Theo-Drama*. Vol. 2: *Theological Dramatic Theory II: The Dramatis Personae; Persons in Christ*. Translated by Graham Harrison. San Francisco: Ignatius Press, 1990.

——. *Theo-Drama*. Vol. 3: *Theological Dramatic Theory III: The Dramatis Personae; Persons in Christ*. Translated by Graham Harrison. San Francisco: Ignatius Press, 1992.

——. *Theo-Drama*. Vol. 4: *Theological Dramatic Theory IV: The Action*. Translated by Graham Harrison. San Francisco: Ignatius Press, 1994.

——. *Theo-Drama*. Vol. 5: *Theological Dramatic Theory V: The Last Act*. Translated by Graham Harrison. San Francisco: Ignatius Press, 1998.

——. *Theo-Logic*. 3 vols. Translated by Adrian J. Walker. San Francisco: Ignatius Press.

——. *Theo-Logic*. Vol. 1: *Truth of the World*. Translated by Adrian J. Walker. San Francisco: Ignatius Press, 2000.

Barber, Michael C. "Pope Francis and the Mother of Mercy." *Columbia Online*, May 1, 2014. www.kofc.org/en/columbia/detail/pope-francis-mother-mercy.html.

Bergoglio, Jorge Mario. *Meditaciones para religiosos*. Mensajero, 2014.

Bolen, Donald. "Mercy." In *A Pope Francis Lexicon*, by Joshua McElwee and Cindy Wooden. Collegeville, MN: Liturgical Press, 2018.

Bonhoeffer, Dietrich. *The Cost of Discipleship*. Edited by R. H. Fuller. New York: Touchstone, 1959.

Borghesi, Massimo. *The Mind of Pope Francis: Jorge Mario Bergoglio's Intellectual Journey*. Translated by Barry Hudock. Collegeville, MN: Liturgical Press, 2018.

Bortoli, Ferruccio de. "Benedetto XVI non è una statua Partecipa alla vita della Chiesa." *Corriere Della Sera*, March 5, 2014.

Boursiquot, Marie-Albert. "Our Lady Undoer of Knots." *Linacre Quarterly* 84 (3): 203–204. www.ncbi.nlm.nih.gov/pmc/articles/PMC5592300/#:~: text=Its%20roots%2C%20however%2C%20go%2.

Dalzell, Thomas. *The Dramatic Encounter of Divine and Human Freedom in the Theology of Hans Urs von Balthasar*. Bern: Peter Lang, 1997.

de Gaál, Emery. *The Theology of Pope Benedict XVI: the Christocentric Shift*. New York: Palgrave Macmillan, 2010.

Faggioli, Massimo. "Polarization in the Church and the Crisis of the Catholic Mind." *La Croix*, November 27, 2017.

Favre, Pierre. *The Spiritual Writings of Pierre Favre*, edited by Edmond C. Murphy, SJ, and John W. Padberg, SJ. St. Louis: Institute of Jesuit Sources, 1996.

Fitzgerald, Michael L. Interview with Gerry O'Connell. *America*, February 3, 2019.

Goulding, Gill, CJ. *A Church of Passion and Hope: The Formation of an Ecclesial Disposition*. London: Bloomsbury, 2016.

———. *Creative Perseverance: Sustaining Life-Giving Ministry in Today's Church*. Ottawa: Novalis, 2003.

Guardini, Romano. "Die Begegnung." In *Begegnung und Bildung*, by Romano Guardini and Otto Friedrich Bollnow. Wurzburg, Germany: Werkbund, 1965.

———. *The End of the Modern World: A Search for Orientation*. Wilmington, DE: ISI Books, 1998.

———. *Learning the Virtues That Lead You to God*. Manchester, NH: Sophia Institute Press, 1998.

———. *Die Lehre des heil: Bonaventura von der Erlösung; Ein Beitrag zur Geschichte und zum System der Erlösungslehre*. Dusseldorf: Schwann, 1921.

———. *The Lord*. Translated by Elinor Castendyk Briefs. Washington, DC: Regnery/Gateway Editions, 1982.

———. *Die menschliche Wirklichkeit des Herrn: Beitrage zu einer Psychologie Jesu*. 3rd ed. Mainz, 1991.

———. *Die Situation des Menschen*. Munich: Akademievorträge, 1953.

———. *Romano Guardini Werke*. Edited by Franz Henrich under the direction of the committee of experts for the literary estate of Romano Guardini with the Catholic Academy in Bayern. Mainz: Matthias Grünewald, and Paderborn: Ferdinand Schöningh, 1955.

Harris, Elise. "This Is How Pope Francis Keeps His Peace amid Vatican 'Corruption.'" *Live with Spirit*, February 9, 2017. www.myspiritfm.com/News ?blogid=8267&view=post&articleid=153069&link=1&fldKeywords=& fldAuthor=&fldTopic=0.

Hodges, Susy. "Pope at Mass: Be Bishops for Your Flock, Not for Your Career." *Vatican News*, May 15, 2018. www.vaticannews.va/en/pope-francis /mass-casa-santa-marta/2018-05/pope-mass-santa-marta-bishops-flock .html.

Horowitz, Jason. "Pope Accepts Resignation of Chilean Bishop Tied to Abuse Scandal." *New York Times*, June 11, 2018. www.nytimes.com/2018/06/11 /world/europe/pope-francis-chile-abuse.html.

Huggett, Joyce. "Why Ignatian Spirituality Hooks Protestants." *The Way Supplement* 68 (1990): 22–34. www.theway.org.uk/back/s068Huggett.pdf.

Ignatius of Loyola. *The Constitutions of the Society of Jesus*. Edited by George E. Ganss. St. Louis: Institute of Jesuit Sources, 1970.

——. *The Spiritual Exercises of St. Ignatius*. Translation and commentary by George E. Ganss, SJ. Chicago: Loyola Press, 1992.

Ivereigh, Austen. "Catholic Dis/Agreement: Pope Francis and the Uses of Disagreement as a Mechanism of Ecclesial Reform, Austen Ivereigh and Eamon Duffey." Part of the 2016–2017 Dynamics of Dis/Agreement lecture series at the Von Hugel Institute, St. Edmund's College, December 2, 2016. www.vhi.st-edmunds.cam.ac.uk/resources-folder/audio-visual.

——. "Pope Francis and the Uses of Disagreement as a Mechanism of Ecclesial Reform." Presentation at the Von Hugel Institute, Cambridge, December 2, 2016.

——. *Wounded Shepherd: Pope Francis and His Struggles to Convert the Catholic Church*. New York: Heny Holt, 2019.

Kasper, Walter. *Mercy: The Essence of the Gospel and the Key to a Christian Life*. Translated by William Mages. New York: Paulist Press, 2013.

——. *Pope Francis' Revolution of Tenderness and Love*. Translated by William Madges. New York: Paulist Press, 2015.

Kreig, Robert, CSC. *Romano Guardini: A Precursor of Vatican II*. Notre Dame, IN: University of Notre Dame Press, 2001.

Lonergan, Bernard, SJ. *Method in Theology*. London: Darton, Longman and Todd, 1975.

——. "Theology and Man's Future." In *A Second Collection*. London: Darton, Longman and Todd, 1974.

McCosker, Philip. "From the Joy of the Gospel to the Joy of Christ: Situating and Expanding the Christology of *Evangelii Gaudium*." *Ecclesiology* 12 (2016): 34–53.

McElwee, Joshua J. "Francis Declares 'The World Is at War' after French Priest's Slaying." National Catholic Reporter, July 27, 2016. www.ncronline.org /francis-declares-world-war-after-french-priests-slaying.

Nichols, Vincent. "St. Brigid's Day Annual Lecture," February 20, 2017. rcdow .org.uk/cardinal/addresses/st-brigids-day-annual-lecture/.

O'Connell, Gerry. "Interview with Archbishop Michael L. Fitzgerald." *America Magazine*, February 3, 2019.

O'Donnell, John. *Hans Urs von Balthasar*. London: Geoffrey Chapman, 1992.

"Our Lady of Aparecida." *Vatican News*, October 12, 2022. www.vaticannews .va/en/saints/10/12/our-lady-of-aparecida.html.

Padberg, John W., SJ, ed. *Constitutions of the Society of Jesus and Their Complementary Norms*. St. Louis: Institute of Jesuit Sources, 1996.

Parolin, Pietro. "Pope Asking Assad to Help Syrian Population." *Vatican News*, July 22, 2019. www.vaticannews.va/en/pope/news/2019-07/card -parolin-pope-asking-assad-to-help-syrian-population.html.

Pita, Antonio. *The Parables of Mercy*. Rome: Pontifical Council for the Promotion of the New Evangelization, 2015.

"Pope Adds Three New Invocations to the Litany of the Blessed Virgin Mary." *Vatican News*, June 20, 2020. www.vaticannews.va/en/pope/news/2020 -06/pope-francis-loreto-litany-new-invocations.html.

"Pope Francis Sends Telegrams In-Flight to Japan," *Vatican News*, November 23, 2019, www.vaticannews.va/en/pope/news/2019-11/pope-francis-telegrams-flight-thailand-japan.html.

"Pope Francis' Remarks at First Session of Synod of Bishops on the Family." *Salt + Light Media*, October 6, 2015. slmedia.org/blog/pope-francis-remarks-at-first-session-of-synod-of-bishops-on-the-family.

"Pope in Santa Marta: Hope Is the Strongest Virtue but the Least Understood." *Rome Reports*, January 17, 2017. www.romereports.com/en/2017/01/17/pope-in-santa-marta-hope-is-the-strongest-virtue-but-the-least-understood/.

"Pope Sends Telegrams to Heads of State on Flight to Panama." *Vatican News*, January 23, 2019. www.vaticannews.va/en/pope/news/2019-01/pope-francis-panama-wyd-2019-telegrams-flyover.html.

"Pope Francis Sends Telegrams In-Flight to Japan." *Vatican News*, November 23, 2019. www.vaticannews.va/en/pope/news/2019-11/pope-francis-telegrams-flight-thailand-japan.html.

"Pope Urges Jesuits to Teach Discernment in Seminaries to Counter Rigidity." *Catholic Voices Comment*, August 26, 2016. cvcomment.org/2016/08/26/pope-urges-jesuits-to-teach-discernment-in-seminaries-to-counter-rigidity/.

Puente, Pablo. Homily to the Conference of Religious, Swanick, UK, January 31, 2001.

Quash, Ben. "The Theo-Drama." In *The Cambridge Companion to Hans Urs von Balthasar*, edited by Edward T. Oakes, SJ, and David Moss. Cambridge: Cambridge University Press, 2004, 143–157.

Rahner, Karl. *The Spiritual Exercises*. London: Sheed and Ward, 1976.

Ratzinger, Joseph. *Behold the Pierced One*. San Francisco: Ignatius Press, 1986.

———. "Guardini on Christ in Our Century." *Crisis*, June 1996.

———. Homily at the Funeral Mass for Pope John Paul II, April 8, 2005. www.vatican.va/gpII/documents/homily-card-ratzinger_20050408_en.html.

———. *Introduction to Christianity*. San Francisco: Ignatius Press, 2004.

Sara, Juan. "*Descensus ad inferos*, Dawn of Hope: Aspects of the Theology of Holy Saturday in the Trilogy of Hans Urs von Balthasar." In *Love Alone Is Credible: Hans Urs von Balthasar as Interpreter of the Catholic Tradition*, edited by David L. Schindler, 209–240. Grand Rapids, MI: Eerdmans, 2008.

Schindler, David L. "On the Catholic Common Ground Project: The Christological Foundations of Dialogue." *Communio* 23, no. 4 (1996): 825–851.

Sosa, Arturo. "Taking the Risk: Making Discernment Central." Address given in the Discerning Leadership Program, Jesuit Curia, Rome, October 28, 2019. discerningleadership.org/releases/father-general-arturo-sosa-s-j-taking-the-risk-making-discernment-central/.

Spadaro, Antonio, SJ. "The Diplomacy and Geopolitics of Mercy? The World of Pope Francis." Presentation at the University of Notre Dame, Indiana, USA, October 2017. nanovic.nd.edu/events/keeley-vatican-lecture/.

Spadaro, Antonio, and Marcelo Figueroa. "Evangelical Fundamentalism and Catholic Integralism: A Surprising Encounter." *La Civiltà Cattolica*, January 12, 2018.

Speyr, Adrienne von. *The World of Prayer.* San Francisco: Igntatius Press, 1985.

Tamayo-Moraga, Sarita. "Buddhist and Ignatian Spiritualities: Reports on a Trial Run of an Interfaith Retreat Based on 'Ignatius and Buddha in Conversation: A Resource for a Religiously Plural Dialog Juxtaposing the Spiritual Exercises of Ignatius and Buddhist Wisdom.'" *Buddhist-Christian Studies* 37 (2017): 131–143. www.jstor.org/stable/44632362#metadata_info_tab _contents.

Touze, Laurent. *Mercy in the Teaching of the Popes.* Vatican: Pontifical Council for the Promotion of the New Evangelization, 2015.

Vallely, Paul. *Pope Francis: Untying the Knots.* London: Bloomsbury, 2013.

Waldrop, Gregory, SJ. "The Dramatic Restoration of the 'Madonna della Strada.'" *America*, December 21, 2009. www.americamagazine.org/faith /2009/12/21/dramatic-restoration-madonna-della-strada.

Zizioulas, John. *Communion and Otherness.* Edited by Paul McPartlan. London: T&T Clark, 2006.

INDEX

Favre, Pierre, 36, 40, 111, 210n57
Francis
    addresses, xiv, 1, 4, 5, 19, 31, 34, 36,
        100, 101, 102, 104, 108
    homilies, 2, 7, 22, 30, 42, 53, 54, 65,
        99, 132
    interviews, 16, 19, 104
    meditations, 9, 10, 19, 27, 79, 141
    See also Christology: of Pope
        Francis; *Evangelii Gaudium*;
        Laudato Si'; *Lumen Fidei*; *Mi-
        sericordiae Vultus*

Guardini, Romano, xv, xvii, 46,
        170n6, 171n16, 172n38
    Christology, 45, 47, 48, 52, 55,
        170n7, 202n6,
    discipleship, 47
    divine love, 98, 176n63
    The End of the Modern World, 98,
        202n6
    influence on Balthasar, 45
    influence on Francis, 45
    liturgy, 49, 172n38
    scripture, 49, 171n25

Ignatius of Loyola, xvii, 18, 22,
        23, 24, 25, 26, 27, 28, 31, 39,
        42, 58, 111, 120, 137, 148n11,
        164n63, 165n70, 164n72, 169n1,
        221n4

John Paul II, xvii, 14, 16, 51, 53, 61,
        53, 61, 66, 125, 139, 146, 148,
        149, 155, 156, 173n48, 175n61,
        212n64, 214n87, 216n112

Kasper, Walter, xvi, 50, 52, 55, 82, 83,
        84, 85, 88, 89, 120, 122, 178n81,
        178n83, 179n89, 194n55, 194n57,
        195n60, 195n66, 197n79, 198n83,
        212n64, 216n110
kenosis, xvi, 60, 69, 70, 71, 72, 73, 74,
        75, 81, 82, 83, 84, 89, 91, 132,

187n2, 188n15, 194n52, 195n58,
        195n60

Laudato Si', 26, 34, 35, 152n37,
        160n12, 203n10
Lonergan, Bernard, 77, 78
Lumen Fidei, xvii
Lumen Gentium, 123, 140

Misera et Misericordia, 45, 61
Misericordiae Vultus, 45, 61, 66,
        147n5

Newman, John Henry, 169n1,
        198n86

Paul VI, 61, 224n9

Rahner, Karl, 160n15
Ratzinger, Joseph. *See* Benedict XVI

Sacred Heart, 41, 42, 43, 44, 143, 168,
        169, 219, 235
Society of Jesus, 22, 30, 41, 42,
        163n59, 221n4
Spadaro, Antonio, 106, 117,
        207n35
Speyr, Adrienne von, 87, 189n22

Trinity
    and distance, 194n55
    divine freedom, 93
    divine love, 44, 47, 70, 73, 77, 81,
        83, 195n59
    in Ignatian spirituality, 58
    and kenosis, xvi, 69, 70, 72, 73, 75,
        77, 82, 83, 86, 86, 89, 92, 93, 95,
        96, 188n15, 193n47
    life in the Trinity, xv, 66, 71, 72, 74,
        132
    and mercy, 72, 73, 75, 76, 83, 92,
        93, 94, 133, 183n138
    and obedience,78, 86, 191n35
    prayer, 87, 134

GILL K. GOULDING, CJ, is professor of systematic theology at Regis College, University of Toronto, and senior research associate at the Von Hügel Institute, University of Cambridge.

Printed in the USA
CPSIA information can be obtained
at www.ICGtesting.com
LVHW021730070923
757535LV00004B/81